W9-BUH-266

ALSO BY SUSAN ORLEAN

The Orchid Thief

Saturday Night

THE BULLFIGHTER CHECKS HER MAKEUP

RANDOM HOUSE NEW YORK

Susan Orlean

THE Bullfighter Checks HER MAKEUP

My Encounters

with Extraordinary

People

Random House and colophon are registered
trademarks of Random House, Inc.

All of the essays in this work have been previously published. For
previous publication information, please see the Author's Note on
page 293.

Grateful acknowledgment is made to Music Sales Corporation for
permission to reprint the following: excerpt from "Things I Wonder" by
Dorothy Mae Wiggin, copyright © 1967 by Music Sales Corporation
(ASCAP) and Hi Varieties Music (ASCAP); excerpt from "Who Are
Parents?" by Dorothy Mae Wiggin, copyright © 1968 by Music Sales
Corporation (ASCAP) and Hi Varieties Music (ASCAP); excerpt from
"Philosophy of the World" by Dorothy Mae Wiggin, copyright © 1969
by Music Sales Corporation (ASCAP) and Hi Varieties Music (ASCAP).
All rights administered worldwide by Music Sales Corporation.
International copyright secured. All rights reserved.
Reprinted by permission.

ISBN 0-679-46298-8

Random House website address: www.atrandom.com
Printed in the United States of America on acid-free paper

2   4   6   8   9   7   5   3

First Edition

Book design by Barbara M. Bachman

For John Gillespie

who makes me so happy

CONTENTS

ENCOUNTERS WITH CLOWNS, KINGS, SINGERS, AND SURFERS

I ALWAYS WANTED TO BE A WRITER. IN FACT, as far as I can recall, I have never wanted to be anything other than a writer. In junior high school I took a career guidance test that suggested I would do well as either an army officer or a forest ranger but I didn't care: I wanted only to be a writer, even though I didn't know how you went about becoming one, especially the kind of writer I wanted to be. I didn't want to be a newspaper reporter, because I have never cared about knowing something first, and I didn't want to write only about things that were considered "important" and newsworthy; I wanted to write about things that intrigued me, and to write about them in a way that would surprise readers who might not have expected to find these things intriguing. During college I kept a journal with a section called "Items Under Consideration," which was a meditation on what I was going to do once I graduated. It was filled with entries like this:

What to Do/Future Plans

Why I Should Go into Journalism

P R O :

Fun!
Interesting!
Writing!
Activity and excitement!
Good people (maybe)
Social value

C O N :

No jobs available
Have to live in NYC for serious work on a magazine
Talent is questionable

Except for some interstitial waitressing, my first job out of college was writing for a tiny magazine in Oregon, and I made it clear at the interview that I would absolutely, positively die if I didn't get hired. After all, I knew being a writer would be "Fun! Interesting!" and full of "Activity and excitement!" I had no experience to speak of, except that I had been the editor of my high school yearbook. When I went to the job interview in Oregon, I brought a copy of the yearbook and a kind of wild, exuberant determination, which was the only thing that could account for my having gotten the job.

What I wanted to write about were the people and places around me. I didn't want to write about famous people simply because they were famous, and I didn't want to write about charming little things that were self-consciously charming and little; I wasn't interested in documenting or predicting trends, and I didn't have polemics to air or sociological theories to spin out. I just wanted to write what are usually called "features"—a term that I hate because it sounds so fluffy and lightweight, like pillow stuffing, but that is used to describe stories that move at their own pace, rather than the news stories that race to keep time with events. The subjects I was drawn to were often completely ordinary, but I was confident that I could find something extraordinary in their ordinariness. I really believed that anything at all was worth writing about if you cared about it enough, and that the best and only necessary justification for writing any particular story was that I cared about it. The challenge was to write these stories in a way that got other people as interested in them as I was. The piece that convinced me this was possible was Mark Singer's profile of three building superintendents that ran in *The New Yorker* when I was in college. The piece was eloquent and funny and full of wonder even though the subject was unabashedly mundane. After I read it, I had that rare, heady feeling that I now knew something about life I hadn't known before I read it. At the same time, the story was so natural that I couldn't believe it had never been written until then. Like the very best examples of literary nonfiction, it was at once familiar and original, like a folk melody—as good an example as you could ever find of the poetry of facts and the art in ordinary life.

My first feature for *The New Yorker* was a profile of Nana Kwabena Oppong, a cabdriver in New York City. Nana's life as a cabbie was the embodiment of ordinariness, but he also happened to have the extraordinary honor of being the king of his tribe, the Ashantis, in the United States. His life seesawed between its two extremes, between the humdrum concerns of daily life, like doing maintenance on his cab and prodding his kids to do their homework and looking for a new apartment, and his royal concerns, like resolving property disputes and officiating at Ashanti ceremonies and overseeing the transportation of deceased members of the tribe back to Ghana so they could be buried in their motherland. I spent months on the story. When I would get together with him, I never knew whether I was meeting with Nana the cabdriver or Nana the king. By the end of our time together, of course, I realized that there was no real difference, and that the marvel was watching him weave together these strands of his life.

Just before I profiled Nana, I had been asked by *Esquire* to write a piece about the child actor Macaulay Culkin, who was ten years old at the time. I don't rule out doing celebrity profiles, but I wasn't in the mood to do one right then and I wasn't very interested in Macaulay Culkin. Then my editor told me that he was planning to use the headline THE AMERICAN MAN, AGE TEN. On a whim, I told my editor that I would do the piece if I could find a typical American ten-year-old man to profile instead—someone who I thought was more deserving of that headline. It was an improbable idea since they had already photographed Macaulay for the cover of the magazine, but my editor decided to take me up on it. I was completely dismayed. First of all, I had to figure out what I'd had in mind when I made the suggestion. Obviously, there is no such thing as a "typical" boy or girl, and even if I could establish some very generous guidelines for what constitutes typicalness—say, a suburban kid from a middle-class family who went to public school and didn't have an agent, a manager, or a chauffeur— there was the problem of choosing one such kid. I considered going to a shopping mall and just snatching the first ten-year-old I found, but instead I asked my friends to ask *their* friends if they knew anyone with a ten-year-old, and eventually I got the name of a boy who lived in the New Jersey suburbs. I liked Colin Duffy right away because he seemed unfazed by the prospect of my observing him for a couple of weeks. He was a wonderful kid, and I still marvel at how lucky I was to have stumbled on someone so endearing, but the truth is that if you set out to write about a ten-year-old boy, any boy would do. The particulars of the story would have been entirely different with a different boy, but the fundamentals would have been the same: An ordinary life examined closely reveals itself to be exquisite and complicated and exceptional, somehow managing to be both heroic and plain.

THERE ARE SO MANY THINGS I'm interested in writing about that settling on one drives me crazy. Usually it happens accidentally: Some bit of news will stick in my mind, or a friend will mention something, and suddenly a story presents itself or a subject engages me. For instance, I decided to profile Felipe Lopez, a star high school basketball player, because I had stumbled across a headline in the paper one day that said CHRIST THE KING AIMS FOR REVENGE. It was one of those headlines that stops you dead in your tracks, and even after you figure it out, you can't quite get it out of your mind. Christ the King turned out to be a Catholic school in New York, and its basketball team was bent on avenging an embarrassing loss to another school. Before reading the story I hadn't realized that there was a Catholic basketball league in the city, and that alone got me interested. But what really hooked me was remembering how ardent people are about high school sports—I guess it was the fierceness of that headline—and that led me to thinking about how a kid who was really good at some sport must lead a very unusual sort of life, and then I started wondering who was the best high school basketball player in the country. I could only hope and pray that he went to a school as evocatively named as Christ the King. As it turned out, Felipe didn't—he went to a school with the very homely name of Rice—but he did live in New York, not far from my apartment, and, like Colin, was happy to have me follow him around.

Some of these stories are about people who are well known, such as the designer Bill Blass and the Olympic figure skater Tonya Harding, and almost all of these were suggested to me rather than having been my own ideas, which tend to be about people who are not yet well known nor ever will be. Bill Blass was suggested to me by Tina Brown, who was editor of *The New Yorker* at the time, and I accepted the assignment when I found out that he still made personal trunk show appearances in small cities around the country, even though most people at his level in the fashion world had long since given it up. I loved the idea of profiling a world-class designer not in New York or Paris or Milan but in Nashville, at a ladies' luncheon in the middle of the week. Writing about Tonya Harding was a different kind of challenge. She had been in the news constantly after the attack on Nancy Kerrigan, and it was hard to imagine that there was a story left about her that hadn't already been told and retold. But I had noticed that all the newspaper stories mentioned she was from Portland, Oregon, which wasn't true: She was from the exurbs twenty miles or so outside of Portland. Because I used to live in Oregon, I knew the two places were entirely different, even antithetical, and I was convinced that Tonya Harding made a lot more sense if you understood something about where she was raised. I assumed that I wouldn't get to interview her when I went out to Oregon, so I interviewed people who cared about her and who lived in her town. It was a little like studying animal tracks and concluding something about a creature from the impression it has left behind. I still wish I could have talked to her, but maybe that will be another story another time.

I LOVE WRITING about places and things almost as much as I like writing about people, and I probably spend half of my time on stories that are primarily about a particular landscape or environment or event. For this book, though, I decided to gather together only pieces that center on people, to present an assembly of the various characters I've profiled so far in my career. There is nothing harder or more interesting than trying to say something eloquent about another person and no process is more challenging. It's much easier to, say, climb Mount Fuji and write about the experience (which I've done) than it is to hang around with a ten-year-old boy or an unemployed Hollywood agent or a famous fashion designer trying to be both unobtrusive and penetrating, and then try to make some sense out of what I've seen. It's just that people are so *interesting*. Writing about them, in tight focus, is irresistible. I am sure that I will continue doing profiles as long as I'm still writing, stepping in and out—lightly, I hope—of other people's lives.

Readers often ask me if I stay in touch with anyone I've written about. It's an understandable question; after all, when you profile people, you spend a lot of time with them, and you do come to know them very well—sometimes even better than people you think of as your friends. But writing a profile is a process that has a beginning, a middle, and an end. Usually when it has ended, the writer and the subject have very little in common except for the fact that they were for a while a writer and a subject. There are some notable exceptions. Robert Stuart, the hairdresser I wrote about in a piece called "Short Cuts," still cuts my hair, so I see him every six to eight weeks. Bill Blass ("King of the Road") invited me to his runway shows for years after my piece ran, so I would see him—from a distance—every fall and spring, when he would come out to take his runway bow. He recently retired, so I won't be seeing him in spotlights anymore. Jill Meilus, the real estate broker ("I Want This Apartment") became a friend, and I have lunch with her now and again; if I sell my apartment, I will probably ask her to handle it. I'm certainly not in touch with Tonya Harding, but I always pay attention when I hear about her in the news; I think she was arrested recently for hitting her boyfriend on the head with a hubcap. As far as I can tell from the coverage of the tennis circuit, the Maleeva sisters ("The Three Sisters") have retired from the professional circuit. Felipe Lopez, after an erratic four years on the St. John's University basketball team, achieved the almost impossible dream of becoming an NBA player. The Jackson Southernaires ("Devotion Road") are still singing gospel and have performed in New York several times since I wrote about them. I've gone to hear them a couple of times. Right after my piece was published, a French movie company made a documentary about them that was shown on European TV. I still read the Millerton *News*, where Heather Heaton was an ace reporter ("Her Town"), but I no longer see her byline, so I assume she's moved on to a bigger paper in a bigger town. The Shaggs ("Meet the Shaggs") played together for the first time in seventeen years after my story came out. I went to the sold-out show and couldn't believe I was seeing it, and I think they couldn't believe it was happening, either. When a young man came up to Dot and showed her his Shaggs tattoo, it was as if time had not just stopped but had doubled back on itself, and the Wiggin sisters were teenagers again in New Hampshire, try-ing their best to play "Philosophy of the World."

Inevitably, though, I lose track of many of the people I've written about, people like Colin Duffy, Nana Kwabena Oppong, Big Lee, Tiffany, Biff, Silly Billy, Leo Herschman, and on and on and on. It's the one part of the job—this "Fun! Interesting! Active! Exciting!" job—that makes me melancholy. I know it is unrealistic and impractical to think I could stay close to everyone I've profiled, and even if I could, we would never be as close as we were when I was writing about them; still, it's hard not to feel attached to people once you've been allowed into their lives. So what I have of them, and always will have, is just that moment we spent together—now preserved on paper, bound between covers, cast out into the world—and they will never get any older, their faces will never fade, their dreams will still be within reach, and I will forever still be listening as hard as I can.

April 10, 2000

THE BULLFIGHTER CHECKS HER MAKEUP

THE AMERICAN MAN,
AGE TEN

*I*F COLIN DUFFY AND I WERE TO GET MAR-
ried, we would have matching superhero notebooks. We
would wear shorts, big sneakers, and long, baggy T-shirts
depicting famous athletes every single day, even in the winter. We would sleep in our clothes. We would both be good
at Nintendo Street Fighter II, but Colin would be better
than me. We would have some homework, but it would
never be too hard and we would always have just finished
it. We would eat pizza and candy for all of our meals. We
wouldn't have sex, but we would have crushes on each
other and, magically, babies would appear in our home. We
would win the lottery and then buy land in Wyoming,
where we would have one of every kind of cute animal. All
the while, Colin would be working in law enforcement—
probably the FBI. Our favorite movie star, Morgan Freeman, would visit us occasionally. We would listen to the
same Eurythmics song ("Here Comes the Rain Again")
over and over again and watch two hours of television every
Friday night. We would both be good at football, have best
friends, and know how to drive; we would cure AIDS and

the garbage problem and everything that hurts animals. We would hang out a lot with Colin's dad. For fun, we would load a slingshot with dog food and shoot it at my butt. We would have a very good life.

HERE ARE THE PARTICULARS about Colin Duffy: He is ten years old, on the nose. He is four feet eight inches high, weighs seventy-five pounds, and appears to be mostly leg and shoulder blade. He is a handsome kid. He has a broad forehead, dark eyes with dense lashes, and a sharp, dimply smile. I have rarely seen him without a baseball cap. He owns several, but favors a University of Michigan Wolverines model, on account of its pleasing colors. The hat styles his hair into wild disarray. If you ever managed to get the hat off his head, you would see a boy with a nimbus of golden-brown hair, dented in the back, where the hat hits him.

Colin lives with his mother, Elaine; his father, Jim; his older sister, Megan; and his little brother, Chris, in a pretty pale blue Victorian house on a bosky street in Glen Ridge, New Jersey. Glen Ridge is a serene and civilized old town twenty miles west of New York City. It does not have much of a commercial district, but it is a town of amazing lawns. Most of the houses were built around the turn of the century and are set back a gracious, green distance from the street. The rest of the town seems to consist of parks and playing fields and sidewalks and backyards—in other words, it is a far cry from South-Central Los Angeles and from Bedford-Stuyvesant and other, grimmer parts of the country where a very different ten-year-old American man is growing up today.

There is a fine school system in Glen Ridge, but Elaine and Jim, who are both schoolteachers, choose to send their children to a parents' co-operative elementary school in Montclair, a neighboring suburb. Currently, Colin is in fifth grade. He is a good student. He plans to go to college, to a place he says is called Oklahoma City State College University. OCSCU satisfies his desire to live out west, to attend a small college, and to study law enforcement, which OCSCU apparently offers as a major. After four years at Oklahoma City State College University, he plans to work for the FBI. He says that getting to be a police officer involves tons of hard work, but working for the FBI will be a cinch, because all you have to do is fill out one form, which he has already gotten from the head FBI office. Colin is quiet in class but loud on the playground. He has a great throwing arm, significant foot speed, and a lot of physical confidence. He is also brave.

Huge wild cats with rabies and gross stuff dripping from their teeth, which he says run rampant throughout his neighborhood, do not scare him. Otherwise, he is slightly bashful. This combination of athletic grace and valor and personal reserve accounts for considerable popularity. He has a fluid relationship to many social groups, including the superbright nerds, the ultrajocks, the flashy kids who will someday become extremely popular and socially successful juvenile delinquents, and the kids who will be elected president of the student body. In his opinion, the most popular boy in his class is Christian, who happens to be black, and Colin's favorite television character is Steve Urkel on *Family Matters,* who is black, too, but otherwise he seems uninterested in or oblivious to race. Until this year, he was a Boy Scout. Now he is planning to begin karate lessons. His favorite schoolyard game is football, followed closely by prison dodgeball, blob tag, and bombardo. He's crazy about athletes, although sometimes it isn't clear if he is absolutely sure of the difference between human athletes and Marvel Comics action figures. His current athletic hero is Dave Meggett. His current best friend is named Japeth. He used to have another best friend named Ozzie. According to Colin, Ozzie was found on a doorstep, then changed his name to Michael and moved to Massachusetts, and then Colin never saw him or heard from him again.

He has had other losses in his life. He is old enough to know people who have died and to know things about the world that are worrisome. When he dreams, he dreams about moving to Wyoming, which he has visited with his family. His plan is to buy land there and have some sort of ranch that would definitely include horses. Sometimes when he talks about this, it sounds as ordinary and hard-boiled as a real estate appraisal; other times it can sound fantastical and wifty and achingly naive, informed by the last inklings of childhood—the musings of a balmy real estate appraiser assaying a wonderful and magical landscape that erodes from memory a little bit every day. The collision in his mind of what he understands, what he hears, what he figures out, what popular culture pours into him, what he knows, what he pretends to know, and what he imagines makes an interesting mess. The mess often has the form of what he will probably think like when he is a grown man, but the content of what he is like as a little boy.

He is old enough to begin imagining that he will someday get married, but at ten he is still convinced that the best thing about being married will be that he will be allowed to sleep in his clothes. His father once observed that living with Colin was like living with a Martian who had done some reading on American culture. As it happens, Colin is not especially sad or worried about the prospect of growing up, although he sometimes frets over whether he should be called a kid or a grown-up; he has settled on the word *kid-up*. Once, I asked him what the biggest advantage to adulthood will be, and he said, "The best thing is that grown-ups can go wherever they want." I asked him what he meant, exactly, and he said, "Well, if you're grown up, you'd have a car, and whenever you felt like it, you could get into your car and drive somewhere and get candy."

COLIN LOVES RECYCLING. He loves it even more than, say, playing with little birds. That ten-year-olds feel the weight of the world and consider it their mission to shoulder it came as a surprise to me. I had gone with Colin one Monday to his classroom at Montclair Cooperative School. The Co-op is in a steep, old, sharp-angled brick building that had served for many years as a public school until a group of parents in the area took it over and made it into a private, progressive elementary school. The fifth-grade classroom is on the top floor, under the dormers, which gives the room the eccentric shape and closeness of an attic. It is a rather informal environment. There are computers lined up in an adjoining room and instructions spelled out on the chalkboard—BRING IN: (1) A CUBBY WITH YOUR NAME ON IT, (2) A TRAPPER WITH A 5-POCKET ENVELOPE LABELED SCIENCE, SOCIAL STUDIES, READING/LANGUAGE ARTS, MATH, MATH LAB/COMPUTER; WHITE LINED PAPER; A PLASTIC PENCIL BAG; A SMALL HOMEWORK PAD, (3) LARGE BROWN GROCERY BAGS—but there is also a couch in the center of the classroom, which the kids take turns occupying, a rocking chair, and three canaries in cages near the door.

It happened to be Colin's first day in fifth grade. Before class began, there was a lot of horsing around, but there were also a lot of conversations about whether Magic Johnson had AIDS or just HIV and whether someone falling in a pool of blood from a cut of his would get the disease. These jolts of sobriety in the midst of rank goofiness are a ten-year-old's specialty. Each one comes as a fresh, hard surprise, like finding a razor blade in a candy apple. One day, Colin and I had been discussing horses or dogs or something, and out of the blue he said, "What do you think is better, to dump garbage in the ocean, to dump it on land, or to burn it?" Another time, he asked me if I planned to have children. I had just spent an evening with him and his friend Japeth, during which they put every small, movable object in the house into Japeth's slingshot and fired it at me, so I told him that I wanted children but that I hoped they would all be girls, and he said, "Will you have an abortion if you find out you have a boy?"

At school, after discussing summer vacation, the kids began choosing the jobs they would do to help out around the classroom. Most of the jobs are humdrum—putting the chairs up on the tables, washing the chalkboard, turning the computers off or on. Five of the most humdrum tasks are recycling chores—for example, taking bottles or stacks of paper down to the basement, where they would be sorted and prepared for pickup. Two children would be assigned to feed the birds and cover their cages at the end of the day.

I expected the bird jobs to be the first to go. Everyone loved the birds; they'd spent an hour that morning voting on names for them (Tweetie, Montgomery, and Rose narrowly beating out Axl Rose, Bugs, Ol' Yeller, Fido, Slim, Lucy, and Chirpie). Instead, they all wanted to recycle. The recycling jobs were claimed by the first five kids called by Suzanne Nakamura, the fifth-grade teacher; each kid called after that responded by groaning, "Suzanne, aren't there any more recycling jobs?" Colin ended up with the job of taking down the chairs each morning. He accepted the task with a sort of resignation—this was going to be just a job rather than a mission.

On the way home that day, I was quizzing Colin about his worldviews.

"Who's the coolest person in the world?"

"Morgan Freeman."

"What's the best sport?"

"Football."

"Who's the coolest woman?"

"None. I don't know."

"What's the most important thing in the world?"

"Game Boy." Pause. "No, the world. The world is the most important thing in the world."

DANNY'S PIZZERIA is a dark little shop next door to the Montclair Cooperative School. It is not much to look at. Outside, the brick facing is painted muddy brown. Inside, there are some saggy counters, a splintered bench, and enough room for either six teenagers or about a dozen ten-year-olds who happen to be getting along well. The light is low. The air is oily. At Danny's, you will find pizza, candy, Nintendo, and very few girls. To a ten-year-old boy, it is the most beautiful place in the world.

One afternoon, after class was dismissed, we went to Danny's with Colin's friend Japeth to play Nintendo. Danny's has only one game, Street Fighter II Champion Edition. Some teenage boys from a nearby middle school had gotten there first and were standing in a tall, impenetrable thicket around the machine.

"Next game," Colin said. The teenagers ignored him.

"Hey, we get next game," Japeth said. He is smaller than Colin, scrappy, and, as he explained to me once, famous for wearing his hat backward all the time and having a huge wristwatch and a huge bedroom. He stamped his foot and announced again, "Hey, we get next game."

One of the teenagers turned around and said, "Fuck you, *next game*," and then turned back to the machine.

"Whoa," Japeth said.

He and Colin went outside, where they felt bigger.

"Which street fighter are you going to be?" Colin asked Japeth.

"Blanka," Japeth said. "I know how to do his head-butt."

"I hate that! I hate the head-butt," Colin said. He dropped his voice a little and growled, "I'm going to be Ken, and I will kill you with my dragon punch."

"Yeah, right, and monkeys will fly out of my butt," Japeth said.

Street Fighter II is a video game in which two characters have an explosive brawl in a scenic international setting. It is currently the most popular video arcade game in America. This is not an insignificant amount of popularity. Most arcade versions of video games, which end up in pizza parlors, malls, and arcades, sell about two thousand units. So far, some fifty thousand Street Fighter II and Street Fighter II Championship Edition arcade games have been sold. Not since Pac-Man, which was released the year before Colin was born, has there been a video game as popular as Street Fighter. The home version of Street Fighter is the most popular home video game in the country, and that, too, is not an insignificant thing. Thirty-two million Nintendo home systems have been sold since 1986, when it was introduced in this country. There is a Nintendo system in seven of every ten homes in America in which a child between the ages of eight and twelve resides. By the time a boy in America turns ten, he will almost certainly have been exposed to Nintendo home games, Nintendo arcade games, and Game Boy, the handheld version. He will probably own a system and dozens of games. By ten, according to Nintendo studies, teachers, and psychologists, game prowess becomes a fundamental, essential male social marker and a schoolyard boast.

The Street Fighter characters are Dhalsim, Ken, Guile, Blanka, E. Honda, Ryu, Zangief, and Chun Li. Each represents a different country, and they each have their own special weapon. Chun Li, for instance, is from China and possesses a devastating whirlwind kick that is triggered if you push the control pad down for two seconds and then up for two seconds, and then you hit the kick button. Chun Li's kick is money in the bank, because most of the other fighters do not have a good defense against it. By the way, Chun Li happens to be a girl—the only female Street Fighter character.

I asked Colin if he was interested in being Chun Li. There was a long pause. "I would rather be Ken," he said.

The girls in Colin's class at school are named Cortnerd, Terror, Spacey, Lizard, Maggot, and Diarrhea. "They do have other names, but that's what we call them," Colin told me. "The girls aren't very popular."

"They are about as popular as a piece of dirt," Japeth said. "Or, you know that couch in the classroom? That couch is more popular than any girl. A thousand times more." They talked for a minute about one of the girls in their class, a tall blonde with cheerleader genetic material, who they allowed was not quite as gross as some of the other girls. Japeth said that a chubby, awkward boy in their class was boasting that this girl liked him.

"No way," Colin said. "She would never like him. I mean, not that he's so . . . I don't know. I don't hate him because he's fat, anyway. I hate him because he's nasty."

"Well, she doesn't like him," Japeth said. "She's been really mean to me lately, so I'm pretty sure she likes me."

"Girls are different," Colin said. He hopped up and down on the balls of his feet, wrinkling his nose. "Girls are stupid and weird."

"I have a lot of girlfriends, about six or so," Japeth said, turning contemplative. "I don't exactly remember their names, though."

The teenagers came crashing out of Danny's and jostled past us, so we went inside. The man who runs Danny's, whose name is Tom, was leaning across the counter on his elbows, looking exhausted. Two little boys, holding Slush Puppies, shuffled toward the Nintendo, but Colin and Japeth elbowed them aside and slammed their quarters down on the machine. The little boys shuffled back toward the counter and stood gawking at them, sucking on their drinks.

"You want to know how to tell if a girl likes you?" Japeth said. "She'll act really mean to you. That's a sure sign. I don't know why they do it, but it's always a sure sign. It gets your attention. You know how I show a girl I like her? I steal something from her and then run away. I do it to get their attention, and it works."

They played four quarters' worth of games. During the last one, a teenager with a quilted leather jacket and a fade haircut came in, pushed his arm between them, and put a quarter down on the deck of the machine.

Japeth said, "Hey, what's that?"

The teenager said, "I get next game. I've marked it now. Everyone knows this secret sign for next game. It's a universal thing."

"So now we know," Japeth said. "Colin, let's get out of here and go bother Maggie. I mean Maggot. Okay?" They picked up their backpacks and headed out the door.

PSYCHOLOGISTS IDENTIFY ten as roughly the age at which many boys experience the gender-linked normative developmental trauma that leaves them, as adult men, at risk for specific psychological sequelae often manifest as deficits in the arenas of intimacy, empathy, and struggles with commitment in relationships. In other words, this is around the age when guys get screwed up about girls. Elaine and Jim Duffy, and probably most of the parents who send their kids to Montclair Cooperative School, have done a lot of stuff to try to avoid this. They gave Colin dolls as well as guns. (He preferred guns.) Japeth's father has three motorcycles and two dirt bikes but does most of the cooking and cleaning in their home. Suzanne, Colin's teacher, is careful to avoid sexist references in her presentations. After school, the yard at Montclair Cooperative is filled with as many fathers as mothers—fathers who hug their kids when they come prancing out of the building and are dismayed when their sons clamor for Supersoaker water guns and war toys or take pleasure in beating up girls.

In a study of adolescents conducted by the Gesell Institute of Human Development, nearly half the ten-year-old boys questioned said they thought they had adequate information about sex. Nevertheless, most ten-year-old boys across the country are subjected to a few months of sex education in school. Colin and his class will get their dose next spring. It is yet another installment in a plan to make them into new, improved men with

reconstructed notions of sex and male-female relationships. One afternoon I asked Philip, a schoolmate of Colin's, whether he was looking forward to sex education, and he said, "No, because I think it'll probably
make me really, really hyper. I have a feeling it's going to be just like what
it was like when some television reporters came to school last year and
filmed us in class and I got really hyper. They stood around with all these
cameras and asked us questions. I think that's what sex education is probably like."

At a class meeting earlier in the day:

Colin's teacher, SUZANNE: Today was our first day of swimming class,
and I have one observation to make. The girls went into their locker room,
got dressed without a lot of fuss, and came into the pool area. The boys, on
the other hand, the *boys* had some sort of problem doing that rather simple
task. Can someone tell me what exactly went on in the locker room?

KEITH: There was a lot of shouting.

SUZANNE: Okay, I hear you saying that people were being noisy and
shouting. Anything else?

CHRISTIAN: Some people were screaming so much that my ears were
killing me. It gave me, like, a huge headache. Also, some of the boys were
taking their towels, I mean, after they had taken their clothes off, they had
their towels around their waists and then they would drop them really fast
and then pull them back up, really fast.

SUZANNE: Okay, you're saying some people were being silly about their
bodies.

CHRISTIAN: Well, yeah, but it was more like they were being silly about
their pants.

COLIN'S BEDROOM is decorated simply. He has a cage with his pet
parakeet, Dude, on his dresser, a lot of recently worn clothing piled haphazardly on the floor, and a husky brown teddy bear sitting upright in a
chair near the foot of his bed. The walls are mostly bare, except for a Spi-
derman poster and a few ads torn out of magazines he has thumbtacked
up. One of the ads is for a cologne, illustrated with several small photographs of cowboy hats; another, a feverish portrait of a woman on a
horse, is an ad for blue jeans. These inspire him sometimes when he lies in
bed and makes plans for the move to Wyoming. Also, he happens to like
ads. He also likes television commercials. Generally speaking, he likes con-
sumer products and popular culture. He partakes avidly but not indiscrim-

inately. In fact, during the time we spent together, he provided a running commentary on merchandise, media, and entertainment:

"The only shoes anyone will wear are Reebok Pumps. Big T-shirts are cool, not the kind that are sticky and close to you, but big and baggy and long, not the kind that stop at your stomach."

"The best food is Chicken McNuggets and Life cereal and Frosted Flakes."

"Don't go to Blimpie's. They have the worst service."

"I'm not into Teenage Mutant Ninja Turtles anymore. I grew out of that. I like Donatello, but I'm not a fan. I don't buy the figures anymore."

"The best television shows are on Friday night on ABC. It's called TGIF, and it's *Family Matters, Step by Step, Dinosaurs,* and *Perfect Strangers,* where the guy has a funny accent."

"The best candy is Skittles and Symphony bars and Crybabies and Warheads. Crybabies are great because if you eat a lot of them at once you feel so sour."

"Hyundais are Korean cars. It's the only Korean car. They're not that good because Koreans don't have a lot of experience building cars."

"The best movie is *City Slickers,* and the best part was when he saved his little cow in the river."

"The Giants really need to get rid of Ray Handley. They have to get somebody who has real coaching experience. He's just no good."

"My dog, Sally, costs seventy-two dollars. That sounds like a lot of money but it's a really good price because you get a flea bath with your dog."

"The best magazines are *Nintendo Power,* because they tell you how to do the secret moves in the video games, and also *Mad* magazine and *Money Guide*—I really like that one."

"The best artist in the world is Jim Davis."

"The most beautiful woman in the world is not Madonna! Only Wayne and Garth think that! She looks like maybe a . . . a . . . slut or something. Cindy Crawford looks like she would look good, but if you see her on an awards program on TV she doesn't look that good. I think the most beautiful woman in the world probably is my mom."

COLIN THINKS A LOT about money. This started when he was about nine and a half, which is when a lot of other things started—a new way of walking that has a little macho hitch and swagger, a decision about the

Teenage Mutant Ninja Turtles (con) and Eurythmics (pro), and a persistent curiosity about a certain girl whose name he will not reveal. He knows the price of everything he encounters. He knows how much college costs and what someone might earn performing different jobs. Once, he asked me what my husband did; when I answered that he was a lawyer, he snapped, "You must be a rich family. Lawyers make $400,000 a year." His preoccupation with money baffles his family. They are not struggling, so this is not the anxiety of deprivation; they are not rich, so he is not responding to an elegant, advantaged world. His allowance is five dollars a week. It seems sufficient for his needs, which consist chiefly of quarters for Nintendo and candy money. The remainder is put into his Wyoming fund. His fascination is not just specific to needing money or having plans for money: It is as if money itself, and the way it makes the world work, and the realization that almost everything in the world can be assigned a price, has possessed him. "I just pay attention to things like that," Colin says. "It's really very interesting."

He is looking for a windfall. He tells me his mother has been notified that she is in the fourth and final round of the Publisher's Clearinghouse Sweepstakes. This is not an ironic observation. He plays the New Jersey lottery every Thursday night. He knows the weekly jackpot; he knows the number to call to find out if he has won. I do not think this presages a future for Colin as a high-stakes gambler; I think it says more about the powerful grasp that money has on imagination and what a large percentage of a ten-year-old's mind is made up of imaginings. One Friday, we were at school together, and one of his friends was asking him about the lottery, and he said, "This week it was $4 million. That would be I forget how much every year for the rest of your life. It's a lot, I think. You should play. All it takes is a dollar and a dream."

UNTIL THE LOTTERY comes through and he starts putting together the Wyoming land deal, Colin can be found most of the time in the backyard. Often, he will have friends come over. Regularly, children from the neighborhood will gravitate to the backyard, too. As a technical matter of real-property law, title to the house and yard belongs to Jim and Elaine Duffy, but Colin adversely possesses the backyard, at least from 4:00 each afternoon until it gets dark. As yet, the fixtures of teenage life—malls, video arcades, friends' basements, automobiles—either hold little interest for him or are not his to have.

He is, at the moment, very content with his backyard. For most intents and purposes, it is as big as Wyoming. One day, certainly, he will grow and it will shrink, and it will become simply a suburban backyard and it won't be big enough for him anymore. This will happen so fast that one night he will be in the backyard, believing it a perfect place, and by the next night he will have changed and the yard as he imagined it will be gone, and this era of his life will be behind him forever.

Most days, he spends his hours in the backyard building an Evil Spider-Web Trap. This entails running a spool of Jim's fishing line from every surface in the yard until it forms a huge web. Once a garbageman picking up the Duffys' trash got caught in the trap. Otherwise, the Evil Spider-Web Trap mostly has a deterrent effect, because the kids in the neighborhood who might roam over know that Colin builds it back there. "I do it all the time," he says. "First I plan who I'd like to catch in it, and then we get started. Trespassers have to beware."

One afternoon when I came over, after a few rounds of Street Fighter at Danny's, Colin started building a trap. He selected a victim for inspiration—a boy in his class who had been pestering him—and began wrapping. He was entirely absorbed. He moved from tree to tree, wrapping; he laced fishing line through the railing of the deck and then back to the shed; he circled an old jungle gym, something he'd outgrown and abandoned a few years ago, and then crossed over to a bush at the back of the yard. Briefly, he contemplated making his dog, Sally, part of the web. Dusk fell. He kept wrapping, paying out fishing line an inch at a time. We could hear mothers up and down the block hooting for their kids; two tiny children from next door stood transfixed at the edge of the yard, uncertain whether they would end up inside or outside the web. After a while, the spool spun around in Colin's hands one more time and then stopped; he was out of line.

It was almost too dark to see much of anything, although now and again the light from the deck would glance off a length of line, and it would glint and sparkle. "That's the point," he said. "You could do it with thread, but the fishing line is invisible. Now I have this perfect thing and the only one who knows about it is me." With that, he dropped the spool, skipped up the stairs of the deck, threw open the screen door, and then bounded into the house, leaving me and Sally the dog trapped in his web.

MEET THE SHAGGS

Things I Wonder (2:12)

DEPENDING ON WHOM YOU ASK, THE SHAGGS were either the best band of all time or the worst. Frank Zappa is said to have proclaimed that the Shaggs were "better than the Beatles." More recently, though, a music fan who claimed to be in "the fetal position, writhing in pain," declared on the Internet that the Shaggs were "hauntingly bad," and added, "I would walk across the desert while eating charcoal briquettes soaked in Tabasco for forty days and forty nights *not* to ever have to listen to anything Shagg-related *ever* again." Such a divergence of opinion confuses the mind. Listening to the Shaggs' album *Philosophy of the World* will further confound. The music is winsome but raggedly discordant pop. Something is sort of wrong with the tempo, and the melodies are squashed and bent, nasal, deadpan. Are the Shaggs referencing the heptatonic, angular microtones of Chinese *ya-yueh* court music and the atonal note clusters of Ornette Coleman, or are they just a bunch of kids playing badly on cheap, out-of-tune guitars? And what about their homely, blunt lyrics? Consider the song "Things I Wonder":

There are many things I wonder
There are many things I don't
It seems as though the things I wonder most
Are the things I never find out

Is this the colloquial ease and dislocated syntax of a James Schuyler poem or the awkward innermost thoughts of a speechless teenager?

The Shaggs were three sisters, Helen, Betty, and Dorothy (Dot) Wiggin, from Fremont, New Hampshire. They were managed by their father, Austin Wiggin, Jr., and were sometimes accompanied by another sister, Rachel. They performed almost exclusively at the Fremont town hall and at a local nursing home, beginning in 1968 and ending in 1973. Many people in Fremont thought the band stank. Austin Wiggin did not. He believed his girls were going to be big stars, and in 1969 he took most of his savings and paid to record an album of their music. Nine hundred of the original thousand copies of *Philosophy of the World* vanished right after being pressed, along with the record's shady producer. Even so, the album has endured for thirty years. Music collectors got hold of the remaining copies of *Philosophy of the World* and started a small Shaggs cult. In the mid-seventies, WBCN-FM, in Boston, began playing a few cuts from the record. In 1988, the songs were repackaged and rereleased on compact disk and became celebrated by outsider-music mavens, who were taken with the Shaggs' artless style. Now the Shaggs are entering their third life: *Philosophy of the World* was reissued last spring by RCA Victor and will be released in Germany this winter. The new CD of *Philosophy of the World* has the same cover as the original 1969 album—a photograph of the Wiggin girls posed in front of a dark green curtain. In the picture, Helen is twenty-two, Dot is twenty-one, and Betty is eighteen. They have long blond hair and long blond bangs and stiff, quizzical half-smiles. Helen, sitting behind her drum set, is wearing flowered trousers and a white Nehru shirt; Betty and Dot, clutching their guitars, are wearing matching floral tunics, pleated plaid skirts, and square-heeled white pumps. There is nothing playful about the picture; it is melancholy, foreboding, with black shadows and the queer, depthless quality of an aquarium. Which leaves you with even more things to wonder about the Shaggs.

Shaggs' Own Thing (3:54)

Fremont, New Hampshire, is a town that has missed out on most every-thing. Route 125, the main highway bisecting New Hampshire, just misses the east side of Fremont; Route 101 just misses the north; the town is neither in the mountains nor on the ocean; it is not quite in the thick of Boston's outskirts, nor is it quite cosseted in the woods. Fremont is a drowsy, trim, unfancy place, rimmed by the Exeter River. Ostentation is expressed only in a few man-size gravestones in the Fremont cemetery; bragging rights are limited to Fremont's being the hometown of the emi-nent but obscure 1920s meteorologist Herbert Browne and its being the first place a B-52 ever crashed without killing anyone.

In the 1960s, when the Wiggin sisters formed the Shaggs, many peo-ple in Fremont raised dairy cows or made handkerchiefs at the Exeter tex-tile mill or built barrels at Spaulding & Frost Cooperage, went to church, tended their families, kept quiet lives. Sometimes the summer light bounces off the black-glass surface of the Exeter River and glazes the big stands of blue pine, and sometimes the pastures are full and lustrous, but ordinary days in southern New Hampshire towns can be mingy and dismal. "Loneliness contributed to severe depression, illness and drunkenness for countless rural families," Matthew Thomas wrote, in his book *History of Fremont, N.H. Olde Poplin: An Independent New England Republic 1764–1997*, which came out last year. "There may have been some nice, pleasant times . . . but for the most part, death, sickness, disease, acci-dents, bad weather, loneliness, strenuous hard work, insect-infested foods, prowling predatory animals, and countless inconveniences marked day-to-day existence."

When I was in Fremont recently, I asked Matthew Thomas, who is forty-three and the town historian, what it had been like growing up there. He said it was nice but that he had been bored stiff. For entertainment, there were square dances, sledding, an annual carnival with a Beano tent, Vic Marcotte's Barber Shop and Poolroom. (These days, there are week-end grass drags out near Phil Peterson's farm, where the pasture is flat and firm enough to race snowmobiles in the summer.) When the Shaggs were growing up, the Fremont town hall hosted ham-and-bean suppers, boxing matches, dog shows, and spelling bees. The hall is an unadorned box of a building, but its performance theater is actually quite grand. It isn't used anymore, and someone has made off with the red velvet curtain, but it still has a somber dark stage and high-backed chairs, and the gravid air of a place where things might happen. In a quiet community like Fremont, in the dull hours between barn dances, a stage like that might give you big ideas.

Who Are Parents? (2:58)

Where else would Austin Wiggin have got the idea that his daughters should form a rock band? Neither he nor his wife, Annie, was musical; she much preferred television to music, and he, at most, fooled around with a Jew's harp. He wasn't a show-off, dying to be noticed—by all accounts he was an ornery loner who had little to do with other people in town. He was strict and old-fashioned, not a hippie manqué, not a rebel, very disapproving of long hair and short skirts. He was from a poor family and was raising a poor family—seven kids on a mill hand's salary—and music lessons and instruments for the girls were a daunting expense.

And yet the Shaggs were definitely his idea—or, more exactly, his mother's idea. Austin was terribly superstitious. His mother liked to tell fortunes. When he was young, she studied his palm and told him that in the future he would marry a strawberry blonde and would have two sons whom she would not live to see, and that his daughters would play in a band. Her auguries were borne out. Annie was a strawberry blonde, and she and Austin did have two sons after his mother died. It was left to Austin to fulfill the last of his mother's predictions, and when his daughters were old enough he told them they would be taking voice and music lessons and forming a band. There was no debate: His word was law, and his mother's prophecies were gospel. Besides, he chafed at his place in the Fremont social system. It wasn't so much that his girls would make him rich and raise him out of a mill hand's dreary métier; it was that they would prove that the Wiggin kids were not only different from but better than the folks in town.

The girls liked music—particularly Herman's Hermits, Ricky Nelson, and Dino, Desi & Billy—but until Austin foretold their futures they had not planned to become rock stars. They were shy, small-town teenagers who dreamed of growing up and getting married, having children, maybe becoming secretaries someday. Even now, they don't remember ever having dreamed of fame or of making music. But Austin pushed the girls into a new life. He named them the Shaggs, and told them that they were not going to attend the local high school, because he didn't want them traveling by bus and mixing with outsiders, and, more important, he wanted them to practice their music all day. He enrolled them in a Chicago mail-order outfit called American Home School, but he designed their schedule himself: Practice in the morning and afternoon, rehearse songs for him after dinner, and then do calisthenics and jumping jacks and leg lifts or practice for another hour before going to bed. The girls couldn't decide which was worse, the days when he made them do calisthenics or the days when he'd make them practice again before bed. In either case, their days seemed endless. The rehearsals were solemn, and Austin could be cutting. One song in particular, "Philosophy of the World," he claimed they never played right, and he would insist on hearing it again and again.

The Shaggs were not leading rock-and-roll lives. Austin forbade the girls to date before they were eighteen and discouraged most other friendships. They hadn't been popular kids, anyway—they didn't have the looks or the money or the savvy for it—but being in the band, and being home-schooled, set them apart even more. Friday nights, the family went out together to do grocery shopping. Sundays they went to church, and the girls practiced when they got home. Their world was even smaller than the small town of Fremont.

This was 1965. The Beatles had recently debuted on American television. The harmony between generations—at least, the harmony between the popular cultures of those generations—was busting. And yet the sweet, lumpish Wiggin sisters of Fremont, New Hampshire, were playing pop music at their father's insistence, in a band that he directed. Rebellion might have been driving most rock and roll, but in Fremont, Dot Wiggin was writing tributes to her mom and dad, with songs like "Who Are Parents?":

> *Parents are the ones who really care*
> *Who are parents?*
> *Parents are the ones who are always there*
> *Some kids think their parents are cruel*
> *Just because they want them to obey certain rules. . . .*
> *Parents do understand*
> *Parents do care*

Their first public performance was at a talent show in nearby Exeter, in 1968. The girls could barely play their instruments. They didn't think they were ready to appear in public, but Austin thought otherwise. When they opened, with a cover of a loping country song called "Wheels," people

in the audience threw soda cans at them and jeered. The girls were morti-
fied; Austin told them they just had to go home and practice more. If they
thought about quitting, they thought about it very privately, because
Austin would have had no truck with the idea; he was the kind of father
who didn't tolerate debate. They practiced more, did their calisthenics,
practiced more. Dot wrote the songs and the basic melodies, and she and
Betty worked together on the chords and rhythms. Helen made up her
drum parts on her own. The songs were misshapen pop tunes, full of shift-
ing time signatures and odd meters and abrupt key changes, with lyrics
about Dot's lost cat, Foot Foot, and her yearning for a sports car and how
much she liked to listen to the radio.

On Halloween, the Shaggs played at a local nursing home—featuring
Dot's song "It's Halloween" in their set—and got a polite response from
the residents. Soon afterward, Austin arranged for them to play at the Fremont town hall on Saturday nights. The girls worried about embarrassing
themselves, but at the same time they liked the fact that the shows allowed
them to escape the house and their bounded world, even if it was just for
a night. At that point, the girls had never even been to Boston, which was
only fifty miles away.

The whole family took part in the town hall shows. Austin III, the
older of the two sons who had been seen in Austin's future, played the
maracas; the other son, Robert, played the tambourine and did a drum
solo during intermission; Annie sold tickets and ran the refreshment stand.
A Pepsi truck would drop off the cases of soda at their green ranch house,
on Beede Road, every Friday night. Even though, according to one town
hall regular, most people found the Shaggs' music "painful and tortur-
ous," sometimes as many as a hundred kids showed up at the dances—
practically the whole adolescent population of Fremont. Then again, there
really wasn't much else to do in Fremont on a Saturday night. The audience danced and chatted, heckled the band, pelted the girls with junk,
ignored them, grudgingly appreciated them, mocked them.

The rumor around town was that Austin forced his daughters to be in
the band. There was even talk that he was inappropriately intimate with
them. When asked about it years later, Betty said that the talk wasn't true,
but Helen said that Austin once was intimate with her. Certainly, the family was folded in on itself; even Austin's father and Annie's mother, after
they were both widowed, became romantically involved and lived together
in a small house on the Wiggin property. The gossip and criticism only

made Austin more determined to continue with the band. It was, after all, his destiny.

I'm So Happy When You're Near (2:12)

"Through the years, this author as town historian has received numerous requests from fans around the country looking for information on 'The Shaggs' and the town they came from," Matthew Thomas wrote in his section about the band. "They definitely have a cult following, and deservedly so, because the Wiggin sisters worked hard and with humble resources to gain respect and acceptance as musicians. To their surprise they succeeded. After all, what other New Hampshire band . . . has a record album worth $300–$500?"

The Beatles' arrival in America piqued Austin. He disliked their moppy hair but was stirred by their success. If they could make it, why couldn't his girls? He wanted to see the Shaggs on television, and on concert tours. Things weren't happening quickly enough for him, though, and this made him unhappy. He started making tapes and home movies of the town hall shows. In March 1969, he took the girls to Fleetwood Studios, outside Boston, to make a record. According to the magazine *Cool and Strange Music!*, the studio engineer listened to the Shaggs rehearse and suggested that they weren't quite ready to record. But Austin insisted on going forward, reportedly telling the engineer, "I want to get them while they're hot." In the album's liner notes, Austin wrote:

> The Shaggs are real, pure, unaffected by outside influences. Their music is different, it is theirs alone. They believe in it, live it. . . . Of all contemporary acts in the world today, perhaps only the Shaggs do what others would like to do, and that is perform only what they believe in, what they feel, not what others think the Shaggs should feel. The Shaggs love you. . . . They will not change their music or style to meet the whims of a frustrated world. You should appreciate this because you know they are pure what more can you ask? . . . They are sisters and members of a large family where mutual respect and love for each other is at an unbelievable high . . . in an atmosphere which has encouraged them to develop their music unaffected by outside influences. They are happy people and love what they are doing. They do it because they love it.

The Wiggins returned to Fleetwood a few years later. By then, the girls were more proficient—they had practiced hundreds of hours since the first recording session—but their playing still inspired the engineer to write, "As the day progressed, I overcame my disappointment and started feeling sorry for this family paying sixty dollars an hour for studio time to record—this?"

I once asked Annie Wiggin if she thought Austin was a dreamer, and after sitting quietly for a few moments she said, "Well, probably. Must have been." If he was, it no doubt got harder to dream as the years went on. In 1973, the Fremont town supervisors decided to end the Saturday night concerts, because—well, no one really remembers why anymore, but there was talk of fights breaking out and drugs circulating in the crowd, and wear and tear on the town hall's wooden floors, although the girls scrubbed the scuff marks off every Sunday. Austin was furious, but the girls were relieved to end the grind of playing every Saturday night. They were getting older and had begun to chafe at his authority. Helen secretly married the first boyfriend she ever had—someone she had met at the dances. She continued living at home for three months after the wedding because she was too terrified to tell Austin what she had done. On the night that she finally screwed up the courage to give him the news, he got out a shotgun and went after her husband. The police joined in and told Helen to choose one man or the other. She left with her husband, and it was months before Austin spoke to her. She was twenty-eight years old.

The Shaggs continued to play at local fairs and at the nursing home. Austin still believed they were going to make it, and the band never broke up. It just shut down in 1975, on the day Austin, who was only forty-seven years old, died in bed of a massive heart attack—the same day, according to Helen, they had finally played a version of "Philosophy of the World" that he praised.

Philosophy of the World (2:56)

Shortly after the newest rerelease of the Shaggs' album, I went to New Hampshire to talk to the Wiggin sisters. A few years after Austin died, Betty and Dot married and moved to their own houses, and eventually Annie sold the house on Beede Road and moved to an apartment nearby. After a while, the house's new owner complained to people in town that Austin's ghost haunted the property. As soon as he could afford it, the new owner built something bigger and nicer farther back on the property, and allowed the Fremont Fire Department to burn the old Wiggin house down for fire-fighting practice.

Dot and Betty live a few miles down the road from Fremont, in the town of Epping, and Helen lives a few miles farther, in Exeter. They don't play music anymore. After Austin died, they sold much of their equipment and let their kids horse around with whatever was left. Dot hung on to her guitar for a while, just in case, but a few years ago she lent it to one of her brothers and hasn't gotten it back. Dot, who is now fifty, cleans houses for a living. Betty, forty-eight, was a school janitor until recently, when she took a better job, in the stockroom of a kitchen goods warehouse. Helen, who suffers from serious depression, lives on disability.

Dot and Betty arranged to meet me at Dunkin' Donuts, in Epping, and I went early so that I could read the local papers. It was a soggy, warm morning in southern New Hampshire; the sky was chalky, and the sun was as gray as gunmetal. Long tractor-trailers idled in the Dunkin' Donuts parking lot and then rumbled to life and lumbered onto the road. A few people were lined up to buy Pick 4 lottery tickets. The clerk behind the doughnut counter was discussing her wedding shower with a girl wearing a fuzzy halter top and platform sneakers. In the meantime, the coffee burned.

That day's Exeter *News-Letter* reported that the recreation commission's kickoff concert would feature Beatle Juice, a Beatles tribute band led by "Brad Delp, former front man of 'Boston,' one of the biggest rock bands New England has ever produced." Southern New Hampshire has regular outbreaks of tribute bands and reunion tours, as if it were in a time zone all its own, one in which the past keeps reappearing, familiar but essentially changed. Some time ago, Dot and her husband and their two sons went to see a revived version of Herman's Hermits. The concert was a huge disappointment for Dot, because her favorite Hermit, Peter (Herman) Noone, is no longer with the band, and because the Hermits' act now includes dirty jokes and crude references.

The Shaggs never made any money from their album until years later, when members of the band NRBQ heard "Philosophy of the World" and were thrilled by its strange innocence. NRBQ's own record label, Red Rooster, released records by such idiosyncratic bands as Jake & the Family Jewels, and they asked the Wiggins if they could compile a selection of songs from the group's two recording sessions. The resulting album, *The Shaggs' Own Thing*, includes the second session at Fleetwood Studios and some live and home recordings. Red Rooster's reissue of *Philosophy of the*

World was reviewed in *Rolling Stone* twice in 1980 and was described as "priceless and timeless." The articles introduced the Shaggs to the world.

Three years ago, Irwin Chusid, the author of the forthcoming book *Songs in the Key of Z: The Curious Universe of Outsider Music,* discovered that a company he worked with had bought the rights to the Shaggs' songs, which had been bundled with other obscure music-publishing rights. Chusid wanted to reissue *Philosophy of the World* as it was in 1969, with the original cover and the original song sequence. He suggested the project to Joe Mozian, a vice president of marketing at RCA Victor, who had never heard the band. Mozian was interested in unusual ventures; he had just released some Belgian lounge music from the sixties, which featured such songs as "The Frère Jacques Conga." Mozian says, "The Shaggs were beyond my wildest dreams. I couldn't comprehend that music like that existed. It's so basic and innocent, the way the music business used to be. Their timing, musically, was . . . fascinating. Their lyrics were . . . amazing. It is kind of a bad record—that's so obvious, it's a given. But it absolutely intrigued me, the idea that people would make a record playing the way they do."

The new *Philosophy of the World* was released last March. Even though the record is being played on college radio stations and the reviews have been enthusiastic and outsider art has been in vogue for several years, RCA Victor has sold only a few thousand copies of *Philosophy* so far. Mozian admits that he is disappointed. "I'm not sure why it hasn't sold," he says. "I think people are a little afraid of having the Shaggs in their record collections."

While I was waiting for the Wiggins, I went out to my car to listen to the CD again. I especially love the song "Philosophy of the World," with its wrought-up, clattering guitars and chugging, cockeyed rhythm and the cheerfully pessimistic lyrics about how people are never happy with what they have. I was right in the middle of the verse about how rich people want what poor people have, and how girls with long hair want short hair, when Betty pulled up and opened the door of my car. As soon as she recognized the song, she gasped, "Do you like this?" I said yes, and she said, "God, it's horrible." She shook her head. Her hair no longer rippled down to her waist and no longer had a shelf of shaggy bangs that touched the bridge of her nose; it was short and springy, just to the nape of her neck, the hair of a grown woman without time to bother too much about her appearance.

A few minutes later, Dot drove in. She was wearing a flowered housedress and a Rugrats watch, and had a thin silver band on her thumb. On her middle finger was a chunky ring that spelled "Elvis" in block letters. She and Betty have the same deep blue eyes and thrusting chin and tiny teeth, but Dot's hair is still long and wavy, and even now you can picture her as the girl with a guitar on the cover of the 1969 album. She asked what we were listening to. "What do you think?" Betty said to her. "The *Shaggs*." They both listened for another minute, so rapt that it seemed as if they had never heard the song before. "I never play the record on my own anymore," Dot said. "My son Matt plays it sometimes. He likes it. I don't think I get sentimental when I hear it—I just don't think about playing it."

"I wonder where I put my copies of the album," Betty said. "I know I have one copy of the CD. I think I have some of the albums somewhere."

The Wiggins have received fan letters from Switzerland and Texas, been interviewed for a documentary film, and inspired a dozen Web sites, bulletin boards, and forums on the Internet, but it's hard to see how this could matter much, once their childhood had been scratched out and rewritten as endless days of practicing guitar, and their father, who believed that their success was fated, died before they got any recognition. They are wise enough to realize that some of the long-standing interest in their music is ironic—sheer marvel that anything so unpolished could ever have made it onto a record. "We might have felt special at the time we made the record," Dot said uncertainly. "The really cool part, to me, is that it's thirty years later and we're still talking about it. I never thought we'd really be famous. I never thought we'd even be as famous as we are. I met a girl at the Shop 'n Save the other day who used to come to the dances, and she said she wanted to go out now and buy the CD. And I saw a guy at a fair recently and talked to him for about half an hour about the Shaggs. And people call and ask if they can come up and meet us—that's amazing to me."

Yet when I asked Dot and Betty for the names of people who could describe the town hall shows, they couldn't think of any for days. "We missed out on a lot," Betty said. "I can't say we didn't have fun, but we missed a social life, we missed out on having friends, we missed everything except our music and our exercises. I just didn't think we were good enough to be playing in concerts and making records. At one point, I thought maybe we would make it, but it wasn't really my fantasy." Her fantasy, she said, was to climb into a car with plenty of gas and just drive—not to get anywhere in particular, just to go.

We ordered our coffee and doughnuts and sat at a table near the window. Betty had her two-year-old and eight-month-old granddaughters,

Makayla and Kelsey, with her, and Makayla had squirmed away from the table and was playing with a plastic sign that read CAUTION WET FLOOR. Betty often takes care of her grandchildren for her son and her daughter-in-law. Things are tight. The little windfall from their recordings helps, especially since Dot's husband is in poor health and can't work, and Betty's husband was killed in a motorcycle accident six years ago, and Helen is unable to work because of her depression.

For the Wiggins, music was never simple and carefree, and it still isn't. Helen doesn't go out much, so I spoke with her on the phone, and she told me that she hadn't played music since her father died but that country and western echoed in her head all the time, maddeningly so, and so loud that it made it hard for her to talk. When I asked Betty if she still liked music, she thought for a moment and then said that her husband's death had drawn her to country music. Whenever she feels bereft, she sings broken-hearted songs along with the radio. Just then, Makayla began hollering. Betty shushed her and said, "She really does have some kind of voice." A look flickered across her face. "I think, well, maybe she'll take voice lessons someday."

Dot is the only one who is still attached to her father's dream. She played the handbells in her church choir until recently, when she began taking care of one of Helen's children in addition to her own two sons and no longer had the time. She said that she's been writing lyrics for the last two years and hopes to finish them, and to compose the music for them. In the meantime, Terry Adams, of NRBQ, says he has enough material left from the Fleetwood Studio recording sessions for a few more CDs, and he has films of the town hall concerts that he plans to synchronize with sound. The Shaggs, thirty years late, may yet make it big, the way Austin saw it in his dreams. But even that might not have been enough to sate him. The Shaggs must have known this all along. In "Philosophy of the World," the song they never could play to his satisfaction, they sang:

> *It doesn't matter what you do*
> *It doesn't matter what you say*
> *There will always be one who wants things the opposite way*
> *We do our best, we try to please*
> *But we're like the rest we're never at ease*
> *You can never please*
> *Anybody*
> *In this world.*

SHOW DOG

*I*F I WERE A BITCH, I'D BE IN LOVE WITH BIFF
Truesdale. Biff is perfect. He's friendly, good looking, rich,
famous, and in excellent physical condition. He almost
never drools. He's not afraid of commitment. He wants
children—actually, he already has children and wants a lot
more. He works hard and is a consummate professional,
but he also knows how to have fun.

What Biff likes most is food and sex. This makes him
sound boorish, which he is not—he's just elemental. Food
he likes even better than sex. His favorite things to eat are
cookies, mints, and hotel soap, but he will eat just about
anything. Richard Krieger, a friend of Biff's who occasionally drives him to appointments, said not long ago, "When
we're driving on I-95, we'll usually pull over at McDonald's. Even if Biff is napping, he always wakes up when
we're getting close. I get him a few plain hamburgers with
buns—no ketchup, no mustard, and no pickles. He loves
hamburgers. I don't get him his own French fries, but if I
get myself fries I always flip a few for him into the back."

If you're ever around Biff while you're eating something he wants to taste—cold roast beef, a Wheatables cracker, chocolate, pasta, aspirin, whatever—he will stare at you across the pleated bridge of his nose and let his eyes sag and his lips tremble and allow a little bead of drool to percolate at the edge of his mouth until you feel so crummy that you give him some. This routine puts the people who know him in a quandary, because Biff has to watch his weight. Usually, he is as skinny as Kate Moss, but he can put on three pounds in an instant. The holidays can be tough. He takes time off at Christmas and spends it at home, in Attleboro, Massachusetts, where there's a lot of food around and no pressure and no schedule and it's easy to eat all day. The extra weight goes to his neck. Luckily, Biff likes working out. He runs for fifteen or twenty minutes twice a day, either outside or on his Jog-Master. When he's feeling heavy, he runs longer, and skips snacks, until he's back down to his ideal weight of seventy-five pounds.

Biff is a boxer. He is a show dog—he performs under the name Champion Hi-Tech's Arbitrage—and so looking good is not mere vanity; it's business. A show dog's career is short, and judges are unforgiving. Each breed is judged by an explicit standard for appearance and temperament, and then there's the incalculable element of charisma in the ring. When a show dog is fat or lazy or sullen, he doesn't win; when he doesn't win, he doesn't enjoy the ancillary benefits of being a winner, like appearing as the celebrity spokesmodel on packages of Pedigree Mealtime with Lamb and Rice, which Biff will be doing soon, or picking the best-looking bitches and charging them six hundred dollars or so for his sexual favors, which Biff does three or four times a month. Another ancillary benefit of being a winner is that almost every single weekend of the year, as he travels to shows around the country, he gets to hear people applaud for him and yell his name and tell him what a good boy he is, which is something he seems to enjoy at least as much as eating a bar of soap.

PRETTY SOON, Biff won't have to be so vigilant about his diet. After he appears at the Westminster Kennel Club's show, this week, he will retire from active show life and work full time as a stud. It's a good moment for him to retire. Last year, he won more shows than any other boxer, and also more than any other dog in the purebred category known as Working Dogs, which also includes Akitas, Alaskan malamutes, Bernese mountain dogs, bullmastiffs, Doberman pinschers, giant schnauzers, Great Danes, Great Pyrenees, komondors, kuvaszok, mastiffs, Newfoundlands, Portuguese water dogs, Rottweilers, Saint Bernards, Samoyeds, Siberian huskies, and standard schnauzers. Boxers were named for their habit of standing on their hind legs and punching with their front paws when they fight. They were originally bred to be chaperons—to look forbidding while being pleasant to spend time with. Except for show dogs like Biff, most boxers lead a life of relative leisure. Last year at Westminster, Biff was named Best Boxer and Best Working Dog, and he was a serious contender for Best in Show, the highest honor any show dog can hope for. He is a contender to win his breed and group again this year, and is a serious contender once again for Best in Show, although the odds are against him, because this year's judge is known as a poodle person.

Biff is four years old. He's in his prime. He could stay on the circuit for a few more years, but by stepping aside now he is making room for his sons Trent and Rex, who are just getting into the business, and he's leaving while he's still on top. He'll also spend less time in airplanes, which is the one part of show life he doesn't like, and more time with his owners, William and Tina Truesdale, who might be persuaded to waive his snacking rules.

Biff has a short, tight coat of fox-colored fur, white feet and ankles, and a patch of white on his chest roughly the shape of Maine. His muscles are plainly sketched under his skin, but he isn't bulgy. His face is turned up and pushed in, and has a dark mask, spongy lips, a wishbone-shaped white blaze, and the earnest and slightly careworn expression of a small-town mayor. Someone once told me that he thought Biff looked a little bit like President Clinton. Biff's face is his fortune. There are plenty of people who like boxers with bigger bones and a stockier body and taller shoulders—boxers who look less like marathon runners and more like weight lifters—but almost everyone agrees that Biff has a nearly perfect head.

"Biff's head is his father's," William Truesdale, a veterinarian, explained to me one day. We were in the Truesdales' living room in Attleboro, which overlooks acres of hilly fenced-in fields. Their house is a big, sunny ranch with a stylish pastel kitchen and boxerabilia on every wall. The Truesdales don't have children, but at any given moment they share their quarters with at least a half dozen dogs. If you watch a lot of dog food commercials, you may have seen William—he's the young, handsome, dark-haired veterinarian declaring his enthusiasm for Pedigree Mealtime while his boxers gallop around.

"Biff has a masculine but elegant head," William went on. "It's not too wet around the muzzle. It's just about ideal. Of course, his forte is right here." He pointed to Biff's withers, and explained that Biff's shoulder-humerus articulation was optimally angled, and bracketed his superb brisket and forelegs, or something like that. While William was talking, Biff climbed onto the couch and sat on top of Brian, his companion, who was hiding under a pillow. Brian is an English toy Prince Charles spaniel who is about the size of a teakettle and has the composure of a humming-bird. As a young competitor, he once bit a judge—a mistake Tina Trues-dale says he made because at the time he had been going through a little mind problem about being touched. Brian, whose show name is Champion Cragmor's Hi-Tech Man, will soon go back on the circuit, but now he mostly serves as Biff's regular escort. When Biff sat on him, he started to quiver. Biff batted at him with his front leg. Brian gave him an adoring look.

"Biff's body is from his mother," Tina was saying. "She had a lot of substance."

"She was even a little extreme for a bitch," William said. "She was rather buxom. I would call her zaftig."

"Biff's father needed that, though," Tina said. "His name was Tailo, and he was fabulous. Tailo had a very beautiful head, but he was a bit fine, I think. A bit slender."

"Even a little feminine," William said, with feeling. "Actually, he would have been a really awesome bitch."

THE FIRST TIME I met Biff, he sniffed my pants, stood up on his hind legs and stared into my face, and then trotted off to the kitchen, where someone was cooking macaroni. We were in Westbury, Long Island, where Biff lives with Kimberly Pastella, a twenty-nine-year-old professional han-dler, when he's working. Last year, Kim and Biff went to at least one show every weekend. If they drove, they took Kim's van. If they flew, she went coach and he went cargo. They always shared a hotel room.

While Kim was telling me all this, I could hear Biff rummaging around in the kitchen. "Biffers!" Kim called out. Biff jogged back into the room with a phony look of surprise on his face. His tail was ticking back and forth. It is cropped so that it is about the size and shape of a half-smoked stogie. Kim said that there was a bitch downstairs who had been sent from Pennsylvania to be bred to one of Kim's other clients, and that Biff could smell her and was a little out of sorts. "Let's go," she said to him. "Biff, let's go jog." We went into the garage, where a treadmill was set up with Biff's collar suspended from a metal arm. Biff hopped on and held his head out so that Kim could buckle his collar. As soon as she leaned toward the power switch, he started to jog. His nails clicked a light tattoo on the rubber belt.

Except for a son of his named Biffle, Biff gets along with everybody. Matt Stander, one of the founders of *Dog News,* said recently, "Biff is just very, very personable. He has a je ne sais quoi that's really special. He gives of himself all the time." One afternoon, the Truesdales were telling me about the psychology that went into making Biff who he is. "Boxers are real communicators," William was saying. "We had to really take that into consideration in his upbringing. He seems tough, but there's a fragile ego inside there. The profound reaction and hurt when you would raise your voice at him was really something."

"I *made* him," Tina said. "I made Biff who he is. He had an overbearing personality when he was small, but I consider that a prerequisite for a great performer. He had such an *attitude*! He was like this miniature *man*!" She shimmied her shoulders back and forth and thrust out her chin. She is a dainty, chic woman with wide-set eyes and the neck of a ballerina. She grew up on a farm in Costa Rica, where dogs were considered just another form of livestock. In 1987, William got her a Rottweiler for a watchdog, and a boxer, because he had always loved boxers, and Tina decided to dabble with them in shows. Now she makes a monogrammed Christmas stocking for each animal in their house, and she watches the tape of Biff winning at Westminster approximately once a week. "Right from the beginning, I made Biff think he was the most fabulous dog in the world," Tina said.

"He doesn't take after me very much," William said. "I'm more of a golden retriever."

"Oh, he has my nature," Tina said. "I'm very strong-willed. I'm brassy. And Biff is an egotistical, self-centered, selfish person. He thinks he's very important and special, and he doesn't like to share."

BIFF IS PRICELESS. If you beg the Truesdales to name a figure, they might say that Biff is worth around a hundred thousand dollars, but they will also point out that a Japanese dog fancier recently handed Tina a blank check for Biff. (She immediately threw it away.) That check notwithstanding, campaigning a show dog is a money-losing proposition for the owner.

A good handler gets three or four hundred dollars a day, plus travel expenses, to show a dog, and any dog aiming for the top will have to be on the road at least a hundred days a year. A dog photographer charges hundreds of dollars for a portrait, and a portrait is something that every serious owner commissions, and then runs as a full-page ad in several dog show magazines. Advertising a show dog is standard procedure if you want your dog or your presence on the show circuit to get well known. There are also such ongoing show dog expenses as entry fees, hair-care products, food, health care, and toys. Biff's stud fee is six hundred dollars. Now that he will not be at shows, he can be bred several times a month. Breeding him would have been a good way for him to make money in the past, except that whenever the Truesdales were enthusiastic about a mating they bartered Biff's service for the pick of the litter. As a result, they now have more Biff puppies than Biff earnings. "We're doing this for posterity," Tina says. "We're doing it for the good of all boxers. You simply can't think about the cost."

On a recent Sunday, I went to watch Biff work at one of the last shows he would attend before his retirement. The show was sponsored by the Lehigh Valley Kennel Club and was held in a big, windy field house on the campus of Lehigh University, in Bethlehem, Pennsylvania. The parking lot was filled with motor homes pasted with life-size decals of dogs. On my way to the field house, I passed someone walking an Afghan hound wearing a snood, and someone else wiping down a Saluki with a Flintstones beach towel. Biff was napping in his crate—a fancy-looking brass box with bright silver hardware and with luggage tags from Delta, USAir, and Continental hanging on the door. Dogs in crates can look woeful, but Biff actually likes spending time in his. When he was growing up, the Truesdales decided they would never reprimand him, because of his delicate ego. Whenever he got rambunctious, Tina wouldn't scold him—she would just invite him to sit in his crate and have a time-out.

On this particular day, Biff was in the crate with a bowl of water and a gourmet Oinkeroll. The boxer judging was already over. There had been thirty-three in competition, and Biff had won Best in Breed. Now he had to wait for several hours while the rest of the working breeds had their competitions. Later, the breed winners would square off for Best in Working Group. Then, around dinnertime, the winner of the Working Group and the winners of the other groups—sporting dogs, hounds, terriers, toys, non-sporting dogs, and herding dogs—would compete for Best in Show. Biff was stretched out in the crate with his head resting on his forelegs, so that his lips draped over his ankle like a café curtain. He looked bored. Next to his crate, several wire-haired fox terriers were standing on tables getting their faces shampooed, and beyond them a Chihuahua in a pink crate was gnawing on its door latch. Two men in white shirts and dark pants walked by eating hot dogs. One of them was gesturing and exclaiming, "I thought I had good dachshunds! I thought I had *great* dachshunds!"

Biff sighed and closed his eyes.

While he was napping, I pawed through his suitcase. In it was some dog food; towels; an electric nail grinder; a whisker trimmer; a wool jacket in a lively pattern that looked sort of Southwestern; an apron; some antibiotics; baby oil; coconut-oil coat polish; boxer chalk powder; a copy of *Dog News;* an issue of *ShowSight* magazine, featuring an article subtitled "Frozen Semen—Boon or Bain?" and a two-page ad for Biff, with a full-page, full-color photograph of him and Kim posed in front of a human-size toy soldier; a spray bottle of fur cleanser; another Oinkeroll; a rope ball; and something called a Booda Bone. The apron was for Kim. The baby oil was to make Biff's nose and feet glossy when he went into the ring. Boxer chalk powder—as distinct from, say, West Highland–white-terrier chalk powder—is formulated to cling to short, sleek boxer hair and whiten boxers' white markings. Unlike some of the other dogs, Biff did not need to travel with a blow dryer, curlers, nail polish, or detangling combs, but, unlike some less sought-after dogs, he did need a schedule. He was registered for a show in Chicago the next day, and had an appointment at a clinic in Connecticut the next week to make a semen deposit, which had been ordered by a breeder in Australia. Also, he had a date that same week with a bitch named Diana who was about to go into heat. Biff has to book his stud work after shows, so that it doesn't interfere with his performance. Tina Truesdale told me that this was typical of all athletes, but everyone who knows Biff is quick to comment on how professional he is as a stud. Richard Krieger, who was going to be driving Biff to his appointment at the clinic in Connecticut, once told me that some studs want to goof around and take forever but Biff is very businesslike. "Bing, bang, boom," Krieger said. "He's in, he's out."

"No wasting of time," said Nancy Krieger, Richard's wife. "Bing, bang, boom. He gets the job done."

After a while, Kim showed up and asked Biff if he needed to go outside. Then a handler who is a friend of Kim's came by. He was wearing a black-and-white houndstooth suit and was brandishing a comb and a can of hair spray. While they were talking, I leafed through the show catalog and read some of the dogs' names to Biff, just for fun—names like Aleph Godol's Umbra Von Carousel and Champion Spanktown Little Lu Lu and Ranchlake's Energizer O'Motown and Champion Beaverbrook Buster V Broadhead. Biff decided that he did want to go out, so Kim opened the crate. He stepped out and stretched and yawned like a cat, and then he suddenly stood up and punched me in the chest. An announcement calling for all toys to report to their ring came over the loudspeaker. Kim's friend waved the can of hair spray in the direction of a little white poodle shivering on a table a few yards away and exclaimed, "Oh, no! I lost track of time! I have to go! I have to spray up my miniature!"

TYPICALLY, DOG CONTESTANTS first circle the ring together; then each contestant poses individually for the judge, trying to look perfect as the judge lifts its lips for a dental exam, rocks its hindquarters, and strokes its back and thighs. The judge at Lehigh was a chesty, mustached man with watery eyes and a solemn expression. He directed the group with hand signals that made him appear to be roping cattle. The Rottweiler looked good, and so did the giant schnauzer. I started to worry. Biff had a distracted look on his face, as if he'd forgotten something back at the house. Finally, it was his turn. He pranced to the center of the ring. The judge stroked him and then waved his hand in a circle and stepped out of the way. Several people near me began clapping. A flashbulb flared. Biff held his position for a moment, and then he and Kim bounded across the ring, his feet moving so fast that they blurred into an oily sparkle, even though he really didn't have very far to go. He got a cookie when he finished the performance, and another a few minutes later, when the judge wagged his finger at him, indicating that Biff had won again.

You can't help wondering whether Biff will experience the depressing letdown that retired competitors face. At least he has a lot of stud work to look forward to, although William Truesdale complained to me once that the Truesdales' standards for a mate are so high—they require a clean bill of health and a substantial pedigree—that "there just aren't that many right bitches out there." Nonetheless, he and Tina are optimistic that Biff will find enough suitable mates to become one of the most influential boxer sires of all time. "We'd like to be remembered as the boxer people of the nineties," Tina said. "Anyway, we can't wait to have him home."

"We're starting to campaign Biff's son Rex," William said. "He's been living in Mexico, and he's a Mexican champion, and now he's ready to take on the American shows. He's very promising. He has a fabulous rear."

Just then, Biff, who had been on the couch, jumped down and began pacing. "Going somewhere, honey?" Tina asked.

He wanted to go out, so Tina opened the back door, and Biff ran into the backyard. After a few minutes, he noticed a ball on the lawn. The ball was slippery and a little too big to fit in his mouth, but he kept scrambling and trying to grab it. In the meantime, the Truesdales and I sat, stayed for a moment, fetched ourselves turkey sandwiches, and then curled up on the couch. Half an hour passed, and Biff was still happily pursuing the ball. He probably has a very short memory, but he acted as if it was the most fun he'd ever had.

THE MAUI SURFER GIRLS

*T*HE MAUI SURFER GIRLS LOVE ONE AN-other's hair. It is awesome hair, long and bleached by the sun, and it falls over their shoulders straight, like water, or in squiggles, like seaweed, or in waves. They are forever playing with it—yanking it up into ponytails, or twisting handfuls and securing them with chopsticks or pencils, or dividing it as carefully as you would divide a pile of coins and then weaving it into tight yellow plaits. Not long ago I was on the beach in Maui watching the surfer girls surf, and when they came out of the water they sat in a row facing the ocean, and each girl took the hair of the girl in front of her and combed it with her fingers and crisscrossed it into braids. The Maui surfer girls even love the kind of hair that I dreaded when I was their age, fourteen or so—they love wild, knotty, bright hair, as big and stiff as carpet, the most un-straight, un-sleek, un-ordinary hair you could imagine, and they can love it, I suppose, because when you are young and on top of the world you can love anything you want, and just the fact that you love it makes it cool and fabulous. A Maui surfer girl named Gloria Madden has that kind of hair—thick red corkscrews striped orange and silver from the sun, hair that if you weren't beautiful and fearless you'd consider an affliction that you would try to iron flat or stuff under a hat. One afternoon I was driving two of the girls to Blockbuster Video in Kahului. It was the day before a surfing competition, and the girls were going to spend the night at their coach's house up the coast so they'd be ready for the contest at dawn. On contest nights, they fill their time by eating a lot of food and watching hours of surf videos, but on this particular occasion they decided they needed to rent a movie, too, in case they found themselves with ten or twenty seconds of unoccupied time. On our way to the video store, the girls told me they admired my rental car and said that they thought rental cars totally ripped and that they each wanted to get one. My car, which until then I had sort of hated, suddenly took on a glow. I asked what else they would have if they could have anything in the world. They thought for a moment, and then the girl in the backseat said, "A moped and thousands of new clothes. You know, stuff like thousands of bathing suits and thousands of new board shorts."

"I'd want a Baby-G watch and new flip-flops, and one of those cool sports bras like the one Iris just got," the other said. She was in the front passenger seat, barefoot, sand caked, twirling her hair into a French knot. It was a half-cloudy day with weird light that made the green Hawaiian hills look black and the ocean look like zinc. It was also, in fact, a school day, but these were the luckiest of all the surfer girls because they are home-schooled so that they can surf any time at all. The girl making the French knot stopped knotting. "Oh, and also," she said, "I'd really *definitely* want crazy hair like Gloria's."

The girl in the backseat leaned forward and said, "Yeah, and hair like Gloria's, for sure."

A LOT OF the Maui surfer girls live in Hana, the little town at the end of the Hana Highway, a fraying thread of a road that winds from Kahului, Maui's primary city, over a dozen deep gulches and dead-drop waterfalls and around the backside of the Haleakala Crater to the village. Hana is far away and feels even farther. It is only fifty-five miles from Kahului, but the biggest maniac in the world couldn't make the drive in less than two hours. There is nothing much to do in Hana except wander through the screw pines and the candlenut trees or go surfing. There is no mall in Hana, no Starbucks, no shoe store, no Hello Kitty store, no movie theater—just trees, bushes, flowers, and gnarly surf that breaks rough at the bottom of the rocky beach. Before women were encouraged to surf, the girls in Hana must have been unbelievably bored. Lucky for these Hana girls, surfing has changed. In the sixties, Joyce Hoffman became one of the first female surf aces, and she was followed by Rell Sunn and Jericho Poppler in the seventies and Frieda Zamba in the eighties and Lisa Andersen in this decade, and thousands of girls and women followed by example. In fact, the surfer girls of this generation have never known a time in their lives when some woman champion wasn't ripping surf.

The Hana girls dominate Maui surfing these days. Theory has it that they grow up riding such mangy waves that they're ready for anything. Also, they are exposed to few distractions and can practically live in the water. Crazy-haired Gloria is not one of the Hana girls. She grew up near the city, in Haiku, where there were high school race riots—Samoans beating on Filipinos, Hawaiians beating on Anglos—and the mighty pull of the mall at Kaahumanu Center. By contrast, a Hana girl can have herself an almost pure surf adolescence.

One afternoon I went to Hana to meet Theresa McGregor, one of the best surfers in town. I missed our rendezvous and was despairing because Theresa lived with her mother, two brothers, and sister in a one-room shack with no phone and I couldn't think of how I'd find her. There is one store in Hana, amazingly enough called the General Store, where you can buy milk and barbecue sauce and snack bags of dried cuttlefish; once I realized I'd missed Theresa I went into the store because there was no other place to go. The cashier looked kindly, so I asked whether by any wild chance she knew a surfer girl named Theresa McGregor. I had not yet come to appreciate what a small town Hana really was. "She was just in here a minute ago," the cashier said. "Usually around this time of the day she's on her way to the beach to go surfing." She dialed the McGregors' neighbor—she knew the number by heart—to find out which beach Theresa had gone to. A customer overheard the cashier talking to me, and she came over and added that she'd just seen Theresa down at Ko'ki beach and that Theresa's mom, Angie, was there too, and that some of the other Hana surfer girls would probably be down any minute but they had a History Day project due at the end of the week so they might not be done yet at school.

I went down to Ko'ki. Angie McGregor was indeed there, and she pointed out Theresa bobbing in the swells. There were about a dozen other people in the water, kids mostly. A few other surfer parents were up on the grass with Angie—fathers with hairy chests and ponytails and saddle-leather sandals, and mothers wearing board shorts and bikini tops, passing around snacks of unpeeled carrots and whole-wheat cookies and sour cream Pringles—and even as they spoke to one another, they had their eyes fixed on the ocean, watching their kids, who seemed like they were a thousand miles away, taking quick rides on the tattered waves.

After a few minutes, Theresa appeared up on dry land. She was a big, broad-shouldered girl, sixteen years old, fierce faced, somewhat feline, and quite beautiful. Water was streaming off of her, out of her shorts, out of her long hair, which was plastered to her shoulders. The water made it look inky, but you could still tell that an inch from her scalp her hair had been stripped of all color by the sun. In Haiku, where the McGregors lived until four years ago, Theresa had been a superstar soccer player, but Hana was too small to support a soccer league, so after they moved there Theresa first devoted herself to becoming something of a juvenile delinquent and then gave that up for surfing. Her first triumph came right away, in 1996, when she won the open women's division at the Maui Hana Mango competition. She was one of the few fortunate amateur surfer girls who had sponsors. She got free boards from Matt Kinoshita, her coach, who owns and designs Kazuma Surfboards; clothes from Honolua Surf Company; board leashes and bags from Da Kine Hawaii; skateboards from Flexdex. Boys who surfed got a lot more for free. Even a little bit of sponsorship made the difference between surfing and not surfing. As rich a life as it seemed, among the bougainvillea and the green hills and the passionflowers of Hana, there was hardly any money. In the past few years the Hawaiian economy had sagged terribly, and Hana had never had much of an economy to begin with. Last year, the surfer moms in town held a fundraiser bake sale to send Theresa and two Hana boys to the national surfing competition in California.

Theresa said she was done surfing for the day. "The waves totally suck now," she said to Angie. "They're just real trash." They talked for a moment and agreed that Theresa should leave in the morning and spend the next day or two with her coach, Matt, at his house in Haiku, to prepare for the Hawaiian Amateur Surf Association contest that weekend at Ho'okipa Beach near Kahului. Logistics became the topic. One of the biggest riddles facing a surfer girl, especially a surfer girl in far-removed Hana, is how to get from point A to point B, particularly when carrying a large surfboard. The legal driving age in Hawaii is fifteen, but the probable car ownership age, unless you're wealthy, is much beyond that; also, it seemed that nearly every surfer kid I met in Maui lived in a single-parent, single- or no-car household in which spare drivers and vehicles were rare. I was planning to go back around the volcano anyway to see the contest, so I said I'd take Theresa and another surfer, Lilia Boerner, with me, and someone else would make it from Hana to Haiku with their boards. That night I met Theresa, Angie, and Lilia and a few of their surfer friends at a take-out shop in town, and then I went to the room I'd rented at Joe's Rooming House. I stayed up late reading about how Christian missionaries had banned surfing when they got to Hawaii in the late 1800s, but how by 1908 general longing for the sport overrode spiritual censure and surfing resumed. I dozed off with the history book in my lap and the hotel television tuned to a Sprint ad showing a Hawaiian man and his granddaughter running hand in hand into the waves.

THE NEXT MORNING I met Lilia and Theresa at Ko'ki Beach at eight, after they'd had a short session on the waves. When I arrived they were standing under a monkeypod tree beside a stack of backpacks. Both of them were soaking wet, and I realized then that a surfer is always in one of two conditions: wet or about to be wet. Also, they are almost always dressed in something that can go directly into the water: halter tops, board shorts, bikini tops, jeans. Lilia was twelve and a squirt, with a sweet, powdery face and round hazel eyes and golden fuzz on her arms and legs. She was younger and much smaller than Theresa, less plainly athletic but very game. Like Theresa, she was home-schooled, so she could surf all the time. So far Lilia was sponsored by a surf shop and by Matt Kinoshita's Kazuma Surfboards. She has a twin brother who was also a crafty surfer, but a year ago the two of them came upon their grandfather after he suffered a fatal tractor accident, and the boy hadn't competed since. Their family owned a large and prosperous organic fruit farm in Hana. I once asked Lilia if it was fun to live on a farm. "No," she said abruptly. "Too much fruit."

We took a back road from Hana to Haiku, as if the main road wasn't bad enough. The road edged around the back of the volcano, through sere yellow hills. The girls talked about surfing and about one surfer girl's mom, whom they described as a full bitch, and a surfer's dad, who according to Theresa "was a freak and a half because he took too much acid and he tweaked." I wondered if they had any other hobbies besides surfing. Lilia said she used to study hula.

"Is it fun?"

"Not if you have a witch for a teacher, like I did," she said. "Just *screaming* and *yelling* at us all the time. I'll never do hula again. Surfing's cooler, anyway."

"You're the man, Lilia," Theresa said tartly. "Hey, how close are we to Grandma's Coffee Shop? I'm starving." Surfers are always starving. They had eaten breakfast before they surfed; it was now only an hour or two later, and they were hungry again. They favor breakfast cereal, teriyaki chicken, French fries, rice, ice cream, candy, and a Hawaiian specialty called Spam Masubi, which is a rice ball topped with a hunk of Spam and seaweed. If they suffered from the typical teenage girl obsession with their weight, they didn't talk about it and they didn't act like it. They were so active that whatever they ate probably melted away.

"We love staying at Matt's," Lilia said, "because he always takes us to Taco Bell." We came around the side of a long hill and stopped at Grandma's. Lilia ordered a garden burger and Theresa had an "I'm Hungry" sandwich with turkey, ham, and avocado. It was 10:30 A.M. As she was eating, Lilia said, "You know, the Olympics are going to have surfing, either in the year 2000 or 2004, for sure."

"I'm so on that, dude," Theresa said. "If I can do well in the nationals this year, then . . ." She swallowed the last of her sandwich. She told me that eventually she wanted to become an ambulance driver, and I could picture her doing it, riding on dry land the same waves of adrenaline that she rides now. I spent a lot of time trying to picture where these girls might be in ten years. Hardly any are likely to make it as pro surfers—even though women have made a place for themselves in pro surfing, the number who really make it is still small, and even though the Hana girls rule Maui surfing, the island's soft-shell waves and easygoing competitions have produced very few world-class surfers in recent years. It doesn't seem to matter to them. At various cultural moments, surfing has appeared as the embodiment of everything cool and wild and free; this is one of those moments. To be a girl surfer is even cooler, wilder, and more modern than being a guy surfer: Surfing has always been such a male sport that for a man to do it doesn't defy any perceived ideas; to be a girl surfer is to be all that surfing represents, *plus* the extra charge of being a girl in a tough guy's domain. To be a surfer girl in a cool place like Hawaii is perhaps the apogee of all that is cool and wild and modern and sexy and defiant. The Hana girls, therefore, exist at that highest point—the point where being brave, tan, capable, and independent, and having a real reason to wear all those surf-inspired clothes that other girls wear for fashion, is what mat-

ters completely. It is, though, just a moment. It must be hard to imagine
an ordinary future and something other than a lunar calendar to consider
if you've grown up in a small town in Hawaii, surfing all day and night,
spending half your time on sand, thinking in terms of point breaks and barrels and roundhouse cutbacks. Or maybe they don't think about it at all.
Maybe these girls are still young enough and in love enough with their lives
that they have no special foreboding about their futures, no uneasy pre-
sentiment that the kind of life they are leading now might eventually have
to end.

MATT KINOSHITA LIVES in a fresh, sunny ranch at the top of a hill in
Haiku. The house has a big living room with a fold-out couch and plenty
of floor space. Often, one or two or ten surfer girls camp in his living room
because they are in a competition that starts at seven the next morning,
or because they are practicing intensively and it is too far to go back and
forth from Hana, or because they want to plow through Matt's stacks of
surfing magazines and Matt's library of surfing videos and Matt's piles of
water sports clothing catalogs. Many of the surfer girls I met didn't live
with their fathers, or in some cases didn't even have relationships with
their fathers, so sometimes, maybe, they stayed at Matt's just because they
were in the mood to be around a concerned older male. Matt was in his
late twenties. As a surfer he was talented enough to compete on the world
tour but had decided to skip it in favor of an actual life with his wife,
Annie, and their baby son, Chaz. Now he was one of the best surfboard
shapers on Maui, a coach, and head of a construction company with his
dad. He sponsored a few grown-up surfers and still competed himself, but
his preoccupation was with kids. *Surfing* magazine once asked him what he
liked most about being a surfboard shaper, and he answered, "Always
being around stoked groms!" He coached a stoked-grom boys' team as well
as a stoked-grom girls' team. The girls' team was an innovation. There had
been no girls' surfing team on Maui before Matt established his three years
ago. There was no money in it for him—it actually cost him many thousands of dollars each year—but he loved to do it. He thought the girls were
the greatest. The girls thought he was the greatest, too. In build, Matt
looked a lot like the men in those old Hawaiian surfing prints—small,
chesty, gravity-bound. He had perfect features and hair as shiny as an
otter's. When he listened to the girls he kept his head tilted, eyebrows
slightly raised, jaw set in a grin. Not like a brother, exactly—more like the

cutest, nicest teacher at school, who could say stern, urgent things without their stinging. When I pulled into the driveway with the girls, Matt was in the yard loading surfboards into a pickup. "Hey, dudes," he called to Lilia and Theresa. "Where are your boards?"

"Someone's going to bring them tonight from Hana," Theresa said. She jiggled her foot. "Matt, come on, let's go surfing already."

"Hey, Lilia," Matt said. He squeezed her shoulders. "How're you doing, champ? Is your dad going to surf in the contest this weekend?"

Lilia shrugged and looked up at him solemnly. "Come on, Matt," she said. "Let's go surfing already."

They went down to surf at Ho'okipa, to a section that is called Pavilles because it is across from the concrete picnic pavilions on the beach. Ho'okipa is not a lot like Hana. People with drinking problems like to hang out in the pavilions. Windsurfers abound. Cars park up to the edge of the sand. The landing pattern for the Kahului Airport is immediately overhead. The next break over, the beach is prettier; the water there is called Girlie Bowls, because the waves get cut down by the reef and are more manageable, presumably, for girlies. A few years ago, some of the Hana surfer girls met their idol Lisa Andersen when she was on Maui. She was very shy and hardly said a word to them, they told me, except to suggest they go surf Girlie Bowls. I thought it sounded mildly insulting, but they weren't exactly sure what she was implying and they didn't brood about it. They hardly talked about her. She was like some unassailable force. We walked past the pavilions. "The men at this beach are so sexist," Lilia said, glaring at a guy swinging a boom box. "It's really different from Hana. Here they're always, you know, staring, and saying, 'Oh, here come the *giiiirls*,' and 'Oh, hello, *ladies*,' and stuff. For us white girls, us haoles, I think they really like to be gross. *So* gross. I'm serious."

"Hey, the waves look pretty sick," Theresa said. She watched a man drop in on one and then whip around against it. She whistled and said, "Whoooa, look at that sick snap! That was so rad, dude! That was the sickest snap I've seen in *ages*! Did you see that?"

They were gone in an instant. A moment later, two blond heads popped up in the black swells, and then they were up on their boards and away.

DINNER AT MATT'S: tons of barbecued chicken, loaves of garlic bread, more loaves of garlic bread. Annie Kinoshita brought four quarts of ice cream out of the freezer, lined them up on the kitchen counter, and watched them disappear. Annie was fair, fine-boned, and imperturbable. She used to be a surfer "with hair down to her frickin' butt," according to Theresa. Now she was busy with her baby and with overseeing the open-door policy she and Matt maintained in their house. That night, another surfer girl, Elise Garrigue, and a fourteen-year-old boy, Cheyne Magnusson, had come over for dinner and were going to sleep over, too. Cheyne was one of the best young surfers on the island. His father, Tony, was a professional skateboarder. Cheyne was the only boy who regularly crashed at Matt and Annie's. He and the girls had the Platonic ideal of a platonic relationship. "Hell, these wenches are *virgins*," Annie said to me, cracking up. "These wenches don't want anything to do with that kind of nastiness."

"Shut up, haole," Theresa said.

"I was going to show these virgins a picture of Chaz's head coming out when I was in labor," Annie yelled, "and they're all, 'No, no, no, *don't!'* "

"Yeah, she's all, 'Look at this grossness!' " Theresa said. "And we're all, 'Shut up, fool.' "

"Duh," Lilia said. "Like we'd even want to see a picture like that."

The next day was the preliminary round of the Quicksilver HASA Competition, the fourth of eight HASA competitions on Maui leading to the state championships and then the nationals. It was a two-day competition— preliminaries on Saturday, finals on Sunday. In theory, the girls should have gone to bed early because they had to get up at five, but that was just a theory. They pillow-fought for an hour, watched *Sabrina, the Teenage Witch* and *Boy Meets World* and another episode of *Sabrina*, then watched a couple of Kelly Slater surfing videos, had another pillow fight, ate a few bowls of cereal, then watched *Fear of a Black Hat,* a movie spoofing the rap music world that they had seen so many times they could recite most of the dialogue by heart. Only Elise fell asleep at a decent hour. She happened to be French and perhaps had overdosed on American pop culture earlier than the rest. Elise sort of blew in to Hawaii with the trade winds: She and her mother had left France and were planning to move to Tahiti, stopped on Maui en route, and never left. It was a classic Hawaiian tale. No one comes here for ordinary reasons in ordinary ways. They run away to Maui from places like Maryland or Nevada or anyplace they picture themselves earthbound, landlocked, stuck. They live in salvaged boxcars or huts or sagging shacks just to be near the waves. Here, they can see watery boundlessness everywhere they turn, and all things are fluid and imperma-nent. I don't know what time it was when the kids finally went to sleep because I was on the living room floor with my jacket over my head for insulation. When I woke up a few hours later, the girls were dressed for the water, eating bowls of Cinnamon Toast Crunch and Honey Bunches of Oats, and watching *Fear of a Black Hat* again. It was a lovely morning and they were definitely ready to show Hana surfing to the world. Theresa was the first to head out the door. "Hey, losers," she yelled over her shoulder, "let's go."

THE FIRST HEATS of the contest had right-handed waves, three or four feet high, silky but soft on the ends so that they collapsed into whitewash as they broke. You couldn't make much of an impression riding something like that, and one after another the Hana girls came out of the water scowling. "I couldn't get any kind of footing," Theresa said to Matt. "I was, like, so on it, but I looked like some kind of kook sliding around."

"My last wave was a full-out closeout," Lilia said. She looked exasperated. "Hey, someone bust me a towel." She blotted her face. "I really blew it," she groaned. "I'm lucky if I even got five waves."

The girls were on the beach below the judges' stand, under Matt's cabana, along with Matt's boys' team and a number of kids he didn't sponsor but who liked hanging out with him more than with their own sponsors. The kids spun like atoms. They ran up and down the beach and stuffed sand in one another's shorts and fought over pieces of last night's chicken that Annie had packed for them in a cooler. During a break between heats, Gloria with the crazy hair strolled over and suddenly the incessant motion paused. This was like an imperial visitation. After all, Gloria was a seasoned-seeming nineteen-year-old who had just spent the year surfing the monstrous waves on Oahu's North Shore, plus she did occasional work for Rodney Kilborn, the contest promoter, plus she had a sea turtle tattooed on her ankle, and most important, according to the Hana girls, she was an absolutely dauntless bodyboarder who would paddle out into wall-size waves, even farther out than a lot of guys would go.

"Hey, haoles!" Gloria called out. She hopped into the shade of the cabana. That day, her famous hair was woven into a long red braid that hung over her left shoulder. Even with her hair tamed, Gloria was an amazing-looking person. She had a hardy build, melon-colored skin, and a wide, round face speckled with light brown freckles. Her voice was light and tinkly, and had that arched, rising-up, quizzical inflection that made everything she said sound like a jokey, good-natured question. "Hey, Theresa?"

she said. "Hey, girl, you got it going *on*? You've got great wave strategy? Just keep it up, yeah? Oh, Elise? You should paddle out harder? Okay? You're doing great, yeah? And Christie?" She looked around for a surfer girl named Christie Wickey, who got a ride in at four that morning from Hana. "Hey, Christie?" Gloria said when she spotted her. "You should go out further, yeah? That way you'll be in better position for your wave, okay? You guys are the greatest, *seriously*? You rule, yeah? You totally rule, yeah?"

At last the junior women's division preliminary results were posted. Theresa, Elise, and two other girls on Matt's team made the cut, as well as a girl whom Matt knew but didn't coach. Lilia had not made it. As soon as she heard, she tucked her blond head in the crook of her elbow and cried. Matt sat with her and talked quietly for a while, and then one by one the other girls drifted up to her and murmured consoling things, but she was inconsolable. She hardly spoke for the rest of the afternoon until the open men's division, which Matt had entered. When his heat was announced, she lifted her head and brushed her hand across her swollen eyes. "Hey, Matt!" she called as he headed for the water. "Rip it for the girls!"

THAT NIGHT, a whole pack of them slept at Matt's—Theresa, Lilia, Christie, Elise, Monica Cardoza from Lahaina, and sisters from Hana named Iris Moon and Lily Morningstar, who had arrived too late to surf in the junior women's preliminaries. There hadn't been enough entrants in the open women's division to require preliminaries, so the competition was going to be held entirely on Sunday, and Iris would be able to enter. Lily wasn't planning to surf at all, but as long as she was able to get a ride out of Hana she took it. This added up to too many girls at Matt's for Cheyne's liking, so he had fled to another boy's house for the night. Lilia was still blue. She was quiet through dinner, and then as soon as she finished she slid into her sleeping bag and pulled it over her head. The other girls stayed up for hours, watching videos and slamming one another with pillows and talking about the contest. At some point someone asked where Lilia was. Theresa shot a glance at her sleeping bag and said quietly, "Did you guys see how upset she got today? I'm like, 'Take it easy, Lilia!' and she's all 'Leave me *alone*, bitch.' So I'm like, 'Whatever.' "

They whispered for a while about how sensitive Lilia was, about how hard she took it if she didn't win, about how she thought one of them had wrecked a bathing suit she'd loaned her, about how funny it was that she even *cared* since she had so many bathing suits and for that matter always had money for snacks, which most of them did not. When I said a Hana girl could have a pure surfing adolescence, I knew it was part daydream, because no matter how sweet the position of a beautiful, groovy Hawaiian teenager might be in the world of perceptions, the mean measures of the human world don't ever go away. There would always be something else to want and be denied. More snack money, even.

Lilia hadn't been sleeping. Suddenly she bolted out of her sleeping bag and screamed, "Fuck you, I *hate* you stupid bitches!" and stormed toward the bathroom, slugging Theresa on the way.

THE WAVES ON SUNDAY came from the left, and they were stiff and smallish, with crisp, curling lips. The men's and boys' heats were narrated over the PA system, but during the girls' and women's heats the announcer was silent, and the biggest racket was the cheering of Matt's team. Lilia had toughened up since last night. Now she seemed grudgeless but remote. Her composure made her look more grown up than twelve. When I first got down to the beach she was staring out at the waves, chewing a hunk of dried papaya and sucking on a candy pacifier. A few of the girls were far off to the right of the break where the beach disappeared and lustrous black rocks stretched into the water. Christie told me later that they hated being bored more than anything in the world and between heats they were afraid they might be getting a little weary, so they decided to perk themselves up by playing on the rocks. It had worked. They charged back from the rocks shrieking and panting. "We got all *dangerous*," she said. "We jumped off this huge rock into the water. We almost got killed, which was great." Sometimes watching them I couldn't believe that they could head out so offhandedly into the ocean—*this* ocean, which had rolls of white water coming in as fast as you could count them, and had a razorblade reef hidden just below the surface, and was full of sharks. The girls, on the other hand, couldn't believe I'd never surfed—never ridden a wave standing up or lying down, never cut back across the whitewash and sent up a lacy veil of spray, never felt a longboard slip out from under me and then felt myself pitched forward and under for that immaculate, quiet, black instant when all the weight in the world presses you down toward the ocean bottom until the moment passes and you get spat up on the beach. I explained I'd grown up in Ohio, where there is no surf, but that didn't satisfy them; what I didn't say was that I'm not sure that at fifteen I had the abandon or the indomitable sense of myself that you seem to need in order to look at this wild water and think, I will glide on top of those waves. Theresa made me promise I'd try to surf at least once someday. I promised, but this Sunday was not going to be that day. I wanted to sit on the sand and watch the end of the contest, to see the Hana girls take their divisions, including Lilia, who placed third in the open women's division, and Theresa, who won the open women's and the junior women's division that day. Even if it was just a moment, it was a perfect one, and who wouldn't choose it over never having the moment at all? When I left Maui that afternoon, my plane circled over Ho'okipa, and I wanted to believe I could still see them down there and always would see them down there, snapping back and forth across the waves.

LIVING LARGE

*T*HE COOLEST PERSON IN NEW YORK AT THE
moment is a man named Fred Brathwaite, who is known
most of the time to most of his friends as Fab Five Freddy,
Fab, Five, or just Freddy. Freddy has a lot of jobs. He has
been, at one time or another, a graffiti artist, a rapper, an
internationally exhibited painter, a video and TV commercial director, a screenwriter, a film scorer, an actor, a lecturer, and a television personality. Currently, he is also
known to millions of viewers as the host of MTV's popular
Saturday-night rap music show, *Yo! MTV Raps.* Freddy also
knows a lot of people. He counts among his friends the late
Andy Warhol, a music promoter who goes by the name
Great Adventure, the painter Julian Schnabel, and the
afternoon manager of a McDonald's on 125th Street in
Harlem. Freddy's tastes range all over the place. In the
course of any given day, he might express enthusiasm
for Italian postmodern painters, a new rap song by Public
Enemy, the oxtail soup served at a dumpy little Haitian
restaurant on Tenth Avenue, the actor who played Grandpa
Munster on *The Munsters,* Malcolm X, high-end stereo com-

ponents, medieval armor, dogs, women, and nicely designed long-haul trucks. Hanging around with Freddy is a multimedia experience.

Freddy has perfect grammar, but, in keeping with his nonstandard tastes, he prefers to use a finely discriminated array of nonstandard English expressions to characterize his regular outbreaks of good feeling. These include:

Fly—implies exceptional stylishness or unusually high achievement. How Freddy described the food at a dinner he attended with representatives of the Ebel watch company at Le Cirque.

Excellent—often refers to a successful business transaction. How Freddy said he felt when he found out he was being hired to play himself in an upcoming movie.

Dope—expresses all-purpose positiveness, especially about something intense or challenging. How Freddy rated a new album by the Jamaican singer Shabba Ranks.

Extra happy—refers to a big, expansive swell of feeling. How Freddy described his emotions upon hearing that his television show would be broadcast in the Soviet Union.

Yo!—the ultimate, all-purpose exclamation, which, depending on inflection, can imply marvelousness or wonderment. How Freddy begins a discussion of what it's like for him to consider that at this fairly early point in his life he is already the host of a hip internationally televised music show, has a deal with Warner Brothers to direct two movies, travels freely among a dozen different worlds, knows famous people, and is famous himself.

PEOPLE RECOGNIZE FREDDY on the street all the time these days, but you get the feeling that even if he weren't televised weekly he would still not be the sort of person to go unnoticed. On camera he can look wiry, but in person he is over six feet tall and more than solidly built. He is thirty-one years old, looks about thirty, and will occasionally assign himself a few years less than that in the telling. He has prominent, round cheekbones, a bow-shaped, wily smile, and a small, nearly forgettable mustache. His hands are large and long-fingered and mobile. He is very adept at the classic B-boy gestures of rap—stiff thumbs, forefingers, and pinkies moved in deliberate, threatening sweeps, ending with arms crossed high, shoulders hunched, and head tilted sassily—but his real body language is more subtle. He walks canted forward, as if he were about to lean over and whisper. His voice is slightly nasal and usually amusing. I can describe neither his eyes nor his hair, because he always wears a hat and sunglasses—indoors and out, night and day. He favors felt fedoras and Jean-Paul Gaultier shades. The rest of his outfits have an equally arresting quality—he always looks camera ready. One time I was with him, he was wearing a scarlet camp shirt with flap pockets, baggy black gabardine pants, red suede oxfords, and a taupe felt fedora. Another time, he was wearing a pumpkin-colored rayon shirt buttoned to the neck, no tie, a string of large amber beads, baggy rust-colored pants, green suede oxfords with thick black soles, and a black silk trench coat. All in all, his style is pretty sui generis.

Summing up what he does for a living, Freddy said recently, "I'm the king of synthesis." There is no such job listed with the United States Bureau of Labor Statistics. Freddy nonetheless synthesizes full time. An ideal Fab Five Freddy project involves several media and several individuals who represent the high and low ends of artistic endeavor or social standing and whose association would be discordant if they were not harmonized by Freddy. His favorite version of such projects at the moment is the cross-pollination of black street culture with highbrow art. Some months ago, describing a trip he took to Italy, he told me, "I wanted to walk by Fellini's house, because I really admire his filmmaking. So I took a huge ghetto blaster, put in a Run-D.M.C. tape, and walked up and down Fellini's street, right in front of his house, blasting rap music. I liked the idea of combining the two experiences."

Freddy describing the rest of his stay in Italy: "Then I went to dinner at the home of the man who runs the Galleria la Medusa in Rome. We were getting together to talk about the graffiti scene, and all that. His house was filled with all these gorgeous Caravaggios and de Chiricos and Italian Futurist paintings. It was, like, yo."

ONE MORNING THIS SPRING, I caught a cab and headed over to pick Freddy up at his apartment. Freddy lives in a modern high-rise on the western edge of midtown Manhattan. Before that, he lived in a tenement on the Lower East Side. When he first achieved notoriety as a graffiti artist, he was living at home with his parents, in Bedford-Stuyvesant. His present apartment has sensational views in three directions, quite a few mirrors, a vacuum-sealed ambience, and, to my eye, a sort of Wall Street yuppie gleam, which makes it exactly not the place I would have expected Freddy to live in. As it happens, though, Freddy appreciates good views and slick buildings. He also has a lot of friends circulating in the neigh-borhood; one evening when he and I were coming back from a *Yo!* taping, we ran into a rapper named Queen Latifah and her manager, both friends of his, in the entranceway.

The things Freddy does and the pace at which he does them make him seem to be all over the place all the time. This is true of many people in New York—and, in particular, of the kinds of people who populate Freddy's various businesses—but Freddy takes being on the move, like everything else he does, to its highest form of expression. A typical day for him might include shooting an episode of *Yo!* on location in the Bronx, then editing one of his music videos at a production facility in midtown, then shopping in SoHo, then meeting people for dinner at the Odeon, then visiting friends at midnight in Bed-Stuy. One afternoon this winter, Freddy called me from Los Angeles. I was actually expecting him to be calling from Japan, where he and rap have lately become hot commodities, both separately and as they are teamed up on *Yo!* Freddy is usually more than happy to travel wherever he has become a hot commodity, and a few weeks earlier he had decided he ought to visit Japan while he was still in vogue, but apparently the trip had fallen through, and instead he had gone to California. In Los Angeles, he was staying at the Mondrian Hotel, a glossy place on Sunset Boulevard whose owners also happen to consider him a hot commodity: Several years ago, they let him live in the hotel for three months in exchange for some of his paintings. Toward the end of the con-versation, I asked Freddy what he'd be doing for the next few days. He rat-tled off a list that included movie, television, advertising, and music projects that would entail traveling to three nations on three continents. When I said that he'd be hard to find, he said, "Oh, not really. I don't know how to drive, so the whole time I'm in L.A., I'll kind of be stuck in my hotel room."

This particular morning in New York, Freddy was first going to a meet-ing about an upcoming music video project, then shooting the episode of *Yo! MTV Raps* that would run the following Saturday night, then working on his Warner screenplay, and then having a meeting about another music video he might be directing. I was late, but Freddy didn't seem to notice: When my cab pulled up, he was sitting in the lobby, absorbed in a maga-zine about expensive stereo equipment. The lobby was busy with people in smart business suits. Freddy was wearing a silky shirt with a pattern of brightly colored fruits and vegetables, zoot-suit-style brown twill pants, tan socks, his green suede oxfords, a satin baseball jacket with the slogan

45 KING on the back, a small leather map of Africa hanging from a rawhide thong around his neck, a newsboy cap of Irish tweed, and steel-rimmed Gaultier shades with little round lenses. He looked stylish. He appeared to be in a good mood. Upon seeing me, he hollered "Yo!" and then laughed— a loud, articulated laugh that sounds like the air brakes on an eighteen-wheeler seizing. On our way out, he accosted his doorman, his concierge, and various people entering the building by cocking his head and calling out "Yo! My *man*!"

"How's it going, Freddy?" his doorman asked.

"Living large, man," Freddy answered, sauntering through the doorway. "Living *very* large."

As we crossed the courtyard, Freddy stopped to greet a neighbor who was walking twin black pugs. "Great dogs," he said, leaning over to pet them. "I love that—matched dogs."

"Brother and sister," the neighbor said. "They're not exactly matched."

"I love the way they look," Freddy went on, disregarding the correction. "That's so *dope*! I should get a dog. It would look fly to walk down the street with twin dogs."

The morning's first meeting was being held at the SoHo offices of the film director Jonathan Demme. Ted Demme, the executive producer of *Yo! MTV Raps*, is Jonathan's nephew, and Jonathan himself is a music enthusiast, who occasionally directs videos for rap groups. This particular meeting had been called by the rapper KRS-One, who recently founded an education project called Human Education Against Lies and was proposing to make a collaborative rap record and video to raise money for it. A group of rappers—L. L. Cool J, Kid Capri, Freddie Foxx, Big Daddy Kane, M. C. Lyte, Queen Latifah, Run-D.M.C., and Ms. Melodie—had already been drafted to rap on the record. The two Demmes, Freddy, and a young director named Pam Jenkins had been invited to direct sections of the video.

Freddy, stretching out in the cab, was smiling to himself. "I'm thinking, Yo, this is pretty *cool*," he said. "Here it is, right after Oscars night, and here I am going to a meeting to direct something with Jonathan Demme. That's some cool fucking shit! Jonathan Demme, you know—director of *Silence of the Lambs*, and everything." He drummed his fingers on the seat. The cabdriver turned his radio up. A toxic smell from New Jersey wafted in one window, mixed with the air freshener on the dashboard, and blew out the other side. It was a bright morning with a wind that came in startling chilly puffs. No rain was imminent. Somewhere across town, a *Yo! MTV*

Raps production assistant was noting with relief that the day's taping could take place outside, as planned. "It's funny, me and Jonathan were No. 1 and No. 2 for a while," Freddy went on. "What I mean is that Jonathan's film *Lambs* is out now, and so is the movie I'd been working on as associate producer, *New Jack City,* and we were No. 1 and No. 2 box office in *Variety* for weeks. We'd still be No. 1 and No. 2, except that the new Teenage Mutant Ninja Turtles movie is out and it bumped us. I'm not dissing it, but it does hurt to be bumped by turtles."

Demme's office is a narrow, cluttered loft on the eighth floor of a building on lower Broadway. It is filled with mismatched chairs and desks, and has the economical look of a student newspaper office, except that hanging on the walls are a huge *Silence of the Lambs* poster and a photograph of a theater marquee announcing a double feature of that film and another Demme production, *Miami Blues.* When we arrived, the meeting was already in progress. The Demmes, KRS-One and his associates, and various technical advisers had pulled their chairs into a circle in the middle of the loft and were discussing the logistical challenges of shooting a video in Harlem with four directors, countless interested onlookers, and a three-thousand-dollar-a-day Steadicam. The conversation stopped when we walked in.

"Fab," Ted Demme said, in greeting.

"Yo," Freddy said.

"Fred," KRS-One said.

"Yo, man," Freddy said. Freddy and KRS have some history. The first video Freddy ever directed was "My Philosophy," a hit for KRS-One and Boogie Down Productions in 1988. When Freddy introduces the video on *Yo! MTV Raps,* he invariably says, with no trace of bashfulness, "Yo, now here's a great video, one of my *favorites.*" When Freddy refers to KRS in conversation, he quite often identifies him as "the heart and soul and conscience and brains and philosophy of rap" and sometimes adds that he is "my main man."

"We'll catch you up," Ted said. "KRS was just talking about his project to advance human consciousness."

"Excellent," Freddy said. He nodded to KRS and sat down, reached for a pen, and nodded genially at the others in the room.

Everyone turned back to the business at hand. I had never previously seen Freddy in any situation where he wasn't the principal object of attention. In this circle, he seemed uncharacteristically unanimated. KRS, a bulky, soft-faced man with a rolling bass voice and a soothing, professorial manner, did most of the talking, describing a plan to distribute 4 million copies of a book he had written challenging the basic assumptions of Western education. "I'm going to drop the book onto the school system," KRS said. "Our goal is to get people thinking. For instance, we put out the statement 'Aristotle was a thief.' The first reaction will be 'What are you talking about?' The next is that it will start people thinking."

"I'll tell you what I've been thinking," Ted Demme responded. "I'm thinking that when kids hear that there are ten major rappers in the neighborhood they're going to go crazy."

A discussion of laminated security passes followed. It was close to noon. Jonathan Demme stood up, excused himself to go to another meeting, and headed for the door. Then Ted Demme stood up, thanked everyone, and said that he and Freddy had to leave for the *Yo!* taping, and that he was available to meet again as the plans proceeded. He then shot Freddy an urgent look.

Freddy stood up and strolled over to the *Silence of the Lambs* poster and paused in front of it. The large face of Jodie Foster framed the back of Freddy's head. "Yo," he said to me after a moment. "Doing something with Jonathan is excellent. I'm *extra* happy I got asked to do this video."

MANY THINGS MAKE FREDDY extra happy. Working with someone well established and successful, like Jonathan Demme, is one of his extra-happiest experiences. He is unabashed about it. In fact, he aspires to it. He started his movie career, in 1980, by telephoning Charlie Ahearn, whose movie *The Deadly Art of Survival* was then being celebrated on the underground film circuit, and asking Ahearn to include him in whatever he was doing next. When he got interested in painting, he cultivated friendships with Jean-Michel Basquiat and Keith Haring. When he did graffiti, he did it alongside the graffiti star Lee Quinones. He scored a movie, when movie scoring caught his attention, with Chris Stein, of the band Blondie. People like Freddy; almost everyone he has sought to attach himself to has said yes. The trade-off is that Freddy has a gift for getting himself and his undertakings, and therefore his collaborators, noticed. He manages, seemingly without effort, to create an aura of noteworthiness. His philosophy of career advancement is not a matter of being a successful hanger-on. It's a philosophy that appreciates mastery and technical proficiency but prizes the knack for courting accomplished, proficient people, the knack for noticing which direction popular culture is heading, the knack for grafting one art form or pop form onto another, the knack for attracting a lot of attention to whatever you do, and the knack for understanding that attracting attention is, ultimately, the real art form of this era. Freddy has all these knacks. There are times when I am of the opinion that Fab Five Freddy is the hip-hop Andy Warhol. And, in fact, Freddy's extra-happiest professional association was with Warhol, whom he refers to as his hero.

This is the path from Bedford-Stuyvesant to Andy Warhol: "My mother is a nurse, and my dad is an accountant. There was always a very heavy music thing in our house. Max Roach is my godfather, and Max and my dad are like brothers. They were beboppers together—black intellectuals. My dad lived in Brooklyn, and he had a posse of musicians like Bud Powell, Cecil Payne, Thelonious Monk, Clifford Brown. They'd hang at his house—everybody called it the Chess Club. My dad's not a musician, but he'd always hang with all these dudes. Bed-Stuy is cool—it's anchored by all these churches in the community. My parents just got cable about a month ago. Before that, I'd send them tapes of *Yo!* so they could see it. I grew up about three blocks from where Spike made *Do the Right Thing.* I kind of slipped out of high school and finished up in this program called City as School, which is for people who are smart but don't want to listen to other people. I was going to Medgar Evers College and I got the idea to be a painter. I'd been tagging my name up, doing graffiti, when I was an adolescent, so that I could start getting known, to popularize myself in the city. That was when all these dudes would tag up their names. My tags were Bull 99 and Showdown 177 and Fred Fab Five. I'd play hooky a lot and go to the Met to look at armor, look at paintings, look at jewelry, and I would think, Yo, *I* want to do this. I didn't want to be a folk artist, I wanted to be a fine artist. I wanted to be a *famous* artist. Somewhere in there, I started reading about Pop art. I was reading a lot of books about art—and some of them were really hard to read and boring and didn't say anything to me, and others sounded cool, and they were about Pop art. I started reading *Interview* and making my plans. I knew you had to have some kind of plan to move into the media."

Freddy's plans to be a famous artist coincided with the Pop art movement's championing of enlightened amateurism in every field. It was then the mid-seventies. By Pop standards, anyone was eligible to make art. Anyone could have a punk band. Anyone could silk-screen Campbell's soup cans. Anything anyone declared to be sculpture was sculpture. Anyone could have his own cable television show and invite his friends to appear on it and just *act like themselves,* and the show would be conceptually com-

plete. This did indeed happen. Glenn O'Brien, a writer and Warhol aco-
lyte, produced a television show on Manhattan's public-access channel
which was called *Glenn O'Brien's TV Party;* it entailed nothing much more
than his inviting his friends to hold a cocktail hour on the air. His friends—
among them Deborah Harry, Chris Stein, David Byrne, and Arto Lindsay—
were members of the social set that Freddy usually describes as "groovy
downtown hipsters." Freddy, who was a fan of Glenn's column in *Interview,* arranged to have Glenn as a guest on a college radio show he was em-
ceeing. Not long afterward, Freddy was seized with the desire to become a
cameraman for *Glenn O'Brien's TV Party.* For two years, he was a cameraman for the show, and also, soon after starting, one of its on-camera personnel, and also, in time, a regular member of the groovy downtown
hipsters and a Warhol devotee. He saw, firsthand, the power of being a
smart spectator and a collector, and the satisfaction of making yourself
and your tastes well known. "Andy was the biggest influence on me,"
Freddy now says. "I hung around with him as much as I could. For me and
Jean-Michel, coming from where we were coming from, being young black
males in this happening downtown scene, we were just operating on another planet, and Andy was it."

Uptown, and in Brooklyn and the Bronx, the notion of populist street
art was nothing new, but the forms it was taking—rapping, break dancing,
and graffiti painting—were. Freddy would often ride the subway to the city
parks in the South Bronx where rappers and break-dancers set up and performed. He was, he says now, just a fan, but a fan with interesting connec-
tions. "I was, like, this person who understood the fine-art thing," Freddy
says. "I was hip enough to hang downtown at places like Danceteria with all
these art people, gallery owners, all the groovy people, but I had the pure
hip-hop roots as well. So this was my synthesis. I was credited with bringing rap downtown. I went onstage and rapped at the Mudd Club, which was
a new wave hangout. I knew I wasn't much of a rapper, but I wanted to fuse
the two worlds, and I figured the audience downtown wouldn't know the
difference if I was or wasn't much of a rapper. I knew whatever I did down
there would look interesting. I wanted people to see this whole hip-hop
street-culture thing bubbling up under their noses."

Freddy's next big synthesis was proposing that graffiti and break dancing and rapping were related forms of street art which, taken as a whole,
defined the new aesthetic of black hip-hop culture. This might seem obvious now, but at the time the three were considered separate, transitory im-
pulses at best and discrete forms of public nuisance at worst. Freddy, being

Freddy, came up with the idea, and then followed it with this proposal: "Damn, put this all in a *movie,* it would be *dope.*" Charlie Ahearn, after being approached by Freddy, agreed that it would be very dope to make a movie about hip-hop. Freddy's relationship with the resulting project, *Wild Style,* is a Freddy classic. As Ahearn now recalls it, Freddy initially planned to co-write the screenplay with him but didn't have the patience to niggle over the fine points of screenwriting, and initially planned to co-direct it but didn't have the patience to labor over the details of film direction. In the end, Freddy helped Chris Stein produce the soundtrack. He also wound up with a major role, even though acting happened to be one of the few job positions in the film he had not been interested in filling.

Ahearn is extremely complimentary when it comes to Freddy's contributions. "First of all, he's the best actor in the film," he says. "He didn't want to be in it. That was my idea. As far as the other stuff, Freddy didn't have the focus at that particular time to write or direct, although he was very interested in doing both. His incredible talents lay more in his charisma, his ability to form relationships with a huge number of people, and to have this unique vision of street culture, and to have the desire to bring the ghetto scene downtown. In a way, he was the one who brought it all together."

Wild Style is the story of a South Bronx graffiti artist who has to decide whether he should remain an anonymous outlaw vandal making street art for nothing or cash in and start selling his graffiti paintings to effete, upscale collectors. Freddy plays a fast-talking, cynical smoothy named Phade, who has no particular job but lots of important positions: He appears to be, at various times, a club manager, a concert promoter, a businessman, a tour guide, a master of ceremonies, a negotiator, and a general all-around operator. When word gets out that a reporter from a downtown newspaper is coming to the South Bronx to write about the graffiti artist and his friends—rappers and break-dancers—most of them are wary. Phade, on the other hand, positions himself to escort the reporter and act as her agent. He laughs at the notion that it would be better to keep hip-hop unexposed. "You serious?" Phade says at one point, sounding incredulous. "Hey, man, it's about time we got some publicity for this goddam rap shit."

FORTY-EIGHTH STREET between Sixth and Seventh Avenues is the professional musicians' block in midtown Manhattan. It is a jammed, jumbled, slightly seedy street, which seems to generate its own constant buzz. The sidewalks are skinny and sooty. Flyers advertising band jobs and guitarists for hire flutter in the gutters. Hand trucks stacked with Bose speakers and Fender guitars line the sidewalks. The buildings are low and plain faced, and have unglamorous storefronts, with amplifiers, mixing boards, guitar strings, and computer consoles piled haphazardly in their windows. It is one place where the fraternity of musicianship prevails over the diffusions of musical genre. As our cab worked its way down the street, I noticed country-and-western guitarists and heavy metallists and soul singers side by side, window-shopping for equipment.

Today's *Yo! MTV Raps* was going to be taped outside Sam Ash Music, one of the biggest stores on the block. *Yo!* is always shot on location. Recent episodes have been filmed under the Brooklyn Bridge, in the Roosevelt Island tram, on 125th Street, and in an airplane flying down to a rap convention in New Orleans. It was Freddy's idea to place the show— that is, the segments consisting of him and his guests, which are interspersed with the videos—somewhere on the street rather than in a studio, to emphasize its immediacy. It is in keeping with Freddy's nature that he enjoys having a crowd watch him work. And it's in keeping with his ability to recognize someone anywhere he goes that on a shoot he often sees someone he knows—either a friend or a famous person. At the *Yo!* shoot on 125th Street, he ran into Afrika Bambaataa, a friend and a famous person. During a shoot on the Roosevelt Island tram, he spotted Grandpa Munster, a famous person but not a friend.

Yo! was the first MTV show to be entirely "remote," and Freddy is irked that other shows on the channel are now imitating him by shooting their host segments outside a studio. "Man, I *thought* of this, I came up with this," he says when he's discussing his imitators. "I hate being copied, man—I made it on my own ideas in this business. I don't got no uncles in the business, if you know what I mean. I'm not dissing it that hard, but my ideas are my *business.*"

Other things were on his mind when the cab was on its way to Sam Ash. "You know what movie's really dope?" he asked Ted Demme, who was riding with us.

"Speak," Ted said.

"*La Femme Nikita,*" Freddy said, chuckling. "I saw that shit *twice,* it made me so extra happy. I'll go peep it again with you, dude, it's so def."

"Yo," Ted said.

The conversation then turned to the Oscars. Freddy expressed admiration for Joe Pesci, the *GoodFellas* star. "You know what I'm wondering, though?" he said, dropping his voice. "I'm wondering this. I was at that restaurant Columbus one night. You know that place, a lot of actors and a lot of hip people go there for burgers, that's the flavor—it's an acting hangout. And I'm there with Veronica, my old girlfriend, and Joe Pesci comes over to our table to say hello, and I'm telling you, for real, he had no hair. So I'm looking at the Oscars last night, and I see him with all that hair, and I'm thinking, Yo! My man! Joe Pesci! Is that a rug, or what?"

"That is too ill," Ted exclaimed. "Joe Pesci is wearing a lid?"

"Yo, I *swear,*" Freddy answered. "I swear! I'm right there at Columbus, and there he is, at my table, in the sight of everyone, not a hair on his bald head."

The two of them laughed wildly and then, after a moment, sat and mused. Then Ted abruptly said, "Yo, Freddy, you have a car, don't you? So this weekend we could peep some locations uptown for the KRS video?"

Freddy shrugged. "I do have a car, but, seriously, I'm not too into running around in it," he said. "It is a lovely vehicle, though—lovely, lovely, love-*ly*. A '57 Chevy, turquoise. It's the color of a Tiffany box."

We were now in front of Sam Ash. So were Moses Edinborough, the show's associate producer and its director; the camera crew; three members of a rap group called Stetsasonic; a scrawny guy with long, tattooed arms who was furiously loading boxes marked PEAVEY AMPLIFIERS into a panel truck; two adolescent boys with the avid, skittish air of truants; a man in dark glasses rotating a cassette tape over and over in one hand; and three Asian tourists, standing at attention. Freddy emerged from the cab and surveyed the gathering crowd with deliberate aloofness. His mood had turned distinctly Garboesque. This was a sea change from the Joey Bishop he had been doing in the cab on the way over and from his Sally Field turn at the morning meeting. We regrouped on the sidewalk. In front of us, Moses was pacing back and forth, wagging a finger at Daddy-O, Stetsasonic's main rapper, and saying with mock seriousness, "Now, I don't want you all to be bugging out here, got that?" Seeing Freddy, he interrupted himself, grinned, and said, "Yo, Fab."

"What's the flavor, Moses?" Freddy said in greeting.

"We're missing half of Stetsasonic, but we're going to start anyway," Moses said. "It's going to be totally def."

Show No. 117A of *Yo! MTV Raps* would eventually consist, like Show No. 1, of an opening (a frantic video montage of rap artists and graphics) and five one-and-a-half-to-two-minute segments of Freddy interviewing his guests (a rapper or a rap group, usually enjoying a current hit), dropped between ten rap videos, which Ted Demme and his staff had selected. The formula has worked well for three years. It is one of MTV's highest-rated blocks of programming. Its viewers span a broad range of age and race. It has spawned a spin-off (a daily late-afternoon studio version, with a former rapper named Ed Lover and the former Beastie Boys DJ Doctor Dré as hosts). So dominant is its position in the rap world these days that its choices of videos and guests prefigure and, in fact, preordain rap hits.

The genesis of the show is uncomplicated: Ted Demme, who grew up on Long Island admiring black street music, and who apprenticed his way through the entry levels at MTV, persuaded the company in 1988 to let him produce a rap video special, with Run-D.M.C. as host. Two facts conspired to make this a logical enterprise: MTV had had great success playing Run-D.M.C.'s "Walk This Way," the first real rap record to be popular with a mainstream white audience, and had recently introduced, also successfully, its first programs offering something other than wall-to-wall videos—a game show and a dance show. A third fact, though, was less encouraging. At that time, despite Run-D.M.C.'s breakthrough, rap was still seen as marginal music: ghetto noise that was little more than mono-tonal chanting in rhyme—sometimes lewd, sometimes militant—to rhythm tracks, usually lifted without ceremony or license from another record. That rap had been around for quite a few years without moving much be-yond its small, young black male audience was equally unencouraging. (The one exception was the white rock band Blondie's 1981 hit "Rapture," a novelty rap that happened to include a reference to Fab Five Freddy.) Nonetheless, MTV's programming department let Demme produce the special, on the strength of Run-D.M.C.'s popularity, and sat up in surprise when it drew a huge audience. In short order, a weekly show was planned. Searching for a host, Demme asked for a recommendation from Peter Dougherty, who is now the director of on-air promotion for MTV Europe but was then a producer with the network. "All the time we were putting the show together, I was imagining Freddy as the host," Dougherty says. The two had met ten years earlier at one of the many groovy-downtown-hipster functions that both frequented—something at the Fun Gallery, or maybe the Roxy, or maybe a party for Keith Haring or Futura 2000 or Warhol. In any case, Freddy had impressed Dougherty as being a legiti-mate Renaissance character and also a bit of a ham. "There used to be these guys fifty years ago or so who knew everyone, did everything, could move around the city with ease. They'd even meet dignitaries at the airport," Dougherty says. "They called themselves Ambassadors of New York. That's what Freddy's like. I mean that in a very positive way." No one else was even auditioned for the job.

WEST FORTY-EIGHTH STREET, in a gathering crowd. "Welcome to *Yo! MTV Raps,* the coolest hour on television," Freddy announced when the camera started running. "Getting ready to hip-hop you right out of your living-room seat right about now." After this introductory segment, Freddy turned to his guests. "I'm here with the *bad* Stetsasonic. My man Daddy-O, what's up?"

"What up, what up, what up, what up! How you been, man?" Daddy-O said.

"What's been going on with Stetsasonic?" Freddy pointed the microphone at Daddy-O.

They bantered about the band's new album, about Stetsasonic's upcoming trip to Africa ("That's real inspirational," Freddy commented. "Going back to the motherland"), about the video that would be played next. They spent a few minutes discussing the burgeoning bootleg-tape trade. Each week, Freddy likes to touch on a serious subject, and bootlegging has been one of his favorites. Otherwise, the interviews are friendly volleys, a little posturing, a lot of promotion, some gossip. Freddy takes care of business, too. During the Stetsasonic taping, he dropped mentions of having attended Nelson Mandela's first American appearance, of having worked on *New Jack City,* and of having directed Stetsasonic's first video, which he assessed thus: "Yo, it's *cool.*"

The three members of the group—the missing Stets never appeared— bounced around in front of the camera and delivered sharp answers to Freddy's wide outside pitches. Nearly every segment was shot in one try. Word is that the early shows were rather raw, Freddy being hyper and jivey, a catalog of distracting mannerisms. These days, he is mostly unselfconscious and funny, displaying good-natured bravado and manicured cool. These days, too, most of his guests are one-take, media-savvy, well traveled, and fine-tuned. Rap has come a long way. It is still a musical genre that requires little in the way of initial capitalization and has an unrefined immediacy that suggests songs written between subway stops, but now it is also a big, profitable, important business. The best-selling album of 1990 (over 10 million copies) was M. C. Hammer's *Please Hammer Don't Hurt*

'Em; one of the top four best-selling singles was the white rapper Vanilla Ice's "Ice Ice Baby"; and a recent survey showed that 24 percent of all active music consumers in this country had bought a rap recording in the last six months. More significant is that over half of those customers were white. Most significant, by pop-culture standards, is that this year the soap opera One Life to Live added a rap group to its cast of regulars.

Still, Freddy's social skills are often called upon in the show. One afternoon, I accompanied Freddy to a Yo! taping in Washington Square Park. His guest was a young rapper called Special Ed, who had an Eraserhead-style fade hairdo, a hit record, and a dreamy, distracted aura that warned of dead air. Freddy was in a particularly chipper mood that day. The interview went something like this:

FREDDY: So, Special Ed, I want to ask you, you've been able to get your message across to a particular audience—that is, the teenage females. What do you think it is about you or your music that's getting through to them?

SPECIAL ED: I don't know.

FREDDY: Any idea of what it is about what you're doing that's hitting that particular demographic?

SPECIAL ED: Nope. (A pause, during which Freddy laughs loudly.)

FREDDY: Yo, Ed, what's the best thing about MTV?

SPECIAL ED: I don't know. I don't have cable.

Stetsasonic is of a different order. At the Sam Ash taping, the comments of the three who were present tumbled on top of one another; at one point, they burst into a spontaneous wild rap. They were articulate and funny, and they never stopped talking. During one of the breaks, they and the camera crew gathered in the back of the Sam Ash store.

"I was just thinking about this dope kung-fu movie," Daddy-O was saying. "It was about this baby who has swords for fists—it was called something like The Avenging Fists."

D.B.C., the group's keyboardist, said, "Uh-uh, that's the one when the baby's got the superpowerful fists. The sword one, that was so ill—it had a different name."

"It was ill! He was in his baby carriage, and it's whip, whip, whip with those swords!"

Freddy, standing nearby, was ignoring the discussion. He said to Moses Edinborough, "You signed on to direct a video? That's excellent. What kind of bread they paying you?"

"Very nice bread," Moses said.

"Do you have a financial adviser?" Freddy asked. The kung-fu conversation continued noisily behind him. "Because, man, you start getting nice bread, you ought to have someone doing something dope with it."

"I'm planning on it, man."

From behind: "I think it was *The Fists of the Avenger,* maybe."

"No, man, that was the *other* one, not the baby but the little boy who was so bad, he was so powerful, he could chop through the door of a safe."

The man who had been standing on the sidewalk fingering a cassette walked into the store and headed toward Freddy, saying, "Man, I *know* what you're doing, I *like* what you're doing. I want you to listen to this tape."

"Chill, brother," Freddy said to him, and he turned back to Moses. "Financial planning. Yo, I recommend it."

WALKING THROUGH TIMES SQUARE on our way back to Freddy's apartment, we were greeted by all sorts of people: teenagers, who whistled and preened to cover up their admiration; a security guard, who looked way too old to be a *Yo!* audience member; a young, buxom, underdressed woman, walking with her uncle or so; more kids. Freddy responded to each of them with a wave or a "Yo!" or a genuine-sounding "How's it going, man?" He was smiling, a little preoccupied, as he walked along. The taping had gone well. It would be a good show. It would make up for last week, when a boxing match on another channel in the *Yo!* time slot— Saturday night from ten to eleven—administered a nasty uppercut to his ratings. Freddy keeps track of the ratings, of the demographics, of the competition, of the number of people who recognize him on the street. Crossing Broadway, he noticed a gigantic Kodak billboard featuring a gigantic likeness of Bill Cosby. The Cos beamed down on the thicket of traffic and jostling crowds. "See that?" Freddy said. "He couldn't walk through here. He's too *big.* He can't live his life. What I have now, as far as fame, is excellent. I'm *known,* but I'm not too known. I can still walk around, I can still eat dinner out. It's not too much. Not yet." Another clump of kids, passing, called out to him. He answered them, and added, "I like having some of this, being able to flex my muscles, but it can be *painful.* Fame can be painful sometimes."

It was four-thirty when we arrived at Freddy's building. As we passed through the lobby, one of the porters, a heavyset man with a grizzled beard, stopped us and told Freddy he had something for him. He led us back to the mailroom and, after some negotiations with a pile of crates, shoved a huge, sagging cardboard box marked MTV in Freddy's direction.

Getting the box upstairs took some doing. Once inside his apartment, Freddy put on a Frank Sinatra compact disc and started digging through the contents of the box. It was full of mail addressed to him in care of the show. We were seated at an antique secretary in his living room. The living room also contained a large-screen television; a black leather couch; a low, wide, biomorphic coffee table; some amusing kitsch collectibles; a photograph of Freddy mugging with Andy Warhol; a photograph of Freddy on the set of *New Jack City*; an issue of *Paper* with a photograph of Freddy and his former girlfriend, the model Veronica Webb, on the cover; an issue of *Details* folded open to a full-page photograph of Freddy; and several telephones. Hanging across from the secretary was a large, lively painting of a martini glass and a goblet. The style was late-seventies graffiti. The artist was Fab Five Freddy. It is one of many paintings he turned out, with alacrity, during his painting phase. "I focused on painting for a while," he says now. "That's when Jean-Michel Basquiat and Keith Haring and I were really tight. I was painting a lot, but when I saw Jean-Michel's career really take off and explode I started wondering when it was going to happen for me." It did happen, sort of. In 1979, he and Lee Quinones had a show at the Galleria la Medusa, in Rome, and in 1985, after including him in several group shows, Holly Solomon gave him a one-man show at her gallery. He had his moment, but he never really threatened to explode. Anyway, by that time he was getting bored with painting. "I got to a point where I was good, but I got tired of the art world," he says. "I was also tired of not being able to reach a wide audience. I wanted to see things I'd thought of filtering out into the whole culture." He says he will paint again, but the painting will be Freddy style: "I won't present it just as painting. Painting now seems small, a little trite, you know? I will come back to it in the next year, and it will be multimedia. I'll have backing from some major corporations, and it will be shown someplace other than a gallery or where you'd ordinarily see painting."

In the box were letters, tapes, records, much-delayed Christmas presents, a box of chocolate truffles from a record company, more letters, more tapes. First, Freddy opened the truffles. Then he started on the letters. "Here's a guy writing to me from Nigeria, this is *excellent*. . . .

Here's a kid writing from jail. . . . Here's more people writing from Nigeria—yo, what's going *on* there in Nigeria? I guess it's time for me to go to Nigeria." He started singing along with "Autumn in New York," and then the phone rang.

"Yo, girl, how you *been*?" he shouted into the phone. As I listened, it became clear to me that the young woman on the line was an employee of a striptease establishment in Times Square called Show World, and that while she was working there the day before, one of her colleagues happened to get hacked to death in the back of the club. Freddy questioned the woman with enthusiasm. At one point, he put his hand over the mouthpiece and whispered to me, "She says the guy who did it was the dead girl's boyfriend. I guess the relationship wasn't going so well, so he decided to murder her." He went back to the call. He cradled the phone under his chin, continued to open the mail, lowered the volume on Sinatra, and turned the television on to *Video Music Box,* an afternoon rap video show on a local cable channel. "Autumn in New York" now appeared to be coming out of the mouths of De La Soul. After a few minutes, Freddy got a call on his other line, so he put the Show World employee on hold and started yelling into the phone: "Yo, I said I'd consider being in the movie for the *marquee* value, but no one's telling me where anything is at!" These negotiations—for Freddy to play himself in an upcoming movie called *Juice*—went on loudly for many minutes. Freddy hung up. Then he took a call from Ted Demme about Mario Van Peebles, who had appeared that afternoon on the daytime *Yo!* saying things about *New Jack City* that Freddy didn't like. Then he dialed an executive at a record company with whom he was negotiating to direct a video of a record by Shabba Ranks. He put the executive on his speaker phone and continued to open mail. The executive's hiccupy exclamations about the brilliance of the proposed video boomed through the apartment. Freddy hung up, called a friend about dinner plans, saying, "Yo, I just got back from Europe, where I was shooting a Colt 45 ad with Billy Dee Williams. I guess Billy Dee wasn't reaching the younger beer drinker anymore, so they brought me in." His friend put him on hold. While he was waiting, Freddy handed me a book that was sitting under a press kit for Digital Underground and said, "I just got this great book on semiotics—it's very interesting shit. You should read it." Salt 'N Pepa appeared on *Video Music Box.* Sinatra off, Salt 'N Pepa on, extra loud. After finishing his call to his friend, Freddy hung up, slouched in his chair for a few moments, then abruptly sat up, grabbed the phone, and tried to retrieve his call from the Show World employee, who by this time would have been on hold for thirty-five minutes. At some point during those thirty-five minutes, she had apparently had feelings of abandonment and hung up. "Damn, *damn*, that's wack," Freddy said, sounding sad. "I lost her."

THE PLAZA HOTEL'S EDWARDIAN ROOM is one of those hushed, dim chambers where everything is so padded and plushy that it seems as if the carpets have carpets. Heavy swag curtains fall across the windows. Heavy linens drape the tables. Everywhere there are little candles, large men, fancy-looking women, trim waiters, glinting platters, mother lodes of silver, and an air of genteel excess. Freddy eats here often, but not in the dining room. He eats in the middle of the kitchen, where Kerry Simon, the young chef who runs the place, keeps a table for a few friends. This is some complicated form of inverted reverse snobbery. The Edwardian Room is not a groovy-downtown-hipster kind of place by any stretch of the imagination, but the chef's table in the kitchen has become a hot ticket these days. When Freddy has dinner here, he is escorted by a delicate, doe-eyed, sweet-natured woman named Paige Powell, who is the advertising director of *Interview* and was formerly a frequent escort of Andy Warhol and Jean-Michel Basquiat. These days, Freddy refers to her as "my social coach." Paige refers to Freddy as "a forward-thinking catalyst who should have broad-reach international exposure." They are clearly fond of each other. Over the last month or so, Paige got Freddy invitations to a dinner for Giorgio Armani and the one for the people from Ebel watches. "I'd like to see him cross-connect," she said to me recently. "He should get to know these people, so they can take his great energy and use it somehow. I can almost imagine him as an anchor on an international news program on CNN, or something."

Our dinner group was to be Paige, Freddy, and Freddy's friend Great Adventure, whose real name is Roy. Great Adventure—handsome, immaculately tailored, broad shouldered—had just returned from Brazil, where he had been promoting rap concerts. He is Freddy's current best friend and the man Freddy describes as his fashion coach, for graduating him from his previous B-boy style to his present amalgam of street and chic. Freddy knows exactly what good turn each of his friends and associates has done for him. It is as if he saw his life as a project to which a number of people have generously contributed. Considering that three of his best friends—Warhol, Haring, and Basquiat—are now dead, such accounting seems these days to have particular meaning.

"Yo, Kerry," Freddy said as we walked into the kitchen. "I know this is *definitely* about to be something beyond food, and totally artistic."

Paige and Great Adventure joined us, and we sat down at a large, round table set a few feet away from the grill. The kitchen was clattery, warm, buttery smelling, industrial looking. The table was set in pure white, with pale flowers and heavy silverware. Sitting at it, I felt as if I'd been encased in a clean, quiet capsule and dropped into the middle of a stew. Freddy, Paige, and Great Adventure were discussing an upcoming concert in Rio when the first course arrived—a construction of squid and fat pellets of Arborio rice, piled together in a way that called to mind a Japanese pagoda.

Freddy whistled, and said, "This is lovely, lovely, love-*ly*. We are definitely living large tonight! Tell me the name of this dish again. I have to remember to describe it to my mother."

"Squid-ink risotto," Kerry said.

"Excellent," Freddy said. "My mother would bug out if she saw this."

Great Adventure started to chuckle.

"Yo, man," Freddy said to him. "Picture a fine squid-ink risotto in Bed-Stuy."

Three hours later, we were still at the table, having eaten risotto, grilled monkfish, roast lobster with corn sauce, and chocolate cake, and having discussed rap in Brazil, the latest Public Enemy record, Andy Warhol, cooking, Freddy's popularity in Japan, Freddy's interest in shooting an episode of *Yo!* in a prison, the president of Fiat, the sisters who own Fendi, the march of the Ringling elephants through Manhattan, Paige's hometown in Oregon, a pajama party some rappers had had in Los Angeles, the Oscars, the Plaza, Leona Helmsley, Andy Warhol again, the Show World murder, and the various ingredients of the various dishes we'd eaten. It made for peppy conversation. Toward the end of the evening, Freddy's attention started to drift, as if he'd flipped to the next page in his datebook. He explained after a minute that he was starting to think of everything he had coming up in the next few days. It was, by his count, about a million things.

"I've got that movie I'm going to be in, and I have to work on the screenplay of this movie I'll be directing, and there's always *Yo!*, and I got to get this video going," he said when we had finally left the Edwardian

Room and were standing outside the revolving doors. It was now dark. A group of women swaddled in mink stoles brushed past us, murmuring as they headed into the hotel. A horse carriage and a cab were double-parked at the bottom of the steps going down to the street. Freddy posed at the top and lit a cigarette. He was wearing his sunglasses and a big tan hat. Back-lit by the Plaza chandeliers, he formed an imposing silhouette. "This black pop-life shit can get hectic sometimes," he said after a moment. "It's cool most of the time, but it can be hectic. Every now and again, to be honest with you, I'm, like, *damn*."

I WANT THIS APARTMENT

*J*ILL MEILUS IS A NEW YORK CITY REAL ESTATE broker. Like Superman, she can see through walls. Walking down a Manhattan street with her is a paranormal experience. "Nice building," you might remark as you pass a handsome but unrevealing prewar facade, to which she might respond that the J-line apartment on the third floor has a new kitchen, that the guy in 8-A is being transferred to Florida and will entertain any offers of more than two hundred thousand dollars, that the super is a chainsmoker, that there is a one-bedroom for sale because the owners are having money troubles or are having twins or made a new fortune or are splitting up. New York is the big show-off of American cities, yet its residential life is almost invisible to the ordinary passerby. Even so, you cannot hide from a real estate broker. The other day, Jill took one of her customers to view a SoHo loft—a nice, $650,000 sort of place, with a lot of windows and chintz upholstery and silver gizmos artfully scattered around. Jill's customer, a television actress, whom I will call Vivian, liked the loft, so she paced off the dimensions and counted the closets, and eventually came upon a locked door beside the kitchen. She told Jill that she wanted to see what was behind it; after all, the price of the loft could be calculated per square inch, let alone square foot, and behind the door were a few of those high-priced inches. Jill considered the request and then sighed. "Vivian, I wish I could show it to you, but I can't," she said. "The owners of the loft are sadomasochists, and that is their dungeon." "Oh," Vivian said. She looked disappointed. After a moment, Jill brightened. "I know that it'd be a great space for a second bathroom," she added, "and the owners do promise to remove the dungeon fixtures as a condition of sale."

The total value of all privately owned apartments in Manhattan is estimated to be $102.7 billion, and about 7 percent of those apartments turn over every year. In 1998, for instance, the combined sales of all cooperative and condominium units came to $7.9 billion. Many of those units are one-bedroom starter apartments, but some are larger, and a few are a lot larger. Last year, the company that Jill works for, the Corcoran Group, sold a pretty big place on Central Park West to Ian Schrager for $9 million, and recently another brokerage had almost closed a deal for a $22 million apartment that occupies the top three floors of the Pierre Hotel, and is being purchased by a Wall Street analyst with a rather pessimistic view of the stock market. The Corcoran Group handles 20 percent of the sales of New York residential real estate. There are about four hundred Corcoran Group brokers, making it the second-largest brokerage in the city—smaller than Douglas Elliman and bigger than the three other major brokerages, Brown Harris Stevens, Halstead Property, and Bellmarc Realty. These are good days to be a real estate broker in New York. Because prices are so high and the volume of sales is so large, brokers in New York are making more than their counterparts in other big, expensive cities, like Houston and Los Angeles. The top broker in New York earned close to $2 million last year, and a typical broker is making sixty thousand and has no trouble finding people who want to sell and people who want to buy.

When I first met Jill, she had just got a new exclusive, a

PREWAR 2BR FOR $279K. GV/PRIME Charming home just steps off Fifth Avenue on best blk. View of brownstones and lots of sun! Seller relocating!

It was actually a cheery but bantam two-bedroom co-op on West Eleventh Street, in Greenwich Village, which another Corcoran broker had sold to a young investment banker two years ago for $160,000. The banker was getting married and moving to Texas. As the apartment's exclusive agent, Jill was handling all the advertising and marketing. Although any broker from any company could show the apartment to customers, Jill had to be present at all showings, and she would split the commission with the eventual buyer's broker. In effect, she was the seller's representative. She would keep the entire commission if she happened to sell one of her exclusives to one of her own customers, because then she would be representing both the seller and the buyer. Everywhere else in the country, brokers typically share listings and can show a house at any time, by themselves, because keys are usually left in a lockbox outside the house which any broker can gain access to. The New York City system is very New York–like: complicated, arcane, and logistically nightmarish. Not only do brokers have to be available to show their exclusives to other brokers and their customers but they also have to be able to take customers to see apartments on the market which other brokers are handling, and this means they have to arrange with those other brokers to see their exclusives. At the moment, Jill had two apartments that were her exclusives, and about a dozen customers who were actively looking to buy, with price limits ranging from around $160,000 to just under $2 million.

Jill is chestnut haired, self-effacing, midsize, and fortyish. She specializes in downtown real estate and has a lot of artists and writers and architects as customers, which means she goes to work wearing big, hairy sweaters and stretch pants rather than an uptown broker's wardrobe of smart black trouser suits and moderate-height heels. She grew up in a suburb of New York and has lived in the city since she began college. She now lives in an insanely huge loft, for which she pays an insanely low rent—so low that she begged me not to print it, knowing how such a thing would make her the object of pure, embittered resentment. Not that having a great place to live wouldn't stir up envy anywhere in the world; it's just that in New York the span between crummy places and fantastic ones is wide. So is the span between the apartment that is an incredible bargain and the one that is wildly overpriced. Only in New York are you likely to find so many identical apartments with so many unidentical price tags. The fact of Jill's living circumstances came to light when I asked her whether selling real estate was like working in a chocolate factory—that is, whether you were tempted to consume the best merchandise yourself. "Most brokers have some kind of good deal," she said sheepishly. "I mean, we get to see everything and we usually end up with something kind of strange and great." Even so, there have to be times when brokers must feel unrequited. One afternoon, I went with Iva Spitzer, a broker with Douglas Elliman, to see a prewar apartment on West Fifty-seventh Street that she was handling. It was quite nice: about fifty-five hundred square feet; eleven rooms or so; a terrace running around the entire apartment; north, south, east, and west views, including a dead-on view of Carnegie Hall; triple-height ceilings; a majestic living room, with cove lighting and a sky scene painted on the domed ceiling; a shuttered napping room; black walnut flooring; a master bathroom bigger than an average bedroom, with the original sunken marble bath and a huge stall shower with sixteen brass shower spigots mounted on the walls and a dinner-plate-size brass showerhead with a few hundred pinpoint spray holes; and a yawningly large professional-quality kitchen with Sub-Zero everything and a stainless-steel fendered range. I could easily imagine living there, until Iva mentioned that it was a rental that happened to be priced at thirty-five thousand dollars a month. I asked if it frustrated her to handle such a place. "No, it's an incredible place, but I don't really see myself here," she said, sounding philosophical. "I see someone like Sean Penn here. Or Puff Daddy."

Real estate can be an aggravating profession. "It's a sort of manic-depressive business," Jill likes to say. "It's always either totally crazy or dead. Things fall through all the time. If you get devastated by stuff like that, you can't go on." Up until twenty years ago, residential real estate in New York City was usually handled by "social brokers"—older women who sold apartments now and then to their friends over afternoon tea or at the hairdresser's. In those years, very little property in Manhattan was actually bought or sold. What few hundred listings existed were handwritten on index cards, collated on knitting needles, and filed in leather binders. The cooperative and condominium conversions that began in the 1970s turned thousands of rental apartments into real estate that could be bought and sold. Suddenly, there was a lot more money to be made, and real estate brokerages began attracting actresses and artists and teachers, people who liked the independence and mobility of the job and were used to a certain amount of unpredictability and rejection, and usually came to real estate after another career. Jill was a chef at a couple of popular New York restaurants before she got her broker's license, eleven years ago. She worked from home for a while after she had a baby, and had returned to her office, in the Flatiron district, a year before we met. Iva Spitzer had also been a chef—at a restaurant in Boston—before going into real estate. Barbara

Corcoran, the owner and founder of the Corcoran Group, had held twenty-six short-term jobs before she started her business; her favorite was waitressing at a diner in New Jersey. She liked it because it was a people job.

EARLY ONE TUESDAY MORNING last month, I went with Jill to the West Eleventh Street two-bedroom. It was the first day she was showing the apartment. She had advertised it in the *Times* over the weekend and had also posted a description of it on the Corcoran Group Web site, and already she had gotten a dozen queries. The apartment house was an elegant eight-story brick box built at the turn of the century, with a curlicued banister running up the stairs and tiny Juliet balconies on each landing, but the interior had been gutted and rebuilt in the early eighties, and the apartments were now stripped down and undetailed, with chalky white drywall walls and hollow-core doors. The seven hundred square feet of the apartment were diced up into a galley kitchen, one full bath, a rectangular living room, one average-size bedroom, and one dwarfish one. Most normal people living in normal cities would probably consider it far too small to live in for the price, but by New York standards it was a sunny, snug, well-located apartment, which would probably sell quickly. In New York, "quickly" means "quickly" and sometimes even "viciously." When the market in New York is heated up, war breaks out. Real estate gets most people agitated, but in New York it seems to provoke a special fervor. Brokers start accepting only sealed bids, and bids offering more than the asking price are taken for granted. So is offering all cash, proposing to forgo the mortgage-contingency clause in the contract, begging to sign a contract on the spot, and tendering press releases and family portraits to plead one's case. One of Jill's colleagues had a customer who bartered for an apartment with rare French movie posters, which he guaranteed would appreciate in value.

The owner of the apartment had already gone to work when we arrived, but she had obviously tidied up before she left. A few fresh magazines were fanned out on her coffee table like a deck of cards, and all the wastebaskets were empty. Her cat was on the sofa, chewing on a piece of wire and daydreaming. It was a chilly but brilliant day and the apartment was filled with light. Right after we settled in, a broker named Jackie called from the lobby, and a moment later she stepped through the door with her customer, a pale young man with a shaved head. The customer surveyed the little living room and then walked to the window and gazed out onto the street.

"Boy, it's really sunny," Jackie said.

"All day," Jill said.

"Such a pretty block," Jackie added.

"Quintessential Village," Jill said. She turned to the young man and told him, "By the way, none of the walls in here are structural, so you can move them all around if you want to."

The customer wandered out of the living room, into the bigger bedroom, and then into the bathroom. "I'm not in a rush to buy," he called over his shoulder. "I've only been looking for about a year." Jackie shot Jill a look.

After a minute, the customer said, "You know, I just realized that I forgot my glasses, so I'm going to have to come back and look another time." He wandered out the front door. Jackie trailed behind, mouthing "I'll call you" to Jill.

"She'll never call," Jill said, closing the door behind them.

A few minutes later, another broker—Bill from Douglas Elliman—appeared at the door, accompanied by another pale young man. This one was carrying a briefcase, which he dropped in the kitchen doorway. When he was out of earshot, his broker whispered to Jill, "Look! That's good! When people put their bags down, it means they plan to stay for a while."

The young man came back into earshot. "Wow, there's a lot of light in here," he said.

"None of the walls are structural, so you can move anything," Jill said. "I mean, if you want to."

"The light is really beautiful," the customer said.

"It's a historic block," his broker added.

"It's beautiful light," the customer said, "and I like the exposed brick." He took another turn around the living room and said, "I love this building! This feels so good!"

"You could take down the wall between the bedrooms," Jill said. "Or between the kitchen and the little bedroom."

The customer wasn't listening. "That's my deal, see. I need light. And this has light. It's awesome. Beautiful. I really like it."

A broker named Edna arrived, leading her customer, a poker-faced young woman who said she worked as a recipe tester for a gourmet magazine. Edna dawdled by the door while the woman scanned the apartment.

Then they huddled in the living room and waited for the young man and the Douglas Elliman broker to leave. Once they had gone, Jill turned to Edna and her customer. "So?" she said.

"I love it," the young woman said. "I want it."

Jill raised her eyebrows.

"I really, really love it," the young woman went on. "By the way, are dogs okay?"

Jill lowered her eyebrows. "No dogs," she said. "Sorry."

Edna clutched at her throat and gasped. "Oh God. No dogs? No dogs? You have *got* to be kidding. Well, there goes my deal. She wants to buy the apartment right now. However, she has a dog."

The young woman started to tremble. "My dog is like . . . *adorable*! She looks like Benji! She's totally quiet! Look, I want this apartment! I really want it!"

Jill asked her if the dog was bigger than a cat. The young woman chewed on her lip for a minute and then said, "Well, I don't know how she would compare to a cat, but if you cut a wheaten terrier in half that's what she looks like. Her name is Hunni, and she licks everybody, and everybody loves her. I can pay all cash for the apartment. I'll pay the asking price. I mean, I really love this place."

"Let me think," Jill said, jiggling her foot. "Okay, maybe I should present it to the co-op board as . . . as a catlike dog named Hunni. Why don't you write a letter to the board and describe her and talk about what she does during the day and what she does during vacations, and then we can present it from there." The young woman looked buoyed, said she would write the letter that day, and offered to bring Hunni over to meet people in the building.

"That might be premature," Jill said. "I'd go with the letter."

The next day, a letter supporting Hunni's residency application arrived by fax at the Corcoran Group offices. Jill passed it along to the co-op board president, who said that Hunni sounded very likable but the answer was still no.

BECAUSE OF THE IDIOSYNCRASIES of the market, New York brokers come to know more about their clients than brokers elsewhere ordinarily do. If you are buying a house in the suburbs, your broker might never know the exact details of your economic circumstances. In New York, most privately held apartments are part of either a co-op or a condominium association. Anybody with enough money can purchase a condominium, but a prospective buyer of a co-op must submit supporting material to the building's board of directors, including letters of reference, a complete statement of net worth, and, often, tax returns going back several years, and then must sit for an interview with the board's admissions committee. Even with a mortgage in hand, a buyer isn't guaranteed a deal until he or she gets the committee's approval. A good broker will help a buyer prepare the board package, which means that he or she will see your letters of reference, figures on your net worth, and your tax returns—details many people consider rather personal. Because New Yorkers move so much—more than other Americans do—they often work with a broker repeatedly. Several of Jill's customers were people who had bought or sold through her before. And, whether it's because prices are so high in the city or because New Yorkers are peculiarly indecisive, it seems to take some people a long, long time to buy a place to live, and they therefore spend a long, long time with their brokers. Two of Jill's active customers had been looking for two years, and a few more had been looking almost as long. In the meantime, their lives had changed, their jobs had evolved, they'd gotten more money, they'd had kids, they'd colored their hair, their marital status had wavered. Some had come to regard Jill as a friend. She worried over them and kept an eye on their psychic real estate as well as on their real real estate. A few of her customers have asked her to play matchmaker if she ever had a customer she thought they'd like.

Jill was fretting that day over Lucy, a customer of hers who worked in film production. Lucy had been looking for an apartment for two years. Jill wanted her to buy the Eleventh Street apartment but despaired that she couldn't commit. "Lucy really needs to get focused," she said, sighing. "She's backed out of a few deals already and she just puts herself through agony every time. We had a talk one day about whether we should keep working together, and whether our relationship was getting to be too much of a burden, but I think we worked it out." Bertram, an architect who'd been looking with Jill for a year, was "a perfectionist, and very apprehensive," Jill told me. "He thinks he wants to live downtown, but I think he should really be looking in Chelsea, considering what he can pay, so we're working on that." Bertram had an accepted offer on a place in Chelsea, but Jill knew him well enough not to consider it a done deal. While she was waiting for another broker to show up at West Eleventh, she checked her voice mail. There was a message from Bertram saying he'd decided to withdraw his offer on the Chelsea place, because he'd heard from a resident of the building that another apartment there had just sold for less than he was offering. "I knew it. He got stressed out," Jill said. "He was so nervous anyway." She also got a message from a customer telling her he'd decided he could spend more, so she could expand the price range as she searched for him; a message from a customer who was preparing his board package and had forgotten to get letters of reference and was in a panic; and a message from an art dealer who had read about Jill on the Corcoran Web site and was interested in the Eleventh Street place.

The Corcoran Group is now selling an apartment a day through its Web site. Barbara Corcoran believes that the Internet will eventually replace much of the work now being done by brokers. A typical person buying an apartment in New York City calls in response to a newspaper ad and then sees an average of fourteen apartments before buying; someone real estate shopping on a computer sees floor plans, photographs, long descriptions, and a biography of the broker before making a call, and then seems to need to see only four apartments before buying. Instead of making brokers obsolete, Internet real estate shopping will make the marketing part of their job more critical, and waste less of their time dragging customers around town. In the meantime, though, being a broker remains a full-time—even a day-and-nighttime—job. As the next broker was heading up to see West Eleventh Street, Jill mentioned that she'd had a terrible dream the night before. She dreamed that she had run into a friend whom she'd been showing apartments to—a real person, whom she really is showing apartments to—and the friend told her that she'd just bought an apartment from another broker. The apartment was in the West Fifties. "It was just awful!" Jill said. "I've been showing her apartments forever. I said, 'Lil! You told me you would never live in the West Fifties!' I couldn't believe it. I think that when I see her I'm going to feel really upset, even though it was just a dream."

THERE WERE TWO BIG STORIES in New York real estate that week. One was that a four-bedroom duplex loft that had been on the market for seven years—an unofficial record for longevity—and had been handled at one time or another by every broker in town (including Jill) had finally been sold. The other was that at a recent closing the attorney had threatened to withhold twenty-five thousand dollars of the broker's commission, so the broker grabbed the contract away from the attorney, which compelled the attorney to smash the broker's arm onto the table, bruising it severely and breaking her watch. A few brokers who had heard this tale suggested that in the future all closings be moderated by a therapist. Iva once remarked that she became the center of attention at any gathering as soon as she mentioned she was a broker; everyone had a horror story or a happy story to recount, and wanted to know whether the market was going up or down and whether a person had gotten a good deal or had been ripped off and whether she knew about Building X or Apartment Y. The experience, she said, was sort of like telling people at a dinner party that you're a doctor, and finding yourself besieged with moles to examine and surgery stories to hear.

"Shopping for apartments, I think, is horrible for most people," Jill said. "They get very emotional." We had taken a break from West Eleventh Street and were walking back to her office. The air was fresh and sweet and cold, and the sky was as blue as a swimming pool, and all the buildings on the block glowed a little in the afternoon sun. We passed a brownstone with wide stairs and a handkerchief-size garden. "Really nice inside," Jill said, nodding toward it. "I showed it to some people last year, and they almost bid on it, but they were thinking of starting a family, and it would have been too small." This made her think of Vivian, who is currently single but wants a two-bedroom. "She's so lovely," Jill said. "And I guess she's optimistic, even though she complains to me how impossible it is to meet men." That made her think of Greg, who is also single, and whose loft she had just gotten as an exclusive, because his next-door neighbor's daughter went to school with Jill's daughter. And that made her think of an apartment for sale on the Upper East Side that Greg might like to buy after she sold his loft. And that made her think of Lucy, for no particular reason except that she thought about her often, and decided she would take her back to see something at London Terrace, a large prewar complex in Chelsea, because, even though Lucy had bid and backed out on something there before, Jill thought she might have finally reached the point where she would just buy something halfway decent, so she could stop looking. Around every corner we turned was another building that Jill knew or had sold something in or had handled in some way. It was as if to her the city's buildings all quivered with change and movement: Her view was like time-lapse photography that reveals commotion in something that otherwise, in quick glances, appears to be entirely still.

A few days later, Jill sent me a message saying that she'd sold the West Eleventh Street apartment to a couple—a film editor and a network news employee—for $270,000; that Vivian had decided not to bid on the loft with the dungeon; that Lucy had agreed to look at London Terrace again; that the art dealer who came to her through the Web site hadn't bid on West Eleventh but wanted Jill to take her around. She had gotten a number of new customers who had answered the ad for West Eleventh, and would lose a few old ones, at least temporarily, once they'd found a place, bought it, and moved. It was business as usual.

DEVOTION ROAD

*T*HE BIGGEST, NICEST THING A TRAVELING GOS-
pel group might pray for is a bus. Usually, gospel groups
consider themselves blessed if they book a show, and truly
blessed if they can also find a way to get there; sometimes
they get the call but they don't have a ride. Flying is rarely
an option, because it costs too much, and because gospel
concerts are often in places that are underserved by airlines, like Demopolis, Alabama, and Madison, Georgia. The
Jackson Southernaires, who have been singing in gospel
programs around the country virtually every weekend for
the last fifty years, used to travel from show to show
crowded into whatever car they could get their hands on,
and they thanked God if the car got them to the program
and back before it broke down. In 1965, they sang in a
gospel competition in Detroit, and a fan of theirs bet a fan
of the Mighty Clouds of Joy that the Southernaires would
win. The Mighty Clouds were heavy favorites but the
Southernaires prevailed, and their fan was so grateful that
he bought them a bus with some of his winnings. The
Southernaires are now on their third bus. In a previous life,

their bus worked for Trailways; now it is painted silver and white, has a license plate that says BUCKLE UP WITH JESUS, and has THE JACKSON SOUTHERNAIRES stenciled in large, loopy script on the back and both sides.

The bus attracts attention. Once, at a diner in Florida, a truck driver who was hauling a carnival ride from Tampa to Birmingham came over to the Southernaires' table, introduced himself, and said, "I heard you-all sing thirty years ago, in a union hall in Suffolk, Virginia, and I been dreaming of meeting you ever since." Then he clapped his hands to his chest and exclaimed, "Thank Jesus for causing me to see your bus!" Another time, in Jackson, Mississippi, which is the group's base of operations, Mack Brandon, the Southernaires' driver, was outside checking the engine and the tires, and a woman pulled over to take a picture of the bus for her gospel scrapbook. She asked Mack to pose beside the front tire. He was in work clothes and didn't feel photogenic, but she persisted. Not long ago, I asked him if he had ever seen the photograph, and he said, "And *how*! That lady and me got engaged."

Sometimes the bus becomes a source of problems. Once, the Southernaires broke down somewhere between Nashville and Louisville and needed three days to raise the money for repairs. Another time, in Richmond, Virginia, the transmission blew up, but, fortunately, Willis Pittman—the lead singer in Willis Pittman and the Burden Lifters—lives in Richmond and is a mechanic, and he fixed the transmission for free. One night, in the middle of Ohio, a tire blew out and they ran out of gas at the same moment. A farmer heard the commotion and came out of his house, then went into his barn, found a tire that fitted the wheel, filled a can of gas, jacked up the bus, replaced the tire, filled the gas tank, pulled them back onto the road with his tractor, and then showed them his Ku Klux Klan membership card and asked them to be on their way.

THE GOSPEL AUDIENCE is probably the poorest of any mass audience in the country, and there are a thousand ways, like working at a Kmart or doing construction, that most gospel singers could make more money than they do singing gospel; and most gospel singers don't make enough from their music to live on. It is a matter of devotion. Gospel music has complicated origins, but it primarily came out of the Southern black Church of God in Christ and the Holiness movement of the Methodist Church; musically, it is a union of English revival hymns and African song styles—call-and-response, moaning, shouting. In the thirties, gospel singers started traveling a circuit of auditoriums, churches, Grange halls, and tent meetings, and through more than half a century the gospel highway has hardly changed. There are gospel records, but for most of the audience gospel is more a form of public worship and performance than something you listen to at home.

Over the past year, the Jackson Southernaires, as they have for most of the last five decades, left home nearly every Thursday and spent the weekend on the road. They sang in almost every state and in Ontario, in places as tiny as Blytheville, Arkansas, and as big as Brooklyn; they sang in half-empty church halls and in packed theaters; and last year, for the first time, they sang in France and were treated like stars. Not long ago, I traveled with the Southernaires on the gospel circuit. The first night on the road, I couldn't sleep, so I sat on the steps at the front of the bus and talked to Mack. We were on our way to Demopolis, Alabama, a run-down town in the center of the state. Mack said, "We're going way out in the country. You wait and see—people'll be coming to the show on mules." Mack has been a gospel bus driver for twenty-five years. He started with Reverend Julius Cheeks and the Sensational Nightingales, and then he drove for Willie Neal Johnson and the Gospel Keynotes, and then, four years ago, he joined the Southernaires. Until 1965, he drove for Trailways. His home is in Roxboro, North Carolina, but he often stays at the Stonewall Jackson Motel, in Jackson, Mississippi. He said that his professional zenith was in 1981, after Willie Neal was nominated for a gospel Grammy, when the Gospel Keynotes rode to the ceremony in a limousine. "It wasn't just the limousine," he said. "When they came to pick me up, I opened the door, and there was Dionne Warwick. It was a completely beautiful experience. I opened the door, I saw Dionne, and I wanted to *die*."

When Mack gets tired, James Burks drives. That's his No. 2 job with the Southernaires; his No. 1 job is to play bass guitar and sing backup. Everyone in the group doubles up. Granard McClendon, the guitar player, who is slim and glib and is a sharp dresser, negotiates for the motel rooms when they pull into a town, and he also chooses which of their six sets of matching uniforms they will wear each night. During my trip with the group, Melvin Wilson sang tenor ("high") and falsetto ("top") and was also the sound engineer. He has satiny dark skin and a plump, pumpkin-shaped face. When Melvin was a teenager, in Robersonville, North Carolina, his father managed a gospel group called the Dynamic Powell Brothers. No one knew that Melvin could sing—not even Melvin. One day, he was riding home with the Dynamic Powell Brothers from a show and he just opened his mouth and let go. His voice was as cool and clear as water; the Dynamic Powell Brothers hired him on the spot. When I traveled with the Jackson Southernaires, the keyboard player was Gary Miles. (Melvin and Gary recently left to join another group, and have been replaced by Tony Nichols and Daryl Johnson.) Gary also hauled equipment out of the bus for shows and hauled it back afterward. In his off-road life, he is an actor. He has been an extra on *Murder, She Wrote* and *Magnum, P.I.* Both times, he was cast as an officious waiter. He has skinny arms, a wide trunk, a nutty laugh, and an air of astonishment.

Maurice Surrell drums and sings and is the Southernaires' enforcer; that is, he writes up members of the group when they infract Southernaire rules. The rules take up fifteen typewritten pages. They were established years ago by Luther Jennings, one of the original Southernaires, who is now retired from gospel and teaches math at a high school in Jackson. Luther wanted the Southernaires to be known as the gentlemen of the gospel circuit, so his rules are strict and the fines are steep: twenty-five dollars for a wrinkled uniform, twenty-five dollars for unshined shoes, a hundred dollars for cursing, a hundred dollars for bringing a young lady to the restaurant where the group is eating, twenty-five dollars for hitting the wrong note in a song. Luther did not believe in leniency; if he transgressed, he fined himself. Luther was also the Southernaires' debt collector. Sometimes concert promoters were so moved by the Southernaires' performances that they misplaced the money they owed the Southernaires. This had a way of irritating Luther, so he usually carried one or more of the guns he owned—a single-action revolver, a bolt-action rifle, a .22, a .32, a Winchester, two .25-caliber revolvers, some twelve-gauge shotguns, two .357s, two .45s, and a couple of dainty handguns—which he could lay down, as if he were setting the table, when he went to collect from the promoter at the end of a show.

The Southernaires have two lead singers—Roger Bryant and Huey Williams. Roger is an ordained minister and an emphatic public speaker, so he is responsible for going onstage before each concert and urging the members of the audience to buy a Southernaires record or video before they leave. He has full cheeks, gap teeth, a sidelong glance, and parchment-colored skin. His hair is puffy and moldable; it looks different every day. His voice is choked and explosive. Onstage, Roger is a pacer, an arm swinger, a hip slapper, a fist shaker, and a screamer. He is now thirty-nine years old. When he was small, he was in a group called the Sunbeam Jrs.

His father, a foundry worker and preacher in Saginaw, Michigan, would stand him up on the kitchen table and beat him to make him sing.

Huey Williams is fifty-five. He has been with the group for twenty-nine years, and now when people think of the Southernaires they mostly think of Huey. He grew up in the country south of Jackson. Before he became a full-time gospel singer, he did construction work in Detroit and in New Orleans, but his enthusiasms are strictly rural. He once told me that people refer to him as the coon-hunting gospel singer. Currently, he has six Walker hounds; they live in big dog pens behind his house, in McComb, Mississippi. On his days off, Huey usually takes the dogs hunting or attends to hunting-related errands. One time when I visited him in McComb, we spent the day driving across the state to the taxidermist, to pick up a bobcat Huey had shot. Huey is a tall man with a broad chest and the steep cheekbones of a Cherokee. He has big dimples, blue eyes, and a thin mustache. He wears two chunky gold rings and a thick gold cuff; his hands are long and elegant, and his nails are smooth and shiny. The first time I met him, he took my chin in his hands, tilted it toward him, and said, "Take a good look at my face. Have you ever in your life seen blue eyes on a black man?" His speaking voice is sometimes brisk and commanding and sometimes whispery and intimate, and always tonic. I have heard him sing in a bass voice, which is so deep that it sounds like burping, and in a shrieking, afflicted tenor, and in a buttery, pliant baritone. When he was around thirty, his voice was so supple he could do anything with it; he believes that at the time he was simply the best singer in the whole world. Before a performance, when he is encircled by his fans, he walks around like Goliath. In the morning, when he wakes up hoarse from the show and creaky from sleeping on the bus, he looks like someone who thinks a lot about retiring. His wife, Mamie, who is a machine operator at a General Motors plant in Mississippi, says, "I'm so used to him traveling I don't know what I'd do if he were here. He's got his dogs, I suppose. But, with him always being away, we don't have time to get into each other's hair."

ON THE ROAD, at truck stops and diners, we ate Reese's peanut butter cups; Reese's Pieces; Sour Cream 'n Onion Pringles potato crisps; 3 Musketeers; chicken, baked, simmered, stewed, smothered, potted in pies, or creamed à la king; chicken-fried steak; chicken-fried chicken; chicken even for breakfast sometimes, if we'd traveled all night after a show and never got dinner. Arriving in Columbus, Georgia, after driving since midnight, we had baked chicken at ten in the morning, which was the earliest I had ever eaten chicken in my life. Most often, the Southernaires take their meals at truck stops, which have telephones at the tables and showers for rent and sometimes Southernaires tapes for sale in racks near the cashiers. "Truck stops have beautiful food," Mack once explained to me. "Besides, we can get the bus serviced at the same time we eat."

Now and then when I was with the Southernaires, I felt we spent more time arranging to eat, stopping to eat, ordering food to go, waiting to eat, and eating than we did at gospel shows. The night I began my travels with them, we left Jackson, drove about twelve miles, then pulled off at a truck stop and had dinner. It was a quarter to one in the morning. None of the Southernaires understood why I found this odd. The truck stop was fairly empty, and the nine of us spread out at five or six tables, so when Huey said grace our "Amen"s ping-ponged around the dining room. When the Southernaires' agent books a date for them, she tries to get the promoter to pay for their hotel and dinner, to supplement the small amount they are paid for the show. Sometimes the promoter offers to cook them dinner instead of underwriting it. In Madison, Georgia, an old man who was a friend of the promoter set up a booth outside the auditorium with paper plates, napkins, an ancient deep fryer, and a Crock-Pot, and started cooking yellow perch and hot dogs for the group to have before the show. When I asked him if the fish was good, he gave me a funny look. Then he slapped a piece of perch across the palm of his hand and said, "Like I said, it don't got no bones."

AT THE CONCERTS, I saw men wearing spats and women wearing hats such as I'd never seen before: a black porkpie with a turquoise veil and bow; a midshipman's white cap with little pearls sewn along the rim; a tricorne of orange faille; a green beanie; a purple derby, worn at a slant; a red saucer that had netting looped around the edge and a piece of stiff fabric shaped like a Dorito sticking straight up from the crown; a fuchsia-colored ten-gallon with an ostrich feather drooping from the hatband. The hats were on elderly ladies, who moved through the crowds like cruise ships. Teenage girls came to the concerts, too, in flowered dresses or in jeans and tank tops, wearing their babies slung on their hips, the way hikers wear fanny packs, or jouncing them absentmindedly, like loose change.

I heard people at gospel concerts call eyeglasses "helpers" and a gravel road "a dirty road," and I heard an infant called "a lap baby," and a gun called "a persuader," and dying called "making it over," and an embarrassed person described as "wanting to swallow his teeth," and a dead person described as someone who was "having his mail delivered to him by groundhogs." Everybody talked about Jesus all the time. He was called a doctor, a lawyer, a lily of the valley, a lamb, a shepherd, joy in the morning, a rock, a road, peace in the evening, a builder, a captain, a rose of Sharon, a friend, a father, and someone who is always on time. I met a man named Porkchop and a man named Midget and a little boy named Royriquez Clarencezellus Wooten. I heard other gospel groups perform: the Christian Harmonizers and the Sensational Harmonizers and the Harmonettes and the Religiousettes and the Gloryettes and the Gospel True Lights and the True Gospel Singers and the Brotherhood Gospel Singers and the Five Singing Sons and the Mighty Sons of Glory and the Fantastic Disciples and the Fantastic Soulernaires and the Fantastic Violinaires and the Sunset Jubilaires and the Pilgrim Jubilees and the Brown Boys and the Five Blind Boys and Wonder Boy and the Spiritual Voices. The concerts were like big public conversations. The exhortations that people called out to the singers most often were "Take your time!" and "Let Him *use* you!" The exhortations that Huey and Roger called out most often were "Do you believe in Jesus?" and "Can I get just one witness?" and "Are you with me, church?" and "You know, God is *able*."

In Madison, Georgia, the Southernaires performed as part of a program given in a school auditorium. As soon as the concert began, a tiny woman in a peach-colored pantsuit got up from her seat and made her way over to the aisle, and then she spiraled around for about an hour, gasping, "Thank you, Jesus! Thank you, Jesus!" with her eyes squeezed shut and her hands flapping in the air. People stepped around her carefully when they went to and from their seats. On the stage, a local group was performing, and one of the singers had raised her arms and turned her palms toward her face as she sang; she had six fingers on each hand, and each nail was painted coral pink. After the song, she leaned over the edge of the stage and said sharply, "Isn't Satan busy? Satan's a stubborn old mule. I remember when I would lay out all night on what they call the disco floor. Then something hit me in the head. The voice I heard, it was just like threading a needle." I saw only one white person besides myself at one concert—she was the desk clerk at the motel where we were staying, and Huey told her if she gave us good rooms he'd give her a free ticket. Huey introduced me to the audience one night, and afterward someone passed me a note that said, "We Welcome You, To Madison, Georgia. From: Hattie." I read it and looked up, and the woman who had written it fluttered her handkerchief at me, and during the next song she crossed the room and kissed me.

MARIANNA, FLORIDA: We arrive at four-thirty in the morning, after driving all night. Granard will try to negotiate a half-day rate at a motel, since we will sleep for only a few hours and then will leave to set up the show, and after the show we'll get back on the bus and start driving to McCormick, South Carolina, for the next show. Even for a gospel group as well established as the Southernaires, every dollar makes a difference. One night, I found a scrap of paper on the bus on which someone had been doing calculations. It said, "Show, $1500. Records $232." When all was said and done, that appeared to be all they would make that evening, and they had to pay for their food and gas and lodging and split the remainder eight ways. The motels we drive by and consider around Marianna are squat, cinder-block buildings on weedy lots. At the first one we try, the night manager comes out and looks at the bus and then he tells Granard the motel is totally booked, even though the parking lot is empty. We stop at another motel, and Granard negotiates for ten minutes, until the clerk gives him a hospitable price. Mack pulls the bus behind the motel, where the parking lot turns into dirt and saw grass. My motel room is stale and dreary. There is a shopping program and a white gospel show on television, and a lizard, paralyzed but pulsating, on one corner of my door.

The next afternoon, the air is completely still. The street leading to Marianna High School is lined with palm trees, and not a frond is moving. The school is a pretty building with Mediterranean inclinations. Its walls are apricot brick. The lawns around it have been roasted. Some little blond girls are playing kickball in front of a bungalow next to the school. A few yards away, a group of old black men wearing short-sleeved white dress shirts and creased fedoras, their pants hiked up to their diaphragms, are standing and talking. When they see the bus, they hitch their pants up even higher and start trotting toward it, waving us around to the side of the school. Mack pulls up to a loading dock and yanks the gears until the bus wheezes and settles down.

Huey stands and stretches, half bent: He is too tall to unfold himself fully in the bus. He nudges Roger, who is listening to his Walkman, and then wipes his forehead, peers out, and says hoarsely, "I always do love Florida."

Through the loading-dock door comes Sister Lula Cheese Vann. She is a husky woman with the haughty bearing of a big shot. She is dressed in a salmon-colored luncheon suit, a dozen rings and pins and bracelets, and a structurally complex salmon-colored hat the size of a breadbox. In her right hand is a flyer for the evening's program. In her left is a quiver of paper fans, which are printed with an essay entitled "How to Get Along with People," and are sponsored by her full-time business, the Vann Funeral Home. By vocation, Sister Vann is a mortician; as an avocation she promotes gospel. She comes to the open door of the bus and says smartly, "Southernaires. Hello. Do you know who I am?"

Huey steps out and says "Sister *Vann*," in his most sultry voice, and shakes her hand. Sister Vann melts a little. The old men form a buzzy circle around them, giving orders and gesturing. Gary and Melvin step out, wearing work gloves, jeans, and T-shirts, and start shoving the equipment out of the belly of the bus. Mack is dragging the record crates up the ramp of the loading dock.

The hall of the school is cool and empty. The front door is propped half open; a wedge of yellow late-afternoon light, of parched lawn, of palms, of shuttered bungalows, of tar-drizzled sidewalk, of little blond girls wandering by is showing through. The hall begins to fill. Mack, setting up the cassette table, is clowning with two young girls in fancy dresses. A brassy-voiced woman walks past them, hauling her teenage daughter by the elbow. "I would like Sister Vann to give her a listen," the woman says to Mack. "Put her on the program. Yes, I would." Brother Alonzo Keys, a handsome chatterbox from Panama City, Florida, who is singing tonight, comes over to pay his respects to Huey and the Southernaires. Sister Gladys Madrick, who will open the gospel program, flounces by, trailed by three skittery young women in lavender dresses. The auditorium is medium-sized and tidy, with smooth gold seats and purple fittings. Three women are already seated, halfway back, and are flapping at one another with Sister Vann's fans.

By seven, Melvin has finished the sound check, so the Southernaires go back to the bus and change into the clothes they will wear for the hour or so before they change into the evening's uniforms—whichever of their six sets Granard has chosen. Melvin has put on a mustard-colored blazer, a mustard shirt, and a black tie. Huey is wearing a turquoise tunic. The last sunlight has deepened and now fades. The neighborhood is dead quiet and dim, except right here, in this little pocket, which is full of noise and commotion, with the school lights flaring, and someone in the auditorium already yelling, and Sister Gladys Madrick's organist starting to play.

THE UNIFORM THAT GRANARD chooses is a black double-breasted suit that they wear with a crisp white shirt, a tie with a purplish gardenia print, and smooth black shoes. Onstage in this uniform, they look polished, natty, and a little grave. Sister Vann introduces them: "I feel blessed. I never, never thought I'd get the Jackson Southernaires here in Marianna, and here they are. The Lord's been good to me." She pauses. "Now, before I start with the Southernaires I want to say to you-all that we got to stop this screaming and *crying* about the price of these tickets. This program costs seven dollars a ticket, and I can tell you, with God as my witness, that this is the cheapest the Jackson Southernaires have ever been anywhere they've gone. So give God a hand, would you, and quit this miserable complaining!" A smattering of applause. Sister Vann smiles wanly. Her funeral home motto is "Concern for the Living, Reverence for the Dead." "I am so glad to be following in God's footsteps," she says. "And I'm glad God put love in my heart and I don't mind sharing it. Now, Marianna, the Jackson *Southernaires*!!"

Maurice taps the drum, and they begin. Each program opens with Roger singing "I've Been Changed." It's a song with a clunky, unlovely beat, but it always rouses the crowd. Singing it, Roger is coiled and ferocious. The auditorium is mostly full now, and the audience is clapping in time. When Roger finishes the song, he steps to one side, and Huey comes forward. "Say 'Amen,' Marianna," he says.

"Amen!"

"Say 'Amen' *again*." Huey flicks the microphone upward, looks forward, and then snaps the microphone to the right and his head the other way. It is a tiny gesture, but vivid—as if he has stolen a look at something and then torn himself away.

"Amen."

"Sing it, Huey. Sing it! Sing it!"

The woman next to me leans over and whispers, "Oh Lord, we got a loud one here."

"Let me ask you something," Huey says, stepping forward. "How many of you here know there is a heaven?"

"A-*men*."

Huey gives his testimony, about the night his house burned to the ground. It is a terrible true story: He lost everything he had, and his son could have died if Huey had not stumbled on him as the family was getting away. Around me, people are nodding and weeping. I have now heard Huey tell this many times—to me in private, and also at several shows— but each time the clenched and anguished look on his face seems fresh. After the story, he always sings "He Will Make a Way," which begins as a sweet, slow, melancholic exchange between singer and chorus, and then rises into a storm. In the last verse, Huey is shouting that God will make a way, that he always makes a way, and then he can't speak anymore, and he starts laughing, and sweat is running down his cheeks, and he turns his eyes upward, and he stares up past the auditorium ceiling, and tears stream down his face.

Huey steps back, exhausted, and Maurice starts the rattling drumbeat for "No Coward Soldier." Roger will take over until the end of the show. He bounds to the edge of the stage and starts singing. The woman next to me, who had taken my hand and held it through most of the show, now releases it gently, as if she were putting a hooked fish back in the water, and turns to me and says, "I'm sorry, baby, but I got to get *loose*." Then she jumps out into the aisle and bends forward from her waist and snaps in a staccato rhythm back and forth as Roger sings.

At that point, I get up and work my way along the row and across the far aisle and stand in the doorway by the side of the stage. It is almost midnight. Someone is frying catfish out front, and the peppery smell thickens the air. Someone with a wheezy cough is standing behind me. A big bug smacks into me, sizzles, and falls. I can see everything from where I am standing: a man in the front row pitched back in his seat and crying without making any noise; twin teenagers in dotted sundresses fanning themselves a few rows behind him; Mack, at the back of the auditorium, sitting on the gray plastic crates that hold the group's records and tapes; a diapered baby in a sailor suit, draped over the shoulder of a slim woman in a yellow sheath; a woman, too wide to sit in an auditorium seat, teetering on a folding chair someone put out for her near the exit door; Roger, on the lip of the stage, taking little explosive bounces on the balls of his feet; Huey, behind him, leaning against the electric piano and running his hand over his hair, his expression a mingling of rapture, fatigue, and distraction, a sort of stillness absorbing him, as if he were in a different, quieter place; a banner over the stage showing the Marianna High School Fighting Bulldog mascot dressed in a snug purple crewneck; a toddler; a wheelchair; a tossed-away flyer; a flash of white in the crowd each time a woman flaps her handkerchief or a man raises his to dab his face—a flash as incandescent as a lit bulb or the luminous envelope of a flame.

Roger jumps off the stage and hollers, "What day did you get the Holy Ghost? Did you get it on a Monday? On a Tuesday? On a Wednesday? Did someone here get it on a Thursday?" One by one, people rise up like bubbles and float toward the stage, grab his hand, shake it hard, and then spin and dance away. He calls for anyone who got the Holy Ghost on Sunday; he sings that God don't need no coward soldiers. He shouts that he wishes he had a witness. He says he knows some people here tonight are going through something. He claps his left hand to his head and then whips it down and pounds his chest. The night is ending. The Southernaires' time is nearly over. They will be back on the bus and on the road to Jackson within the hour. The music is roaring. A little breeze is picking up outside, lifting bits of grass and gravel and blowing them away. Roger stamps his foot and screams, *"We will surely meet again someday!"*

AFTER THE PARTY

*M*IDMORNING, ON A BLUSTERY DAY IN NEW York, Sue Mengers is in her New York hotel, the Lowell, killing time. She doesn't know where she's going from here. She has an apartment in Paris and a house in Beverly Hills, a room key in Manhattan, the story of Hollywood of the late sixties and seventies in her head, and no particular plans. She fidgets around the room. She wants to open the window for you or lend you a sweater if it's open too much or get you cappuccino and a nice breakfast even if the temperature is perfect and you want nothing to eat. She has the fussy, buzzing restlessness of someone who wants to be occupied doing something for someone else. Her phone rings. "Yes, hello," she says, answering impatiently. "No, no, I don't want to go to the Russian Tea Room. I was there the other day, and it was so . . . stressful." She coughs and listens, staring hard at the floor. "Okay, we can do the Russian Tea Room. We can do it."

She will be having lunch with Helen Gurley Brown, an old friend. After that, she's not sure. She doesn't think she'll stay long in New York. "New York is such a working

place," she says. "If you're here but you're not working, it's hard to fit in."
She will probably go back to Paris. She doesn't talk about going back to
Los Angeles. For almost two decades, she was one of the most powerful
agents and most commanding hostesses in Hollywood. She rose fast in a
business that was then dominated by men. She outmanned many of them:
She was the toughest negotiator, the bluntest adversary, the nerviest deal
maker. In her years at Creative Management Associates, which then became International Creative Management, from 1967 to 1986, she made
a lot of movies happen. She represented, among others, Candice Bergen,
Faye Dunaway, Brian De Palma and Anthony Perkins. Then she lost one
big client, and then another, and her way of doing business—all personality, no strategy—started to seem an anachronism. She no longer fits in.
She hasn't had more than a few people over for dinner since 1986. She
doesn't want to go to screenings anymore; she doesn't want to go to big
parties. As she tells it, Hollywood is a club that she loved to belong to, yet
you can tell she never felt she really belonged. For a while, people appreciated her usefulness, which is not the same as belonging, although for a
stretch it can look the same. She was tactless and contemptuous, and
made enemies needlessly, either because she knew in her heart that someday she would no longer belong and so indulged a preemptive bitterness or
because she believed she'd belong forever and so could afford to do anything. She coughs again. She says, "I feel just like the Queen Mother, because I have this association with Hollywood but no function there
anymore. I'm just like her." She smooths her hair, looks away, and then
says, "Only not as rich."

AS SOON AS you talk to Mengers, you can imagine that on the phone,
making deals, she must have been formidable. Her voice is a pebbly alto
with a little tremor that snags on a syllable now and again. She has a powerful way with a pause. She speaks deliberately, stamping everything she
says with plain, braggy boldness. She didn't learn English until she was six
years old, after her family escaped the Holocaust and emigrated from
Hamburg to New York; the pause and the deliberateness may not be pur-
poseful affect so much as the result of elocution lessons she was given as
a child to banish her accent. She is small, rounded, with a sweet smile, a
doll's nose, tiny feet, and a head of silky blond hair. Being a blonde is a
theme in her personal history. A lot of her stories are punctuated this way:
"And here I was, this blonde . . ." "They weren't expecting this blonde . . ."

When she got out to Hollywood, in 1968, after working as a theater agent for CMA in New York, the only blondes were in the movies, not making deals. She eventually made it into the movies, only she was played by a blonder blonde—Dyan Cannon, who portrayed Mengers in the 1973 movie *The Last of Sheila.*

NO ONE EVER ASKED her to the movies. "I would have Jack and Anjelica over," she says. "It was for a purpose. They were not my *friends.* It was never 'Oh, Sue, it's Anjelica, let's go have dinner, let's go out and see something.'" She knew everyone. She would bully her way through a day of meetings, storm out of a few of them. Then she would put on a little party. "It was my power base. A man in this business would not have had to put on a party. Someone with another power base would not have had to entertain." She didn't make an issue of it—and she even declined a request to help organize Women in Film. She just gave more parties, the best parties. People clamored to come to her parties. "They didn't come because they were my *friends,*" she says. "They didn't come because they were so impressed with my warmth as a hostess." Her parties were celebrated—perfectly cast, staged, and choreographed. "I never had too many actresses who would feel competitive, and I would have enough studio heads so the actors could meet the important people. I never invited anyone who wasn't successful. I was ruthless about it. It was all stars. I would look around my living room at all of them, and even *I'd* be impressed with myself. The parties were great." But the parties were chores. "The parties were always given to accomplish something. I never just *had* people over. I had them over for a reason. I never had a good time for a minute."

She was incurably starstruck. "I was this kid from New York who had never left the city, who had never been to California, who had no plan, who thought she would end up as, possibly, a secretary. I came to Hollywood, and it was magic, absolute magic. There were stars everywhere. They were exactly as they appeared in the movies." She still managed to be an inflexible snob. "I had *no* interest in unknowns. Anyone can sign an unknown. Only a big agent can sign a big star. I was sent Dustin Hoffman when he was starting out. My attitude was: What do I want with this short, inarticulate, mumbling actor? I sent a sarcastic note to that effect. I was only interested in superstars."

For a long time, she was in love with her business. "I thought being an agent was better than being president of the United States," she says. "I couldn't imagine more to life than getting a good part for Nick Nolte." She now believes she wasted her life on her business. "I never had children," she says. "I didn't think I could both be a great agent to Barbra Streisand and be a mother to a kid. I chose Streisand. I wouldn't choose Streisand if I could do it again." She was naïve and was finally betrayed. "I never thought of it as work. I loved it. I was good at it because I loved it so much. I never imagined that any of these actors and actresses would ever get old. I never imagined they would ever leave me."

The most fun she had was working with Barbra Streisand. "It was totally time-consuming but totally stimulating," she says. "We did *What's Up, Doc?* and *A Star Is Born.* How can I get a dig in on Jon Peters? Let's just say that much of the time I spent on Barbra was spent trying to control Jon." Mengers had arranged for Streisand to star in *All Night Long,* directed by Jean-Claude Tramont, who is Mengers's husband, and also starring Gene Hackman, another of Mengers's clients. It was rumored that Streisand was furious when the movie failed, and decided, in 1981, to leave her. Other clients followed. Mengers's ruthless exclusivity failed her. She had no one in reserve once her big clients left, because she had never had time for anyone other than big clients. She says, "I overdosed on the industry. I lost it. I lost my enthusiasm. It got to be less fun. The actors stopped being *movie stars.* I found myself becoming irritable. Suddenly, all anyone could talk about was hardware. I wasn't a visionary, like Mike Ovitz. I never was interested in producing, or in sitting in a room with a group of Japanese businessmen talking about the sale of Sony. I wanted to help the stars. I'm not so knocked out by Mike Ovitz. What he does isn't being an agent. If Mike Ovitz quit the business and opened a chain of karate schools tomorrow, there is not one picture that would stop shooting. It just wouldn't matter that much. Maybe it was my age that made me burn out. Maybe because I did what I did so intensely. Men usually work as agents and then move on to the studios, because they find nurturing people and servicing them too demeaning. When I started, everyone was hot—Redford, Streisand, Jack Nicholson. But then it becomes harder. It's hard to force yourself to be an agent, because you have to get it up all the time to assure your client that he's not cold even when he is."

Once her exodus of clients started, Mengers began to be less useful. She says she felt underappreciated. She quit ICM in 1986. "I never missed it, I swear to you." She managed to stay away only two years. She returned for a disastrous three years at William Morris, during which none of her old clients would come back to her. "I genuinely tried to sign people, but the reputation of William Morris was such that people would flee from it. I had no idea. Many of my past clients, like Christopher Walken and Farrah Fawcett and Jonathan Demme, had fled *in horror* from William Morris and weren't interested in coming back again. I managed to sign Richard Pryor, and that was it. I tried to play the part of the enthusiastic agent, but the juice was gone. My specialness was always my total love of talent. That thing was gone."

She left the industry in 1991, undoubtedly for good. She says, "I do wish I'd gotten richer. But otherwise Hollywood doesn't owe me shit."

SHOOT THE MOON

WHITE MEN IN SUITS FOLLOW FELIPE LOPEZ everywhere he goes. Felipe lives in Mott Haven, in the South Bronx. He is a junior at Rice High School, which is on the corner of 124th Street and Lenox Avenue, in Harlem, and he plays guard for the school basketball team, the Rice Raiders. The white men are ubiquitous. They rarely miss one of Felipe's games or tournaments. They have absolute recall of his best minutes of play. They are authorities on his physical condition. They admire his feet, which are big and pontoon-shaped, and his wrists, which have a loose, silky motion. Not long ago, I sat with the white men at a game between Rice and All Hallows High School. My halftime entertainment was listening to a debate between two of them—a college scout and a Westchester contractor who is a high school basketball fan—about whether Felipe had grown a half inch over Christmas break. "I know this kid," the scout said as the second half started. "A half inch is not something I would miss." The white men believe that Felipe is the best high school basketball player in the country. They often compare him

to Michael Jordan, and are betting he will become one of the greatest basketball players to emerge from New York City since Kareem Abdul-Jabbar.
This conjecture provides them with suspended, savory excitement and a
happy premonition. Following Felipe is like hanging around with someone
you think is going to win the lottery someday.

At the moment, Felipe is six feet five. He would like to be six feet
seven. His shoes are size twelve. He buys his pants at big-and-tall-men
stores. His ears, which are small and high-set, look exaggeratedly tiny, because he keeps his hair shaved close to his skull. He has blackish brown
eyes and a big, vivid tongue—I know this only because his tongue sometimes sticks out when he is playing hard, and against his skin, which is very
dark, it looks like a pink pennant. His voice is slurry; all his words have
round edges. He is as skinny as a bean pole, and has long shins and thin
forearms and sharp, chiseled knees. His hands are gigantic. Walking down
the street, he gets a lot of looks because of his height, but he is certainly
not a horse of a kid—not one of those man-size boys who fleshed out in
fifth grade and whose adult forms are in place by the time they're thirteen.
He is all outline: He doesn't look like a stretched-out average-size person—
he looks like a sketch of a huge person which hasn't yet been colored in.

On the court, Felipe's body seems unusually well organized. His move-
ments are quick and liquid. I have seen him sail horizontally through thin
air. High school players are often rough and lumbering, and they mostly
shoot flat-footed, but Felipe has an elegant, buoyant game. He floats
around the edge of the court and then springs on the ball and sprints away.
When he moves toward the basket, it looks as if he were speed skating, and
then, suddenly, he rises in the air, lingers, and shoots. His shot is smooth
and lovely, with a loopy arc. Currently, he averages twenty-six points and
nine rebounds per game, and he is within striking distance of the all-time
high school scoring record for New York State. He has great court vision,
soft hands, a brisk three-point shot, and the speed to take the ball inside
and low. He is usually the fastest man in the fast break. He can handle the
ball like a point guard, and he beats bigger players defensively, because of
his swiftness and his body control. When he is not on a court, though, the
way he walks is complicated and sloppy. He seems to walk this way on purpose, to make light of his size and disguise his grace.

Before I met Felipe, people told me I would find him cuddly. Everything I knew about him—that he is a *boy,* that he is a *teenage* boy, that he
is a six-foot-five-teenage-boy *jock*—made this pretty hard to believe, but it

turns out to be true. He is actually the sweetest person I know. At some point during our time together, it occurred to me that he could be a great basketball hustler, because he seems naïve and eager—the ideal personality for attracting competitive big shots on the basketball court. It happens that he is not the least bit of a hustler. But he is also not nearly as naïve and eager as he appears. He once told me that he likes to make people think of him as a clown, because then they will never accuse him of being a snob. He also said that he likes to be friendly to everyone, so that no one will realize he's figuring out whom he can trust.

Felipe spoke no English at all when he moved to New York from the Dominican Republic, four years ago, but he quickly picked up certain phrases, including "crash the boards," "he's bugging out," "get the hell out of the paint," and "oh, my goodness." Now he speaks English comfortably, with a rich Dominican accent—the words tumble and click together, like stones being tossed in a polisher. "Oh, my goodness" remains his favorite phrase. It is a utility expression that reveals his modesty, his manners, his ingenuousness, and his usual state of mind, which is one of pleasant and guileless surprise at the remarkable nature of his life. I have heard him use it to comment on the expectation that he will someday be a rich and famous player in the NBA, and on the fact that he was recently offered half a million dollars by people from Spain to put aside his homework and come play in their league, and on the fact that he is already considered a seminal national export by citizens of the Dominican Republic, who are counting on him to be the first Dominican in the NBA, and on the fact that he is growing so fast that he once failed to recognize his own pants. Sometimes he will use the phrase in circumstances where his teammates and friends might be inclined to say something more dynamic. One night this winter, I was sitting around at school with Felipe and his teammates, watching a videotape of old Michael Jordan highlights. The tape had been edited for maximum excitement, and most of the boys on the team were responding with more and more baroque constructions of foul language. At one point, Jordan was shown leaping past the Celtics center Robert Parish, and someone said, "Yo, feature that, bro! He's busting the Chief's face."

"Busting his fucking face," another one said.

"Busting his goddam big-ass face."

"He's got it going on. Now Jordan's going to bust his foul-loving big-ass mama's-boy dope black ass."

On the tape, Jordan slammed the ball through the hoop and Parish crumpled to the floor. While the other boys were applauding and swearing, Felipe moved closer to the television and then said, admiringly, "Oh, my goodness."

FELIPE'S LIFE IS unusually well populated. He is very close to his family. He is named Luis Felipe, after his father. His older brother Anthony is one of the managers of the Rice High School team. Anthony is a square-shouldered, avid man of twenty-five who played amateur basketball in the Dominican Republic and in New York until his ankle was badly injured in a car accident. Until last month, when he was laid off, he worked at a Manhattan print shop and had a boss who appreciated basketball and tolerated the time Anthony spent with the team. Anthony is rarely away from Felipe's side, and when he is there he is usually peppering him with directions and commentary in a hybrid of Spanish and English: "*Felipe, mal, muy mal! Cómo estás* you go so aggressive to a layup?" A couple of times a month, Anthony makes the rounds of Felipe's teachers to see if his B average is holding up. "If he's not doing well, then I go back and let my people know," Anthony says. "It's nice, it's beautiful to be a superstar, but if he doesn't work hard he doesn't play." Once, Felipe's father forbade him to travel to a tournament because he had neglected to wash the dishes. This made Felipe cry, but in hindsight he is philosophical about it. "He was right," he says. "I didn't do my dishes." Felipe is also close to Lou DeMello, his coach at Rice, and to Dave Jones, his coach with the Gauchos, a basketball organization in the Bronx which he plays for during the summer, and to Louis d'Almeida, the founder of the Gauchos. Felipe says he sometimes gets basketball advice from his mother, Carmen, and from Maura Beattie, a teacher at Rice who tutors him in English. Neither of them plays. "You know what, though?" Felipe says. "They know something." His primary hobby is sleeping, but his other pastime is talking on the phone for hours to his girlfriend, who is an American, a resident of Brooklyn, and a basketball fan.

Sometimes his life seems overpopulated. He has so far received four crates of letters from college coaches and recruiters pitching woo at him. Some make seductive mention of the large seating capacities of their arenas. Basketball camp directors call regularly, saying that they would like Felipe Lopez to be in attendance. Officials of Puerto Rico's summer basketball league have requested the honor of his presence this summer. There are corporate marketing executives who would very much like to be his friends. Not everyone crowding into his life wishes him well. There are people who might wittingly or unwittingly mislead him. Felipe has been warned by his father, for example, never to have sex without a condom, because some girls who pretend to like him might really have appraised him as a lucrative paternity suit. Last year, Felipe and another player were invited to appear in a Nintendo television commercial, and the commercial nearly cost them their college athletic eligibility, because no one had warned them that accepting money for a commercial was against NCAA regulations. There are people who are jealous of Felipe. There are coaches whose hearts he has broken, because they're not at one of the colleges Felipe is interested in—Florida State, Syracuse, St. John's, Seton Hall, North Carolina, Georgia Tech, UCLA, Indiana, Arizona, Ohio State, and Kansas. There are coaches who put aside all other strategy except Keep Felipe Lopez Away from the Ball. Some opponents will go out of their way to play him hard. There are kids on his own team who have bitter moments about Felipe. And there are contrarians, who would like to get in early on a backlash and look clairvoyant and hype-resistant by declaring him, at only eighteen and only a junior in high school, already overrated. His response to all this is to be nice to everyone. I have never seen him angry, or even peeved, but when he isn't playing well his entire body droops and he looks completely downcast. It is an alarming sight, because he looks so hollowed out anyway.

"Wait till this kid gets a body," Coach DeMello likes to say. During practice, DeMello will sometimes jump up and down in front of Felipe and yell, "Felipe! Make yourself *big*!" The best insult I ever heard DeMello hurl at Felipe was during a practice one afternoon when Felipe was playing lazily. DeMello strode onto the court, looked up at Felipe, and said acidly, "You're six-five, but you're trapping like you're *five-eleven*." Anthony Lopez can hardly wait until Felipe gets a body, so sometimes during the off-season he will take him to the steep stairway at the 155th Street subway station, in the Bronx, and make him run up and down the hundred and thirty steps a few times to try to speed the process along. Felipe is less than crazy about this exercise, although he appreciates the advantages that more bulk might give him: "When I first came here, I could tell the guys were looking at me and thinking, Who is this skinny kid? Then they would say, 'Hey, let's'—excuse my language—'bust his ass.' "

Felipe's body is an unfinished piece of work. It gets people thinking. Tom Konchalski, a basketball scout who follows high schools in the Northeast, suggested recently that if Felipe ever wanted to give up basketball he could be a world-class sprinter. Coach DeMello said to me once that, much as he hated to admit it, he thought Felipe had the perfect pitcher's body. Felipe's mother told me that even though Felipe is now a fast-break expert, she thought he should sharpen his ability to penetrate to the basket and go for the big finish—say, a windmill slam dunk. I once asked her whose style of play she wanted Felipe to emulate, and she pointed to a picture of Michael Jordan and said, in Spanish, "If he would eat more, he could be like the man who jumps."

Felipe's father, who played amateur baseball in the Dominican Republic, thought he saw in his son the outlines of a first baseman, and steered Felipe toward baseball when he was little. But Felipe was hit in the nose by a wild throw, and decided that, in spite of its popularity in the Dominican Republic and the success Dominican ballplayers have had in the United States, baseball was not his game. Maura Beattie, his English tutor, is an excellent tennis player, and one day, just for fun, she took Felipe with her to the courts. She was curious to see if someone with Felipe's build and abilities could master a racquet sport. He beat her. It was the first time he'd held a tennis racquet in his life. Another time, the two of them went to play miniature golf in Rockaway, and Felipe, who had never held a putter before, made a hole in one. Some of this prowess can be attributed to tremendous physical coordination and the biomechanical advantages of being tall and thin and limber. Felipe Lopez is certainly a born athlete. But he may also be one of those rarer cases—a person who is just born lucky, whose whole life seems an effortless conveyance of dreams, and to whom other people's dreams adhere. This aura of fortune is so powerful that it is easy to forget that for the time being, and for a while longer, Felipe Lopez is still just an immigrant teenager who lives in a scary neighborhood in the South Bronx and goes to high school in Harlem, where bad things happen every day.

Currently, there are 518,000 male high school basketball players in the United States. Of these, only 19,000 will end up on college teams—not even 4 percent. Less than 1 percent will play for Division One colleges—the most competitive. The present NBA roster has 367 players, and each year only 40 or 50 new players are drafted. What these numbers forebode is disappointment for many high school basketball players. That disappointment is disproportionate among black teenagers. A recent survey of high school students by Northeastern University's Center for the Study of Sport in Society reported that 59 percent of black teenage athletes thought they would continue to play on a college team, compared with 39 percent of white teenagers. Only 16 percent of the white athletes expected that they would play for the pros; 43 percent of the blacks expected that they would, and nearly half of all the kids said they thought it would be easier for black males to become professional basketball players than to become lawyers or doctors. Scouts have told me that everyone on the Rice team will probably be able to get a free college education by playing basketball, and so far all the players have received recruiting letters from several schools. The scouts have also said that it will require uncommonly hard work for any of the boys on the team other than Felipe to ascend to the NBA.

Every so often, scouts' forecasts are wrong. Some phenomenal high school players get injured or lazy or fat or drug-addled or bored, or simply level off and then vanish from the sport, and, by the same token, a player of no particular reputation will once in a while emerge from out of nowhere and succeed. That was the case with the NBA all-stars Karl Malone and Charles Barkley, who both played through high school in obscurity; but most other NBA players were standouts starting in their early teens. Most people who follow high school basketball teams that are filled with kids from poor families and rough neighborhoods encourage the kids to put basketball in perspective, to view it not as a catapult into some fabulous, famous life but as something practical—a way to get out, to get an education, to learn the way around a different, better world. The simple fact that only one in a million people in this country will ever play for the NBA is often pointed out to the kids, but that still doesn't seem to stop them from dreaming.

Being told that you might be that one person in a million would deform many people's characters, but it has not made Felipe cynical or overly interested in himself. In fact, his blitheness can be almost unnerving. One evening when we were together, I watched him walk past a drug deal on 125th Street and step off the curb into traffic, and then he whiled away an hour in a fast-food restaurant where several ragged, hostile people repeatedly pestered him for change. He hates getting hurt on the court, but out in the world he is not very careful with himself. When you are around him, you can't help feeling that he is a boy whose body is a savings account, and it is one that is uninsured. But being around him is also to be transported by his nonchalant confidence about luck—namely, that it happens because it happens, and that it will happen for Felipe, because things are meant to go his way. This winter, he and the Rice Raiders were in Las Vegas playing in a tournament. One evening, a few of them went into a casino and attached themselves to the slot machines. Felipe's first quarter won him a hundred quarters. Everyone told him to stop while he was ahead, but he continued. "I wanted to play," he says. "I thought, I had nothing before I started, now I have something, so I might as well play. So I put some more quarters in, and—oh, my goodness!—I won twelve hundred more quarters. What can I say?"

AT THREE O'CLOCK one afternoon this winter, I went over to the high school to watch Felipe and the Rice team practice. I hadn't met Felipe before that afternoon, but I had heard a lot about him from friends who follow high school basketball. As it happens, Felipe's reputation often precedes him. Before he moved to this country, he was living in Santiago, in the Dominican Republic. The Lopez family had been leaving the Dominican Republic in installments for thirty years. A grandmother had moved to New York in the sixties, followed by Felipe's father in 1982, and then, in 1986, by his mother and Anthony. For three years, Felipe stayed in the Dominican Republic with another older brother, Anderson, and his sister, Sayonara. At age eight, he started playing basketball in provincial leagues, sometimes being bumped up to older age-groups because he was so good. He already had a following. "I would hear from a lot of Dominicans about how good he was getting," Anthony says now. "It made me curious. When I left him in the Dominican Republic, he was just a little kid who I would boss around. He was my—you know, my delivery guy." When more visas were obtained, in 1989, Felipe and Sayonara moved to New York. Anthony took Felipe to a playground near the family's apartment and challenged him one-on-one, decided that the rumors were true, and then took him to try out for the Gauchos. Lou d'Almeida says that people were already talking about Felipe by then. Many high school coaches had intelligence on Felipe by the time he started school. Lou DeMello first saw him in a citywide tournament for junior high players. Felipe was in the Midget Division. "He looked like a man among boys," DeMello says now. "If I could have, I would have taken him then and started him *then* on the Rice varsity. I swear to God. At the time, he was in eighth grade."

Rice High School is a small all-boys Catholic school, which was founded in 1938 and is run by the Congregation of Christian Brothers. It is the only Catholic high school still open in Harlem. Currently, it has about four hundred students. Tuition is two thousand dollars a year, which many of the students can afford only with the help of scholarship money from private sponsors, including some basketball fans. At school, students have to wear a tie, real trousers, and real shoes, not sneakers. There is also a prohibition against beepers. The school is in a chunky brick building with a tiny blind entrance on 124th Street, close to some Chinese luncheonettes, some crack dealers, and some windswept vacant tenements. A lot of unregulated commerce is conducted on the sidewalks nearby, and last year a business dispute in an alley across from the school was resolved with semiautomatic weapons, but the building itself emanates gravity and calm. Inside, it is frayed but sturdy and pleasant. There is an elevator, but it often isn't working; the gym, which occupies most of the top two floors of the school, is essentially a sixth-floor walk-up. The basketball court is only fifty-five feet long instead of the usual ninety-four, and the walls are less than a foot away from the sidelines. It would qualify as regulation-size in Lilliput. Rice has to play its games in a borrowed gym—usually the Gauchos' facility, in the Bronx.

At the time Coach DeMello first heard about Felipe Lopez, the Rice Raiders had a win-loss record of eight and thirteen, tattered ten-year-old uniforms, and an inferiority complex. Catholic League basketball in New York City is a particularly bad place for any of these. Since the early eighties, the Catholic schools in New York have had ferocious rivalries, fancy shoes and uniforms from friendly sporting goods companies, and most of the best players in the city. College teams and the NBA are loaded with New York City Catholic League alumni: Jamal Mashburn, now at Kentucky, attended Cardinal Hayes; the Nets' Kenny Anderson and the Houston Rockets' Kenny Smith went to Archbishop Molloy; the Pacers' Malik Sealy, Syracuse's Adrian Autry, and North Carolina's Brian Reese all went to St. Nicholas of Tolentine; the Pistons' Olden Polynice attended All Hallows; Chris Mullin, of Golden State, went to Xaverian; Mark Jackson, now of the Clippers, went to Bishop Loughlin. Rice had won the city Catholic school championship in 1966 and proceeded to become steadily undistinguished over the next few decades. Four years ago, Lou DeMello took over as head coach. First, he persuaded Nike—and later Reebok and Converse—to donate shoes and uniforms to the team. Then he started scouting Midget Division players who might have a future at Rice. The Gaucho coaches have a cordial relationship with DeMello and began pointing players like Felipe his way. Last year, the Rice Raiders reached the finals of the city championship. This year, they are ranked in the top twenty high schools nationally—the first time they have been ranked there for twenty-seven years.

Coach DeMello is short and trim, and has bright eyes and a big mustache and an air of uncommon intensity, like someone who is just about to sneeze. His usual attire consists of nylon warm-up suits that are very generously sized. The first time I saw him in street clothes, he looked as if someone had let his air out. He speaks with a New York accent, but in fact he was born in Brazil, and played soccer there. His motivational specialty is the crisp reprobation wrapped around a sweet hint of redemptive possibility—stick before carrot. When addressing the team, he is prone to mantra-like repetitions of his maxims, as in "Listen up. Listen up. I want you to go with your body. Go with your body. Go with your body. I want you to keep your foot in the paint. Your foot in the paint. Your foot in the paint. In the paint. And put the ball on the floor. The ball on the floor. On the floor."

This particular afternoon, Coach DeMello was especially hypnotic. The team was getting ready for its first out-of-town tournament of the year, the Charm City/Big Apple Challenge, in Baltimore, which would be played in the Baltimore Arena and televised on a cable channel. The Raiders would be facing Baltimore Southern High School, one of the best teams in the area. When I arrived at the Rice gym, the Raiders had been scrimmaging for an hour. Now, during a break, Coach DeMello was chanting strategy. "You guys are in a funk," he said. Someone dropped the ball, and it made an elastic *poing!* sound and rolled to the wall. "Gerald, hold the ball," DeMello went on. He clasped his hands behind his back. "Hold the ball. Okay. You guys are in a funk. You got to get your head in the game. Your head in the game. We're going up against a serious team in Baltimore. They do a hell of a job on help. A hell of a job. A. Hell. Of. A. Job. We need leaders on the floor. Leaders on the floor. All we want to do is contain. Contain. Contain. So you better hit the boards. Hit the boards. The boards."

Everyone nodded. The Rice Raiders are Felipe, Reggie Freeman, Yves Jean, Gerald Cox, Melvin McKey, Scientific Mapp, Gary Saunders, Gil Eagan, Kojo Lockhart, Rodney Jones, Robert Johnson, and Jamal Livingston. Melvin, the point guard, is usually called Ziggy. Jamal, the center, is known as Stretch. Gerald, who also plays center, is known as G-Money. Scientific, the reserve point guard, is known as Science. All of them are known, familiarly, as B, which is short for "bro," which is short for "brother." During practice, they are solemn and focused. During a game, they are ardent and intense, as if their lives depended on it. Before and after each game, they stand in a circle, make a stack of their right hands, and shout, "One, two, three, Rice! Four, five, six, family!"

Most of the Raiders live in the Bronx or upper Manhattan. Once, after a game, I rode in the van with an assistant coach as he dropped the team members off at their homes. A few of them lived in plain, solid-looking housing projects and some in walk-ups that, at least from the outside, looked bleak. No one lived in a very nice building. Some of the kids have families that come to all their games and monitor their schoolwork; some have families that have fallen apart. Six of the twelve live with only their mothers. Ziggy lives with his uncle, and the five others have a mother and a father at home. Each of them has at least one person somewhere in his life who arranges to send him to attend a disciplined and serious-minded parochial school. Sometimes it's not a parent; the Gauchos, for instance, send a number of basketball players to school. The coaches and teachers I met at Rice are white. Most of the teachers are Catholic brothers. The basketball team is all black, and none of its members is Catholic, although Gary told me once that he was thinking of converting, because "being Catholic seems like a pretty cool thing." There is currently a debate in the Catholic Church about financing schools that used to have Catholic students from the surrounding parish but are now largely black and non-Catholic, their purpose having shifted, along with neighborhood demographics, from one of service to the Church to one of contribution to the inner city. The debate may also have a flip side. I had heard that for a time one player's father, a devout Muslim, was unhappy that his son was being coached by a white man. But Coach DeMello resisted being drawn into an argument about something no one on the team ever paid attention to, and the crisis eventually passed. I didn't think of race very often while I spent time with the team. I thought more about winning and losing, and about how your life could be transformed from one to the other if you happened to be good at a game.

The seniors on the team are Yves Jean, Gerald Cox, and Reggie Freeman. Yves has signed a letter of intent to go to Pitt-Johnstown, which is a Division Two school; Gerald and Reggie are going to the University of South Carolina and the University of Texas, respectively, which are both in Division One. Yves grew up in Lake Placid. He was more fluent in ice fishing than in basketball when he moved to New York, but he is big and strong and has learned the game well enough, even as a second language. Usually, he looks pleasantly amazed when he makes a successful play. Gerald and Reggie are handsome, graceful players who would have been bigger stars this year if it weren't for Felipe. Gerald is dimpled and droll and flirtatious. Reggie has a long, smooth poker face and consummate cool. At times, he looks rigid with submerged disappointment. I remember Coach DeMello's telling me that when Reggie was a sophomore he was waiting patiently for Jerry McCullough, then the senior star, to leave for college, so that at last he would be the team's main man. Then Felipe came. Reggie and Felipe now have a polite rapport that fits together like latticework over their rivalry.

The team is a changeable entity. Some of the kids have bounced on and off the squad because of their grades. One of the players has had recurring legal problems. The girlfriend of another one had a baby last year, and because of that he missed so much school that for some time he wasn't allowed to play on the team. When I first started hanging around with the Raiders, Rodney Jones wasn't on the roster, having had discipline problems and some academic troubles. Sometimes the boys get sick of one another. They practice together almost every day for several hours; they travel together to games and tournaments, which can sometimes last as long as two weeks; and they see one another all day in classrooms, at the Gaucho gym, and on the street. Usually, they have an easy camaraderie. During the other times, as soon as they are done with practice they quickly head their own ways.

"Are you guys listening to me? Are you listening?" DeMello was saying. He was now joined by Bobby Gonzalez, an assistant coach, who was nodding and murmuring "Uh-huh" after everything he said. Gonzalez handed DeMello a basketball. DeMello curled it to his left side, and then held his right hand up, one finger in the air, as if he were checking wind direction. "One more thing. One more thing. If there's one player you guys want to be looking up to right now, I'll tell you who it is."

"Uh-huh," Bobby Gonzalez said.

"That guy is Reggie Freeman. Reggie Freeman." No expression crossed Reggie's face. Felipe, who was standing on the other side of the circle, flexed his neck, rotated his shoulders, and then stood still, a peaceful expression on his face. "Reggie is the most unselfish player here. He is the most unselfish. I want you to remember that. He's grown a lot. That's who you should be looking at. Okay."

"Uh-huh."

DeMello bounced the ball hard, signaling the end of practice. The boys circled and counted: "One, two, three, Rice! Four, five, six, family!" They straggled out of the gym, talking in small groups.

"I never been to Baltimore."

"Let me ask you something. You think Larry Bird's a millionaire?"

"Larry Bird? I don't know. A millionaire. Magic's a millionaire."

"Magic's a millionaire, and he didn't have fifty-nine cents to buy himself a little hat and now he's going to die. The man's stupid."

"I don't know if Larry Bird's a millionaire. I do know he's never been to Harlem, and he's never done the Electric Slide."

FELIPE ON HIS DEVELOPMENT as a player:

"Back in my country, I was just a little guy. I tried to dunk, but I couldn't. I tried and I tried. Then, one day, I dunked. Oh, my goodness. Three months later, I was dunking everything, every way—with two hands, backwards, backwards with two hands. I can do a three-sixty dunk. It's easy. You know, you jump up backwards with the ball and then spin around while you're in the air—and *pow!* I'm working all the time on my game. If Coach DeMello says he wants me to work on my ball handling, then I just work at it, work at it, work at it, until it's right. In basketball, you always are working, even on the things you already know.

"When I come to this country, I was real quiet, because I didn't speak any English, so all I did was dunk. On the court, playing, I had to learn the words for the plays, but you don't have to talk, so I was okay. My coach used his hands to tell me what to do, and then I learned the English words for it. There aren't too many Spanish kids at school. I know a lot of kids, though. I meet kids from all over the country at tournaments and at summer camps. If you do something good, then you start meeting people, even if you don't want to. Sometimes it's bouncing in my head that people are talking about me, saying good things, and that some people are talking about me and saying bad things, saying, like, 'Oh, he thinks he's all that,' but that's life. That's life. I don't like when it's bouncing in my head, but I just do what I'm supposed to do. I'm quick. I broke the record for the fifty-yard dash when I was in junior high school—I did it in five point two seconds, when the record was five point five seconds. I also got the long-jump record. It feels natural when I do these things. In basketball, I like to handle the ball and make the decisions. I can play the big people, because of my quickness. But I got to concentrate or the ball will go away from me. At basketball camp, I'm always the craziest guy—people always are walking around saying, 'Hey, who's that Dominican clown?' But on the court I don't do any fooling around. I got to show what I got.

"In life, I don't worry about myself. My brother will run defense for me. I got my family. Some kids here, I see them do drugs, messing around, wasting everything, and I see the druggies out on the street, and I just, I don't know, I don't understand it. That's not for me. I got a close family, and I got to think about my family, and if I can do something that will be good for my whole family, then I got to do it. I think about my country a lot—I want to go there so bad. In Santiago, everyone knows about me and wants to see me play now. If I'm successful, the way everyone talks about that, I'd like a big house there in Santiago, where I could go for a month or two each year and just relax."

AFTER PRACTICE, Felipe and I walked down 125th Street in a cold rain. First, he bought new headphones for his tape player from a Ghanaian street peddler, and then we stopped at Kentucky Fried Chicken to eat a predinner dinner before heading home. He was dressed in his school clothes—a multicolored striped shirt, a purple-and-blue flowered tie, and pleated, topstitched baggy black cotton pants—and had on a Negro League baseball cap, which he was wearing sideways and at a jaunty angle. In his book bag were some new black Reebok pump basketball shoes; everyone on the team had been given a pair for the Baltimore tournament. Felipe was in a relaxed mood. He has traveled to and played in big tournaments so often that he now takes them in stride. He has become something of a tournament connoisseur. One of his favorite places in the world is southern France, where he played last spring with the Gauchos. He liked the weather and the countryside and the fact that by the end of the tour French villagers were crowding into the gyms and chanting his name. This particular evening, he was also feeling pleased that he had finished most of the homework he needed to do before leaving for Baltimore, which consisted of writing an essay for American history on *Brown v. Board of Education* and the Fifteenth Amendment, preparing an annotated periodic table of the elements, and writing two poems for his Spanish class.

One of his poems was called *"Los Dientes de Mi Abuela,"* which translates as "The Teeth of My Grandmother." Sitting in Kentucky Fried Chicken, he read it to me: " *'Conservando la naturaleza se ve en aquella mesa los dientes de mi abuela, que los tenía guardados para Navidad.'* " He looked up from his notebook and gestured with a chicken wing. "This is about an old grandmother who is saving her special teeth for Christmas. In my country, it's funny, old people will go around without their teeth. So in the poem the grandmother is saving the teeth for Christmas, when she'll be eating a big dinner. The teeth are brilliant and shiny. Then she gets impatient and uses them to eat a turkey at Thanksgiving—'GRRRT . . . *suena la mordida de la abuela al pavo.*' " The other poem Felipe had written was about a man about to enter prison or some other gloomy passage in his life. It is called *"La Primera y Última Vez . . ."* As he began reading it, an argument broke out in front of the restaurant between a middle-aged woman in a cream-colored suit and two little boys who were there on their own. First, the boys were just sassy, and then they began yelling that the woman was a crack addict. She balled up a napkin and threw it at them, shouting, "Why don't you respect your elders? What are you doing out at night all alone? Why don't you get your asses home and watch television or read a fucking book?" Felipe kept reciting his poem, raising his voice over the commotion. When he finished, he said, "It's a sadder poem than the one about the grandmother. I like writing poems. In school, I like to write if it's in Spanish, and I like to draw, and I like math. I'm good at math. I like numbers. How do I write the poems? I don't know how. They just come to me."

Done with dinner, we went back out onto 125th Street and caught a cab up to Felipe's apartment. The apartment was in a brick walk-up, on a block with half a playground, a bodega, some unclaimed auto parts, and the depopulated stillness of urban decay. Walking up the four flights to the apartment, we passed an unchaperoned German shepherd napping in the vestibule, a stack of discarded Chinese menus, and someone's garbage, which had toppled over in a doorway. Felipe took the stairs three at a time. He used to dribble up and down the staircase until the neighbors complained that it was driving them crazy. For that reason and many others, the Lopezes were looking forward to moving as soon as they possibly could. Ironically, Felipe has been discouraged from playing in Puerto Rico this summer, on the ground that the basketball league there has a reputation for attracting prostitutes and drug use, when the fact is that spending the summer in Puerto Rico would help him get out of a neighborhood that attracts prostitutes and drug use.

One reason I decided to go home with Felipe was that I thought it might reveal something I hadn't yet seen in him—impatience or embarrassment at living a very humble life when he has been assured that such a rich and celebrated one is virtually in his grasp. That turned out to be not at all the case. In fact, Felipe loves to have people come over to his apartment. That night, he had invited Coach DeMello and his tutor, Maura Beattie, to drop by. When we arrived, they were already there. So were Mrs. Lopez; Felipe's brother Anderson, who moved to this country last year; Anderson's girlfriend, Nancy; Anthony; and Felipe's father. Felipe's sister, Sayonara, was expected as soon as she was through with a meeting at church. The Lopezes are an exceptionally good-looking and unusually large-scale family. Felipe's father, a construction laborer, is broad-chested, dignified, and well over six feet tall. His mother, Carmen, who works in the Garment District, is leggy and vigorous. She competed in track and volleyball as a girl in the Dominican Republic. That night, she was wearing a long flowered dress and black Reeboks. In the Dominican Republic, the Lopezes had a middle-class life. In this country, that life did not change so much as compress. All its hallmarks—Luis's exacting discipline, Carmen's piety, the children's sense of honor and obligation—came over intact, and then intensified in contrast to the disorder of the neighborhood they found themselves in.

The Lopez apartment was a warren of tiny dark rooms. One wall in the living room was covered with plaques Felipe had won—among them the *Parade* All-American High School Boys Award, the Five-Star Basketball Camp Most Promising Player, and the Ben Wilson Memorial Award for Most Valuable Player at ABCD Basketball Camp—and one corner of the room was filled by an old broken television set with what looked like a hundred basketball trophies on top. There was also a new television set, a videocassette recorder, a shelving unit, a huge sofa, a huge easy chair, a huge coffee table, some pretty folk-craft decorations from the Dominican Republic, some occasional tables, big billowy curtains, several floor lamps, and a life-size freestanding cardboard cutout of Michael Jordan. It was an exuberant-looking place. It was also possibly the most crowded place I'd ever been in. The television was tuned to a Spanish soap opera when we walked in, and Maura Beattie and Coach DeMello were sitting beside it, ignoring the show and eating pizza. The Michael Jordan cutout was propped up behind DeMello, blocking the back door. Anderson and Nancy were squeezed together on the couch, looking at one of Felipe's scrapbooks, and Anthony was pacing around the room and talking to his father, who was reclined in the easy chair. Felipe said hello to his mother and they chatted for a minute in Spanish, and then she led him to a seat at the kitchen table and set a stockpot in front of him that was filled with chicken stew. There seemed to be a lot of people coming and going, and the conversation perked along:

DeMELLO: I'll never forget when Anthony brought Felipe to Rice. He couldn't speak a word of English. I thought, How on earth is this kid going to take the entrance exams? Maura, do you remember that?

Ms. BEATTIE: I'm a math teacher. I'm not an English tutor. But I figured this would be something interesting to do. I didn't want the Lopezes to realize I wasn't really a tutor.

ANTHONY (*walking through the kitchen*): Felipe, are you ready for tomorrow? You got your books with you? You planning to play?

NANCY (*translating for Carmen Lopez*): She says Felipe would rather play than eat. Otherwise, he don't give her no torment.

DeMELLO: You should see the tape of the commercial Felipe and Robert Johnson did for Nintendo. They had a lot of fun, a lot of fun. Someone gave them bad advice, though, and it almost cost Felipe his eligibility. He turned down the money, and the commercial has to stop playing when he gets into college.

Ms. BEATTIE: You want more pizza? Should we get more pizza? Felipe, would you eat more? He doesn't eat. I don't think he eats.

NANCY: Would you look at this, all these trophies! Felipe, you got all these trophies?

ANDERSON (*to Nancy*): One of those is mine. Yeah, really. Nancy, look in the middle of the table and you'll find mine.

ANTHONY: Everything everybody tells you is so beautiful—you know, be on TV, score thirty points, be the MVP, have the fame, all right—but you got to pay attention. There are a lot of rules. The NCAA rule is that no coaches can talk to him while he's a junior. They're willing, they're dying to talk to him, but that's not going to happen. When he's ready, we'll meet and talk and see. I had these dreams to be a great player, and I had my ankle broken, so it was all over for me. Felipe is my chance to see it happen for someone in my family, but it's going to happen the right way.

FELIPE (*coming in from the kitchen with Sayonara, just back from church*): Mommy, hey, Mommy, didn't I grow all these inches over here? One day, remember, I went to my closet and found these little pants and I said, "Mommy, whose pants are these?" They were only this big—just little short pants—and she said, "Felipe, those are your pants!" I couldn't believe it! I couldn't believe I ever wore those pants! I just looked at them and thought, Oh, my goodness.

DeMELLO: Hey, Felipe, are you ready for tomorrow? Because anyone who isn't ready with their homework done, Brother is going to hear about it, and we're not going to be going to any other tournaments. Are you ready?

FELIPE: DeMello, I got one thing I got to do tomorrow. I got to type my essay.

SAYONARA: Felipe, I think you're better at basketball than at typing.

NANCY (*translating for Carmen Lopez*): She says he has to do the essay. She says they're so proud of him, and with the help of God he'll go to the top, he'll be a great dunker. That's what she imagines for him in five years. For now, though, they don't soup him up. He has to do right. They still walk to Felipe—they're not running.

WE DROVE TO BALTIMORE the next night in a car rented by the tournament sponsors and a van used by the school. The tournament sponsors were also providing rooms for the whole team in a posh hotel downtown. The following day, after breakfast, the Raiders went for a pregame practice. The Baltimore Arena is big and windy, and it had a depressing effect on the team. They ran some bumbling fast-break drills and then had shooting practice for forty-five minutes, banging the balls against the rim. The clanking sound floated up and away into the empty stands. Coach DeMello called them together toward the end of practice. "I don't know where you guys are," he said. "I don't know where you guys are. You got to get your heads here by tonight. By. Tonight. This team, this team is going to give us something. They've got No. 53, he's a beef, he's six-five. Six. Five. And there's a fast point guard. He looks really young, he's probably a sophomore, but he does a hell of a job on help. They don't gamble. They get a lot of shots off. They help and recover." Pause. "Help and recover. Help and recover. And, Felipe, I saw you start to drop your head because you missed some shots. I don't want to see that. I want to see you lift your head and go on. All right, let's head out. I want everybody to relax and be dressed and in my room at 6:00 P.M., understand? Understand? Okay. Okay."

The arena is near Inner Harbor, a swank shopping development in downtown Baltimore, so everybody walked over there to get some pizza and kill time. Twelve tall black boys, wearing bright yellow-and-green warm-ups, the pants hanging low and almost sliding off their hips, made for a sight that was probably not usual at Inner Harbor. Shoppers were executing pick-and-rolls to avoid them. In the mall, there were dozens of stores open, but the boys seemed reluctant to go into them. We ended up in a sporting goods shop that specialized in clothes and accessories with college and professional team logos. Felipe disappeared down one of the rows. Kojo posted up in front of a rack of jackets, took two down, looked at the price tags, and then put them back. Reggie and Gerald found hats featuring their future colleges. "Yo, I like this one," Gerald said. "It's fly, but what I really want is a fitted Carolina hat. They only have the unfitted kind."

Reggie glanced at him and then said, "Why don't you wait till you get to Carolina, man? They going to have everything you want, man, just *wait*."

"I don't want to wait." Gerald put on an unfitted hat—the kind with an adjustable strap across the back—and flipped the brim back. Gary Saunders came over and looked at him. Gary is a sophomore. An air of peace or woe seems to form a bumper around him. Some people think he will eventually be as good as Felipe, or even better. He pulled Gerald's brim and then rocked back on his heels and said, sadly, "I wish I had a hat head. I can't wear a hat. I look dumb in a hat." Felipe walked by, wearing three hats, with each brim pointing in a different direction. He was smiling like a madman. He admired himself in the mirror and then took the hats off. "I've had enough," he said to no one in particular. "Now I'm going to my room."

SOME THINGS at the tournament did not bode well. For instance, the program listed the team as "Rice, Bronx, N.Y." instead of placing the school in Manhattan. Also, Jamal Livingston had decided to shave his head during the afternoon, and the razor broke after he had finished only one hemisphere. The resulting raggedy hairdo made him look like a crazy person. He was so unhappy about it that he told Coach DeMello he wouldn't play, but Science finally persuaded him, saying, "Stretch, you look cool, man. You're down with the heavy-metal crowd now." The Raiders got their first look at the Southern players as they warmed up. They were big kids, and they looked meaty, heavy-footed, and mean. Damon Cason, the point guard DeMello had warned the Raiders about, had powerful shoulders and a taut body and a merciless look on his face. Beside him, Felipe looked wispy and hipless. Warming up, he was silent and unsmiling. The fans were loud and found much to amuse them. When Jamal stepped onto the court, they began chanting "*Hair*cut! *Hair*cut! *Hair*cut!" and then switched to a chant of "Rice-A-Roni!" and then back to "*Hair*cut!" every time Jamal took a shot.

The game begins, and in the opening moments I focus only on Felipe. Rice wins the tap, but Southern scores nine quick points and looks ready to score more. Three Southern players are guarding Felipe. They struggle after him on the fast breaks, but he slips by and, still skimming along, makes a driving layup from the right. Then a fast-break layup, off a snappy pass from Ziggy. Then, thirty-two seconds later, a driving layup from the left side. The guards are looking flustered and clumsy. Felipe gets a rebound, passes to Reggie, gets the ball back, and then suddenly he drifts upward, over the court, over the other boys, toward the basket, legs scissored, wrists cocked, head tilted, and in that instant he looks totally serene. Right before he dunks the ball, I have the sensation that the arena is silent, but, of course, it isn't; it's just that as soon as he slams the ball down there is a crack of applause and laughter, which makes the instant preceding it seem, by contrast, like a vacuum of sound, a little quiet hole in space.

The final score is Rice 64, Southern 42. Leaving the floor, Felipe is greeted by some of the white men, who have come down to Baltimore to watch his game. One of them comments on how well he played and wants to know what he did all afternoon to prepare. Felipe is mopping his face with a towel. He folds it up and then says, "Oh, my goodness, I didn't do much of anything. I sat in my room and watched *Popeye* on television and listened to merengue music. I just felt good today."

THE LAST TIME I spent with the team was the night before they were to leave on a trip to two tournaments—the Iolani Classic, in Honolulu, and the Holiday Prep Classic, in Las Vegas. The flight to Hawaii was so early that Coach DeMello decided to have the boys sleep at the school. After practice, they spent a few hours doing homework and then ordered in pizzas. Reggie had brought a big radio from home and set it up under a crucifix on the second floor, tuned to a station playing corny soul ballads. Coach DeMello had set up a video player and lent the team his NBA highlight tapes. "You guys going to keep it together up here?" he said. "Let's keep it together up here."

One of them yelled out, "Hey, Coach, I got to ask you something. Are there any girls in Hawaii our age?"

Someone told Reggie to turn off the radio, because the music was awful.

Reggie said, "Bro, you bugging."

"It's stupid, man. Find something better."

"Get your own radio, bro. Then you can be the DJ."

"Reggie Freeman's got a problem."

"Hey, Gary, where'd you get that shirt?"

"Macy's."

"Macy's! What, you rich or something?"

"Put on the tape. I want to see Bird and Magic play."

"Bird's a white guy."

Gerald turned on the video player and put in the tape.

"Bird could be a purple guy, bro. He's got a game."

"Here's Magic. This is the gospel, B, so you better listen up."

They sat in rapt attention, replaying some of the better sections and reciting the play-by-play along with the announcer, Marv Albert. After a few minutes, I realized that Felipe wasn't sitting with us, so I wandered down the hall, looking for him. Except for the vestibule where the boys were camping, the school was still and empty. I went upstairs to the gym. One window was broken, and a shaft of light from outside was shooting in. Someone's jersey was looped over the back of a chair in the corner, and it flapped in the night breeze. I walked from one end of the court to the other. My footsteps sounded rubbery and loud on the hardwood. After a moment, I heard a grinding in the hallway, so I walked back across the court and out to the hall. The elevator door opened, and there was Felipe, his shirttail hanging down, his hat on backward, his hand on the controls.

"Were you looking for me?"

"I was."

"I don't want to hang with the guys." He started to let the door slide shut, then pushed it open and leaned against it, grinning. "I just want to fool around. I don't want anyone to find me. I know what I got to do when we get to Hawaii. I just want to go up and down tonight."

Early the next morning, they left for Hawaii. They had a luau for Christmas, won three out of four games, flew to Las Vegas, ate too much casino food, again won three out of four games, and won a lot of quarters in the slot machines. The blustery, bright day they got back to New York, they celebrated Felipe Lopez's eighteenth birthday.

. . .

THE REST OF THE SEASON was a breeze until February, when Gil, Jamal, Kojo, and Rodney were taken off the team on account of bad grades. Still, going into the city Catholic school championship, the Raiders had a record of nineteen and four. They then played St. Francis and won, 72–54, to get to the quarterfinals, and then beat Molloy, 46–36, to advance to the next round. On a cold night last week, they played Monsignor McClancy and lost in the last few minutes, 39–36, and so their season came to a close. The white men were following Felipe in every game. He had been playing so well and so steadily for the last few months that it now was as if some mystery had lifted off him and he was already inhabiting the next part of his life, in which he gets on with the business of making the most of his talent and polishing his game. In the meantime, the white men started taking note of a few young comers, like Gary Saunders, and also some skinny wisp of a kid at Alexander Burger Junior High. He's only an eighth grader, but he already dunks. They think he's worth watching. What they say is that he might be another Felipe someday.

SHORT PEOPLE

BRIEF ENCOUNTER

*O*F ALL THE GUYS WHO ARE STANDING AROUND bus shelters in Manhattan dressed in nothing but their underpants, Marky Mark is undeniably the most polite. For instance, even though he is very busy getting ready to go to Japan for a promotional tour, Marky took the time to call from Los Angeles the other day just to chat about his new role, as the Calvin Klein Underpants Boy. Heretofore, Marky has been known only as a young white rap star and the leader of Marky Mark and the Funky Bunch. Underwear has always figured in his performances, but it is only in the last few weeks that Marky has ascended to the status of lingerie luminary, and he admitted on the phone that he's still getting used to the job.

Marky was actually a little late in calling, but he offered the perfect excuse: He had spent the morning at the gym doing some upper-body work, and it had taken longer than he expected. Who could begrudge him that? After all, if photographs of you nearly naked were plastered everywhere—this happens to be Marky's current situation—

then upper-body work is exactly the sort of thing you would be wise not to neglect. Nonetheless, Marky was apologetic. "I'm really, really sorry," he said. "I hope I didn't screw up your day, or anything."

In the ads, which were photographed by Herb Ritts, Marky looks like a horny and impudent sixteen-year-old pleased with his pecs, his abs, and his underwear. In reality, he is twenty-one and slightly bashful. Now, about his thing. Since he was a little kid, Marky has favored gigantic pants riding very low on his hips. "I can't move around in tight pants," he said. "I've always been into the baggy thing." One night, when his brother Donnie Wahlberg, who is one of the New Kids on the Block, came to watch him perform, Marky decided to pull down his pants. "I just did it as a joke," he says. "But the crowd went crazy, and the next thing you know, it was like 'Hey, ain't you the kid who pulls his pants down?' "

Is he planning to pull his pants down in Japan?

"I don't know," he said. "I don't want to cause some mad commotion."

Just then, someone came into Marky's hotel room, and he turned away from the phone and called out, "Yo, everybody's in the crib today!" Then Marky got back on the phone and said, "I'm sorry to interrupt. That was my brother Donnie and my road manager, and they were crackin' on me because I haven't taken a bath in three days, so I'm a little greasy and I smell like a dog."

Back to pants removal. Marky has always favored Calvin Klein briefs, and earlier this year he was asked to pose in ads for the company's underwear line. The rest is bus shelter history. "It's some crazy shit seeing the posters of me in my underwear all over the place," Marky said. "But the pictures are really me, you know?" He admitted that he'd left town right before most of the posters went up, so up to now he had missed the full effect of seeing himself in briefs at large. "I think it'll probably be cool," he said. "It's not that big a thing for me. After all, I've pulled my pants down in front of millions of people millions of times."

BIG

THERE ARE OTHER big chairs making the rounds these days, but Bob Silverstein's Big Chair is something a little different. For one thing, Bob Silverstein's Big Chair comes apart. This was Bob's idea. No one else has had this idea. The other big chairs are merely big, whereas Bob's Big Chair is big-plus-transportable—meaning that it can be broken down into four separate, easily moved pieces. The other things that make it different are—well, quite frankly, Bob would rather not say. The line of work Bob Silverstein is in—novelty photo opportunities for street fairs and corporate functions—thrives on technical innovation and conceptual ingenuity, and maintaining these requires an uncommon degree of confidentiality, and it just so happens that Bob Silverstein has gotten big in the novelty photo business by being uncommonly confidential.

The exact dimensions of Mr. Silverstein's Big Chair are really nobody's damn beeswax, but if you go to any of the street festivals where the Big Chair is showing up this summer, you can get a good unauthorized look at it for yourself. The Big Chair is a Colonial-style wing chair with roll arms and a dust ruffle; it's upholstered in nubbly blue-and-brown plaid fabric; and it's extremely large. The dimensions—well, forget about getting specific, but Mr. Silverstein will allow that the chair might possibly be from three and a half to four times as big as a normal chair. The Big Chair's purpose is to make people sitting in it look unbelievably small when Bob takes their picture. The picture goes into a cardboard frame and then goes home with the back-to-normal-size people. Let's say, for instance, that the Big Chair could make someone sitting in it look from three and a half to four times as small as normal. Maybe even smaller. Whatever. A lot of people can fit into the Big Chair for group photos. Maximum capacity is undoubtedly quite a large number. It's maybe a number divisible by five, maybe not. It might be around eight or so.

A certain weekend some time ago, the Big Chair was set up at the Christopher Street Fair, and Bob Silverstein was working the booth. Mr. Silverstein is a stocky man with short sandy hair, a lot of freckles, muscular forearms, and a wide-open, expressive, totally revealing face. If you frequent street festivals in New York or in various other places, such as certain other states nearby—no names, no way—you may have seen him around. He's been doing the Big Chair for two years. Before that, he had a booth where you could be photographed with life-size cutouts—Ronald Reagan, the Pope, Hulk Hogan, and twenty-two other celebrities, all of whom he threw in the trash a few days before coming to the Christopher Street Fair, because, as far as he's concerned, cutouts are totally over. Mr. Silverstein figures that the Big Chair has one more season and then it's going in the trash, too. In the meantime, he's working on something else—something big in the business sense of big rather than big in the Big Chair sense of big, which he will be introducing as soon as the Big Chair is no longer big in the business sense of big. Here's a crazy idea: How about Mr. Silverstein's giving a little hint about this new project? "Are you totally kidding?" Mr. Silverstein said when he heard this crazy idea. "No, thanks. I have no plans to divulge anything about it at this time. When it's ready, you'll know about it, believe me."

Until this next big idea is ready for unveiling, Mr. Silverstein is keeping busy with the Big Chair. How busy? This, too, is the sort of nonpublic information that Mr. Silverstein will not be divulging at this time—or any time soon, for that matter—because indiscreet divulging is exactly how a big street fair booth thing goes from being big to being in the trash. In any case, Mr. Silverstein's Big Chair business card says BIG CHAIR PHOTO: HAVE THE CHAIR AT YOUR AFFAIR. These affairs could be Bar Mitzvahs, sweet sixteen parties, or other events that are strictly the private concern of the individuals involved, and absolutely no one else's, or they could be corporate in nature. "Not to mention any names, but take a bank, for instance—a particular bank might call and say they are having some of their employees, such as, say, their head tellers and their managers, at a gathering," Mr. Silverstein said. As he was saying this, he was assisting a couple in matching Gay Pride T-shirts into the Big Chair and surrounding them with Big Chair props—a giant pink baby bottle, a giant blue baby bottle, and a much-larger-than-life coloring book. "They will have the employees at a particular hotel, and they will contract with us to take a set number of photos," Mr. Silverstein went on. "By the way, I also have a robot, Zoniff the Robot, who can also be hired for corporate events." Interrupting himself, he asked the couple if they wanted the giant beer bottle in the Big Chair with them, too. "No, thanks," the larger of them responded. "We don't want the beer bottle. We want to look like little tiny babies."

It occurred to us that there might be more than one Bob Silverstein Big Chair, so that one could be dispatched to a corporate event while another might be at, say, the Italian Festival at Steeplechase Park. Okay—just as a for instance, then, approximately how many Bob Silverstein Big Chairs might there be in existence in the known universe at this particular point in time?

"A few," Mr. Silverstein answered. "A couple. There are several. Some. Hey—who, exactly, needs to know?"

Next question: Why do people like the Big Chair, really?

"I can't say," Mr. Silverstein said. "They just love it. Right now, it's in. It's a fun idea."

A line was forming at the Big Chair booth. At the head of the line was a group of women wearing Lycra tank tops, faded blue jeans, and studded dog collars.

"Nice fabric," one of the women said to Mr. Silverstein as she climbed up to the chair. "Did you make this chair?"

"I made the chair," he said. "I conferred with an upholsterer on the fabric."

"It's a really big chair," she said.

"That's what everyone says," he said.

HALL OF FAME

AT THE MOMENT, the Rock and Roll Hall of Fame is about two inches high, is made of plastic, and is stored in the architectural model shop at I. M. Pei & Partners' Madison Avenue offices. Someday soon, the Rock and Roll Hall of Fame will be built in Cleveland, and then it will be much bigger—it will have a two-hundred-foot tower, a huge, tent-shaped glass atrium, a music and film library, exhibits, listening rooms, performance spaces, and all sorts of tributes to its inductees. "We are far, far from finished," Mr. Pei, who is designing the building, told us the other day. "Still, everyone seems to want to know about it. My family are more excited about the Rock and Roll Hall of Fame than they are even about my work on the Louvre."

Mr. Pei is known for making big, dignified buildings, like the east wing of the National Gallery in Washington, and he confessed that in the beginning he had had doubts about the new project. "When the committee from the Rock and Roll Hall of Fame Foundation came and asked me to design the building, I was taken aback," he said, throwing his hands in the air the way the Solid Gold Dancers sometimes do. "I told them, 'You know, I'm not a fan. I'm really not.' When I thought of rock and roll, all I thought of was my kids, and with me it was always 'Kids, turn it down! Turn it *down!*' But the people on the committee said that it didn't matter that I wasn't yet a fan, and I was greatly encouraged. And so I started my musical education."

Mr. Pei, who says he prefers classical music, is seventy years old, compact, black haired, and dapper. When we met him, he was wearing a rich dark suit and a floral tie, and eyeglasses with round, thick black frames. He uses a square black lacquer table for a desk, and all the notes and papers on it, we noticed, were in perfectly squared-off piles. After a few minutes, four architects who are also working on the Hall of Fame and who took part in the rock-and-roll education of Mr. Pei came in. They were Craig Rhodes, the project manager (partial to Eurythmics, Kate Bush, and reggae, and currently nurturing an interest in blues), Sophia Gruzdys (major fan of Pink Floyd, Led Zep, Jimmy Yancey), Christopher Rand (into Bach, but sympathetic to the concept of rock and roll), and Michael Rose (seventies-power-pop casualty and ashamed of it, but he's only twenty-two).

"I'm a rock-and-roll fan from way, way back, so when I heard that we might do the project I immediately called Mr. Pei and said, 'Well, I'm available,' " Mr. Rhodes said as he sat down.

"Yes, this is one project I had no trouble staffing," Mr. Pei added. "No trouble at all. But first I had to know if I was right for it. I had to know what rock and roll was. American music to me is like a tree, and I wondered if rock and roll was just a branch or part of the trunk of the tree. If rock and roll was just a branch, I wasn't interested. So I turned to Craig, and he made tapes for me. He culled the most important music for me to hear. It was *fascinating*."

"We also sat together and talked quite a lot," Mr. Rhodes said. "Mr. Pei asked me a lot of questions. We spoke about who Elvis was, and the Beatles, and he asked me about the future of rock and roll. I told him that there were so many evolutionary parallel streams now that you couldn't exactly say what rock and roll was. Actually, I couldn't answer a lot of his questions. But I did make him these tapes, and I put on country and western, and blues, and psychedelic bands. I included some Grateful Dead, and I even put on the Sex Pistols. I put on some disco, too, although I don't think much of it."

Ms. Gruzdys leaned across the table and said to Mr. Rhodes, "Donna Summer? You put on *Donna Summer?*"

"No, it was Silver Convention—'Fly, Robin, Fly,' or something like that," Mr. Rhodes answered. "I don't really remember."

Ms. Gruzdys said, "You know, I had this dream of taking Mr. Pei to some East Village place, like CBGB. The idea of him there was an amazing concept."

Mr. Pei said, "I found all the music on Craig's tape quite remarkable. Then the people from the foundation took me on a trip to New Orleans and Memphis, which convinced me that I should undertake the project."

We asked Mr. Pei what he did when he was in Memphis.

He took a short, sharp breath and said, "*Elvis.* And we went into those music halls on Beale Street. Some of them had old music posters hanging up that were made of metal. I loved those metal music posters. I became quite fascinated by them." Mr. Pei tapped Mr. Rhodes on the knee. "Craig, we must have some of those old metal posters for our building."

Mr. Pei's secretary came into the room and handed him a note. As he was reading it, he started to laugh, and said, "Can you imagine? This is from my symphony hall client in Dallas! Here are the two ends of a spectrum—the symphony and rock and roll!"

Mr. Rhodes produced a large white box, which he told us the team members called their sushi box of models. He turned the box over, and nine tiny Halls of Fame fell on the table. "See these forms that are sort of *exploding* off the main tower?" he said, fingering one of the little buildings. "We're trying to depict an explosion—to show that rock and roll has a dangerous and expansive feeling."

"I did go to Graceland, but it's not a model for us at all," Mr. Pei said. "It is true Americana, but our building will talk about something very different."

Mr. Pei told us that his crash course in rock and roll had left him with a taste for the genre, and that he is especially fond of the Beatles, early Dylan, Chuck Berry, and Fats Domino. He hasn't yet extended his study to bands like Throbbing Gristle and Twisted Sister. He also said that as soon as he felt that his education was ready to enter another phase he'd gone to see some live performances, starting with Paul Simon at Radio City Music Hall and Genesis at the Meadowlands. At the Hall of Fame Foundation induction ceremony and concert recently, he had especially liked Little Richard. "What a performer!" he said. "Was he always like that?"

NONSTOP

"MY NAME IS PETER BENFAREMO, but everyone calls me the Lemon Ice King of Corona. That's been the name of my business since 1946. What's my business? We have Italian-style ices in twenty-nine flavors. You don't see the sign in the front? Just like it says: 'Benfaremo the Lemon Ice King of Corona. Ices with Real Pieces of Fruit in It.' Excuse me a minute. Hey, Louie! There's a guy up at the counter who's picking up eleven cans of ices for his store! Sir, let me see your list. Okay—lemon, raspberry, mint, cantaloupe, pistachio. All right, Louie will get them for you. Louie! *Louie!* Anyway, I grew up here in Corona, and my father had a little store right here, at 108th Street and Fifty-second Avenue, and he was making a few little fruit ices, nothing big. After I got out of the army, I started this store next to him. I knew it was my calling. I was wounded in the war in Europe, and I thought to myself, Hey, you're going to die right here. Instead, I didn't. This was my destiny.

"You were wondering how I got the name Lemon Ice King. Look, I don't know—I didn't set out to go and get it. It just came to me. You ever hear of the Sultan of Swat? The Yankee Clipper? Those are baseball names. They just came about. Well, Lemon Ice King is the same thing. It just came about. I don't know who first called me the Lemon Ice King. Maybe I did. Anyway, that's who I am now. I'm famous. I'm famous and I'm infamous, I always say. I'm famous because of my merchandise, and I'm infamous because I fight with everyone. Everyone's always on me all the time. 'Mr. Benfaremo, can I have an extra this, and a couple of that, and can I have a sixty-nine-cent ice in a dollar-size cup?' And my attitude is: Look, I can't be doing for everybody all the time. I'll fight with anyone. Excuse me a second. Hey, who's this guy? Yes, you. Can I help you?"

"Yes, Mr. Benfaremo. I'm interested in carrying your ices in my store."

"Look, let me ask you one question. Can't you see I'm talking to someone? Do I look like I can take care of you now? No. I cannot. I am with this person, and when I'm done I can discuss this with you. I only have two hands, right? You don't want to wait? No? Fine. Okay, good-bye. See that? See? He's got some little store and he wants to carry *my* merchandise, and I should suddenly bow down and holler with pleasure? Good riddance. Louie, where's Anthony? Anthony! I need you up front. *Anthony!*

"Now, where was I? You were asking what this round thing above the name of the store is. I don't know what it is. It's a Mexican hat. Why a hat? I don't know, maybe it's like the hat my father used to wear. Who thought of it as the store symbol? Who knows? Who knows who thought of the symbol for General Electric? It was just a good idea, that's all. Everything in the store is exactly the way it was when I first started the business. Psychologically, it's very important to keep it that way. People come and see the same things—the Lemon Ice King of Corona T-shirts on display here, and the jars of nuts on display on the back wall, and the list of flavors on the counter—and it absolutely must stay the same. Someday, someone will take this over from me, and they have to agree to keep it exactly the same or I'm not going to give it to them. It has to be my way. I won't let them desecrate it. I'm getting ready to get out, though. I'm seventy years old. I'm not made of steel. Today, I don't feel so good. Most likely, I'll die here. My heart's pumping like crazy. I need a rest already. Hey, look at this guy at the counter with the watches. Hey, you, how much you want for those things?"

"Nice watch, fifteen dollars."

"Fifteen dollars? Whaddya, pulling my leg? Forget about it. Two dollars, maybe. Anyway, come back later. What is he, kidding? *Fifteen* dollars? Anthony, hey, where've you been? Anthony? Louie, get Anthony up front, it's getting busy. See? What did I tell you? It never stops. I work all night and all day. I haven't gone for a walk in the park in thirty-four years. Last time I went, my son was eight months old. It's time for me and Mrs. Benfaremo to have some fun in life. You know something? I have never in my life—never, and I am seventy years old—bought a brand-new car. I'm doing fine, but personally I don't need to flash it around. My '78 Chevy takes me exactly the same place a brand-new Cadillac would take me.

"Let me tell you something. Wait a minute. *Louie!* Tell the new kid not to put the containers in the freezer that way. He's new. He doesn't know. He has to learn. What's this pulling up? Oh, the UPS truck. Never a dull moment around here. Let me see that order. *Anthony!* I didn't tell you to take your boots off, did I? I want you to leave them on for when you go back into the freezer later. Anyway, what I was going to tell you is that to succeed at something you need to have desire. You need the motivation. I am totally unique. No one in this entire country has the merchandise we have. Also, I am practical. I will not make certain flavors. Mango I won't make. Weird stuff I won't make. Some guys who worked for me a couple of years ago, they broke off on their own, and started making the oddest-ball-flavored ices in the world—mango this and banana-something that—and, of course, eventually they went out of business. I found out some guy was carrying their merchandise and carrying mine also in his store, and I said to him, 'No way you're carrying both. Carrying both! You can drop dead.' And you know what? Three weeks later, he did. No kidding. But I had nothing to do with it. He had heart trouble. The fact is, though, I am very vindictive. I am. You might think: Peter Benfaremo, he's a short guy, he's a plumpy guy, what can he do to hurt me? Well, I have my ways.

"Come on back here and I'll show you where we make the merchandise. Step over these boxes. These are boxes of macaroni. I make macaroni for the boys who work for me sometimes, for their lunch break. Anthony! Where's the new kid? What's he doing? *Anthony!* Here's where we make the ices. You know, it took me three years to make grape ice. You want to know why? Because I couldn't make grape to my satisfaction, that's why. Here, taste this. You say it's good? Of course it's good. I never eat the stuff. Oh, I used to eat pineapple occasionally. Now I never eat it. What would I need to eat it for? I know what it is. You wonder what it's been like being the Lemon Ice King of Corona? It's been a big thing, a very big thing. That's the truth. I was born for this."

BUTTONS

DIANA EPSTEIN RECENTLY BOUGHT seventeen thousand buttons, sight unseen, from the city of Tempe, Arizona, and the other day she invited us over to watch as she opened boxes, suitcases, and an entire trunk full of the buttons to find out what she now owned. Ms. Epstein is in the business of buying buttons—she is the founder of Tender Buttons, on East Sixty-second Street, which is the only buttons-only store in America—and she has traveled far and wide to find stock for the shop. In the past, she and her partner, Millicent Safro, have tracked down buttons in Egypt, Russia, Finland, and Italy; in a château outside Paris; in a Quonset hut outside London; in a cave in Brussels; in a campground in Massachusetts; and in a little town near a beefalo ranch in West Virginia. But the lot from Tempe is the first pig in a poke she has ever bought. "I have a feeling these buttons will be either very appealing or very awful," she told us soon after we arrived at her shop. "I'm a little nervous, because I paid thirty-six hundred dollars for the buttons and right after I won the auction I got a letter from a woman in Arizona saying that the collection was nothing but rusty old buttons. All I knew when I put in my bid was that a wealthy woman in Tempe had willed her button collection to a museum in town, and the museum had given it to the city to auction. I couldn't go to Tempe to see the buttons, but I had my mind set on getting them. Now I'm about to see whether my intuition was brilliant or demented."

Ms. Epstein, an exuberant woman with round shoulders and short silvery hair, led us upstairs to her office. It was full of buttons—in bowls, boxes, drawers, crates, and bags. Before we broke into the shipment from Tempe, Ms. Epstein showed us some of her old favorites: Eskimo buttons of ivory in the shape of seals and walruses; Victorian glove buttons with tiny daguerreotype portraits of babies; large, yellowish 1940s buttons made of Lucite salvaged from Second World War bombers; and one big brass button with the famous Currier & Ives print of skaters in Central Park stamped on it, which, she told us, is considered the rarest picture button in the world. Then she said, "Here are my real pets," and handed us little Bakelite buttons in the shape of hearts and matchsticks. "I always liked buttons, and I always liked the word *buttons*, but I never intended to get into the button business. I was in publishing. At lunch, I used to go to a funny old button store on the East Side, where I'd get good four-hole buttons for my clothes. One day, I heard that the owner had died and the contents of the store were for sale. I thought it would be great to go through all those buttons. That's all I really wanted to do—just go through the buttons. So I bought the contents, and when I went to collect them I realized that there were so many buttons that I'd have to rent the store just to go through them. So, suddenly, I had a button store." She cottoned to the button business right away, she said. "It was the middle of the sixties, and I was interested in the nature of performance and art, and all that," she went on. "I liked the philosophical notion of focusing on something so small when everything else was so big. Paintings were big. Buildings were big. It appealed to me that buttons were thought of as useless, everyday objects. I liked the found-art nature of it."

The store manager, Zachary Stewart, came upstairs and said, "Diana, I know this is highly unlikely, but I have a guy on the phone who wants to know if we have any hand-painted ivory buttons of faces."

"We do, we *do*," Ms. Epstein said. "I couldn't resist—I stuck my hand in one of the suitcases yesterday and guess what I pulled out." She handed him a crumbly blue cardboard box that said VITAMINS PLUS on the outside. Inside were six Oriental heads, each wearing a different expression and a different ornate hat. Mr. Stewart shook his head in amazement.

Now Ms. Epstein decided that it was time to dig into the rest of the collection, and she threaded her way between boxes and crates to a corner of the room where a small steamer trunk, two ratty-looking suitcases, and two crumpled cartons were stacked. She rubbed her hands together and then dragged out one of the suitcases and opened it.

"Oh, this is nice!" she said, spreading out a red cloth on which dozens of black glass buttons were sewn. "I should send this to Diana Vreeland. The woman who owned these must have been a real old-time collector." She turned back to the suitcase and started passing buttons to us. "Here's a display card of good carved pearl buttons. I'd say they're from 1880. And this is a display card, very nice, of picture buttons of birds." She rummaged through some more display cards, mumbling, "Oh, here are some bug buttons. Oh, more birds," and then stood up and said, "The cards are too easy. Let's look at a bag."

Ms. Epstein reached into the suitcase, took out a dusty plastic bag full of buttons, and sat down at a table, so she could spill them out and pan them. As she was cutting open the bag, she said, "You know, I still wear only plain four-hole buttons. I think it would be a bit ostentatious of me to wear something more spectacular. Of course, I never, ever wear zippers. I don't believe in them. I don't like the sound or the act of zipping. And I won't even say the word *Velcro* if I can help it."

While she was talking, she was sifting through the pile of buttons. Now she said, "Here's a picture button. Oh, my! This is a very rare button. It's a picture of a rabbit meeting a frog. Oh, my gosh, here's *another* one! Maybe there's a set. This collector had good taste." She held up a small brass button and said, "This is an overalls button. It says 'Stronghold Steve' on it. I love work-clothes buttons. They used to have wonderful, poetic sayings on them. It was as if they were a bit of an escape dream for the working class. Here's a big tin button. That's good for me—I sell my huge buttons to Prince for cuff links. Some of these are a little rusty. We'll have to soak them in Pepsi. Oh, I think this is going to be a fantastic bunch of buttons."

Mr. Stewart came upstairs again and said, "Diana, I've got a guy on the phone who would like to sell you three hundred military buttons."

"That's about two hundred and ninety too many," Ms. Epstein replied. "Tell him no. Oh, *look!*" She slapped her forehead. "This is one of the rarest black glass buttons in the world!" She handed us something small and shiny with a scene of two people on a toboggan molded into it. "A button collector might pay fifty dollars or more for that. That's incredible. Let's open another bag." She swept the buttons on the table into a box and took another dusty bag out of the suitcase.

"This one isn't full of glamorous buttons," she said after scanning the pile. "These are very old buttons that are interesting for historical reasons—for the way they're made. A lot of them are men's trouser buttons. You can see the whole history of men's fashions through trouser buttons alone."

She picked out a small tin button and said softly, "This is what I love about buttons. Each one is like a tiny, evocative event." She held up the button, which had a bit of green thread still wrapped tightly in its sewing holes. "A Boy Scout button, maybe fifty years old," she said. "I wonder where this Scout is now."

THE HUSTLE

THE OTHER DAY, we found out that Frank Stella, who for thirty years has deconstructed pictorial structure and challenged representational art with his formalist paintings, is a C-level squash player. He claims to be a D-level player, which in squash's ranking system would make him an advanced beginner, but people who are intimate with his game insist that he's really a C. These people also say that anyone new to Mr. Stella's squash game should be warned that he is a genius practitioner of the hustle—that is, the classic and artful maneuver of saying you're worse than you are, getting your opponent to drop his guard, and then beating the pants off him. To this, Mr. Stella just says, "Oh, phooey."

If you ask Mr. Stella about squash, which he prefers to art as material for general discussion, he will probably come very, very close to telling you that he has played for only five years, but then he will catch himself and admit that he was *going* to tell you that, because he's such a *lousy* player and it would sound better than the truth, which he has now decided to tell you, and the truth is that he's actually been playing for *eight* years, and he ought to be ashamed of himself for even *thinking* of lying as crassly as he planned to do.

He admits he was once told by one of the people he plays with that he runs like a weasel.

Mr. Stella has a large show of his artwork on display right now at the Museum of Modern Art, but what he had on his mind the other day was squash. At the Palladium nightclub, which is right near his studio, the fifty-thousand-dollar Rolex United States Open Squash Championships were being held—an event he helped organize. He made a poster for the tournament, and arranged for a photograph of one of his pieces—a gigantic, colorful form made of painted cones and swirls of metal—to be used on the program; it was his idea, too, to hold the tournament on the dance floor of the Palladium. He also appeared in a special exhibition match that was part of the tournament, besides playing his usual, thrice-weekly game. "Frank's *very* involved with squash this week," Paula Pelosi, his assistant, told us. "He's happy to talk about it at great length."

Mr. Stella explained that he thinks that squash and art have little or nothing in common—except for something or other about a blank canvas, and that's not anything he'd care to elaborate on. But he did have a few no-

tions on how the two pursuits compare, and he revealed them to us when
we visited him in his studio before heading over to the Palladium with him
to watch the semifinal matches—between Chris (Muscle Man) Dittmar
and Ross (Iron Man) Norman, and between Jahangir (Emperor) Khan and
Jansher (Rubber Man) Khan.

"At least, in painting, experience counts for something," Mr. Stella
said, and then he grinned and wiggled a big cigar between his fingers. He
was wearing a white cardigan with a U.S. Open insignia patch, blue jeans,
and beat-up tennis shoes, and had a pair of eyeglasses strapped to his head
with a stretch band. He's small and wiry—about half the size of one of the
new art pieces hanging in his studio—and often has an impish look on his
face. "In squash, what happens is that you get a lot of experience but you
also get *old*," he went on. "Maybe I could have been better at one time, but
I have had a *lot* of injuries. Of course, they're the sort of injuries other people might consider trivial, but I like to think of them as crippling. When I
started playing, I have to admit, I really thought I would become a great
player. I really *wanted* to become a great player. I really *hoped* I'd become
a great player. In art, you can keep getting better, but in squash you hit
your level and that's just about it. Curtains. You're finished. I hit my limit
at about forty minutes of mediocre playing."

One thing that isn't mediocre about Mr. Stella's squash is his racquet.
He had Ben, the guy who strings racquets over at the Park Place Squash
Club, string it with nylon in five different bright colors instead of the single subdued color that most people use. The result is a squash racquet
Mondrian would have been proud of. Mr. Stella says he did this to bring a
little glamour to his game, but confesses that he hoped it might also serve
to confuse and intimidate his opponents. He said it hasn't worked—the
trouble is that most of them consider his racquet of many colors to be a
sort of sissy affectation.

Just then, Bob Swan, whose company fabricates the metal parts of Mr.
Stella's works, came into the studio with two friends. He walked around
the place, looking at the sculptures and rapping his knuckles on the metal
parts he'd cast. "This is ours," he said to his friends, and then he turned
toward Mr. Stella and said, "Hey, Frank! Come on—let's go see some
squash!"

At the Palladium, Mr. Stella had the triple distinction, as far as we
could tell, of being just about the only man not wearing a suit and tie; the
only one hiding a cigar (smoking wasn't allowed); and the only one who
called out unsolicited coaching tips from his seat. He directed most of his

suggestions to Chris Dittmar, a red-haired, thick-calved Australian, who Mr. Stella hoped would win the tournament. He said, at various times, "Come on, Chris! Wake *up!*" and "Hey, Chris, *concentrate!*" and "Come on, wake up, you *turkey!*" and "If I'd known this was going to be on television, I would have told him to get a haircut." Mr. Stella could barely take his eyes off the ball, but when it looked as though Mr. Dittmar had clinched the match, he did turn to us and say, "Boy, isn't that just *great?*" During one of the breaks, he said that he really got a kick out of seeing world-class squash players. We asked him whether, if he had the choice, he'd rather be remembered as an artist or as a great squash player. He said, "Oh, I'd rather be an artist. I'm too old to be a great squash player. At my best, I'm a D. In fact, I can hardly walk."

MOON TRIP

AT THE VERY MOMENT the New York street festival season was beginning to seem like one gigantic Pennsylvania funnel cake, we ran across the Big Lee Moon Trip. The Moon Trip is not for sale. It is not a Simpsons T-shirt, a slap bracelet, a neon green ripstop-nylon hip pouch, a souvlaki sandwich, a Dianetics handbook, a six-pack of tube socks, a neon-pink terry-cloth-covered hairband, a pair of fake gold Cleopatra hoop earrings, a calzone, a recently boosted and repackaged cassette player, or fudge. The Moon Trip is, therefore, a street festival anomaly.

The Moon Trip is an amusement ride, forty-five years old and currently bright red with yellow racing stripes. It is shaped like a huge beach bucket, is lined with seats (capacity eighteen), and is suspended from a ten-foot-high steel sawhorse mounted on a red Chevy one-ton pickup. Its only motion is back and forth, like that of an oversize porch swing. It is not, technically speaking, scary. At no point in the Moon Trip's functioning does a three-dimensional hologram of Michael Jackson come into view. It does not have two hundred feet of vertical drop or four thousand feet of coiled steel track or a computer-plotted course of corkscrews and double loops. It more closely recalls something that might have emerged after several hours in the basement workshop with some sheet metal, some rivets, and some 1945 issues of *Popular Mechanics*. Its only moving parts are Big Johnny, Little Johnny, and Doug—three Jack La Lanne–style guys who take turns loading the kids and rocking the bucket—and Big Lee, who every weekend from the spring through the late fall pilots the Moon Trip to street festivals, block parties, and the occasional executively produced Bar Mitzvah.

Every now and again, Big Lee considers adding another ride to his lineup—the Whip, maybe—but for the moment he likes to describe his capital improvement plans as being at a standstill. Recently, at the Atlantic Antic, in Brooklyn, he explained his position. "For the time being, the Moon Trip is plenty," he said. "I used to have the pitch game, the novelties, the fishbowl games, the tossing the plates, the parakeets—the whole you-name-it. Now I've got the Moon Trip, and we sell helium balloons. Sum total. The Whip is a maybe, but, right now, just a maybe. A Ferris wheel is another maybe. Currently, I'm sticking with the Moon Trip. It occupies my mind."

A tall woman with a distracted manner walked up to Big Lee, who was sitting on an upended milk crate several yards away from the Moon Trip—a position that allowed him, with a minimum of movement, to manage the balloon concession and make change for his son Mark, who was selling Moon Trip tickets. The Moon Trip is often the only ride at a street festival. That was the case at the Atlantic Antic, and it had attracted a fidgety crowd of about forty kids. The parents stood in a disorderly semicircle a few feet away from the truck. One mother was saying, to no one in particular, "Tito just had a Sno-Kone. I hope this doesn't turn into a disaster."

The distracted woman asked Big Lee if he was interested in buying a king- or queen-size cotton comforter. He ignored her. Then an Asian woman carrying a small spotted dog and a Batman balloon came up to him and asked if she could get stronger gas put in the balloon for free.

Big Lee shook his head and said, "Sorry. These days, everyone's in business."

Monday through Friday, the Moon Trip is stored at an undisclosed site in South Brooklyn, and Big Lee runs a parking lot at an undisclosed site in downtown Brooklyn. Twenty-five years ago, he was running a different parking lot, went broke, started driving a cab, and then answered an ad for a Whip helper. He drove the Whip for six months. That job, besides providing Big Lee with gainful employment, partly satisfied a theretofore thwarted dream he'd had of running away to the circus.

"I always had this idea," he said, pointing at the Moon Trip, which was now loaded with eighteen kids, all screaming in syncopation with its swings. "Nothing sentimental. I knew there was money in it was all. When I was driving the Whip, I got to know where the amusement people hang around, which is a slightly different location from where I hang around. The man who owned the ride had a Mister Softee concession. He just had the ride lying around. I took my savings and I bought it. It was called the Swing Away then. I changed the name myself. *Moon* I thought of because they had just sent someone to the moon at that time. *Trip* I just picked at random, and because people talked a lot about trips in those days."

For a decade or so, Big Lee provided most of the muscle power for the Moon Trip. Then he hired his helpers and acquired the physique of some-one often in repose. He is now about fifty years old, and has slicked-back black hair, a saggy smile, ruddy coloring, and less than perfect posture. He usually wears a pastel polo shirt, jeans, and a thick silver neck chain to the festivals. Big Johnny wears a Playboy pendant. Little Johnny wears hoop earrings. Doug wears a baseball cap. Mark says, "I'm in school studying rec-reational therapy. What do you think—I'm going to make this my *career*?"

While filling a balloon, Big Lee decided to outline his business philos-ophy. First, pick the paint colors for the Moon Trip yourself, so you make sure they're cheerful. Second, you can get rid of the tossing the plates, the pitch game, the parakeets—the whole you-name-it—but balloons will al-ways be good to you. Third, don't pick weaklings as helpers. Fourth, don't hang around any particular festival too long, because people will get to know you. Fifth, don't tell your neighbors that you have a ride, because they'll be asking you to bring it over every other night for barbecues, pool parties, Jennifer's sweet sixteen bash, or whatever. Sixth, wash and Simo-nize the Moon Trip once a week, so it always looks presentable. Finally, push *hard*, because the louder the kids scream, the easier it is for people to find you at the festivals.

"Also, don't put fat kids on the bottom row," he added. "I got two fat ones stuck there once. Now I say eighteen will fit, *depending*. But this is a good moneymaker ride. It's actually *fun*. I go up in it once every year to see how it's doing. It's old-fashioned, but it has a broad range. I always say, 'The Moon Trip—for kids of all ages, master of none.' "

Behind him, Big Johnny had stopped the ride in midswing so that a lit-tle boy with a flattop could disembark.

"He got scared," Big Johnny called to Big Lee, and he added, under his breath, "Man, by the time I get home I don't even want to see my *own* kids."

Big Lee shrugged. "It's almost the end of the season," he said. "Just a few more festivals. Then we go south. I mean, *I* go south. The Moon Trip stays here."

MUSHER

THESE ARE THE QUESTIONS that Susan Butcher, Alaskan dog musher and two-time winner (and record holder) of the eleven-hundred-mile Iditarod Trail Sled Dog Race, is asked most often: How cold does it get in Alaska? How cold is it in Alaska *right now*? Is your house cold? What does caribou taste like? What's your dog's name? Susan's first four answers are: Very, very cold. Not too bad. Doesn't feel that way to me. Really good.

The last question has approximately a hundred and fifty answers, because Susan has approximately a hundred and fifty Alaskan Husky sled dogs, who live outside her log cabin in the Alaskan bush. Such a large number of animals strikes many people as unusual, and even unmanageable, so sometimes, instead of "What's your dog's name?," she is asked if she actually bothers to name all her dogs.

The people who ask that are not fellow mushers—dogsled drivers—but, rather, the kind of people (including us) who came to the Plaza Hotel last week to see Susan receive the Women's Sports Foundation's Professional Sportswoman of the Year Award, and who find the circumstances of Susan's life nearly unimaginable: the dozens of dogs, the rigors of sled racing, the near isolation. (For much of the year, the only human being she sees is her husband, David Monson.) Susan, who told us she much prefers two days on a dogsled to two days in the Plaza Hotel, has accrued so much fame as a musher that she is used to being a curiosity, and she is gracious enough to answer even the most elementary dogmushing, Alaska, or life-in-the-bush question with only a trace of exasperation. "Of course I name all the dogs," she explained. "I name some after places and some after people. Then, for a while, I'll have themes, like the names of book characters. One of my studs is Crackers, so another theme is to name his puppies after cracker brands. Another stud is Granite, and a lot of his puppies have rock names. I know every dog by name. I know every dog's parents. I know every dog's grandparents. I know which one has a cold, and which one didn't eat well last night, and I know each one's personality and where he likes to be scratched. You have to understand, this is all I care about, and this is all I think about. I don't understand anything else, and I don't care about anything else. I'm with the dogs twelve or sixteen hours a day, seven days a week. They're my friends and my family and my livelihood."

As she was talking, Susan kept glancing at her dog Fortuna, whom she had brought with her from Alaska to donate to the Women's Sports Foundation for a benefit auction. Fortuna is six years old and raced in the 1984 Iditarod, but now, according to Susan, she wants to be a pet. To us she didn't seem to like being in New York any more than Susan did, but she looked happier once she'd discovered the nice sled dog living in the Plaza Baroque Room's mirrored columns. "She misses her friends," Susan told us. "She thinks she's finally found another dog." She leaned over. "Hey, For*tuna*, good girl," she cooed. "*Good* girl!"

Susan is thirty-two and has a long black braid and very pale blue eyes. For a normal day of mushing, she wears polypropylene underwear, layers of Thinsulate and GoreTex outer garments, a beaver hat, a wolverine muff, wolfskin gloves, and sealskin mukluks. For the press conference, she wore jeans and a cotton T-shirt that said "Purina ProPlan," which is a type of dog food put out by one of her sponsors. For the foundation's evening black-tie cocktail party, she said, she was going to wear a long gingham skirt, a black satin shirt, and an ivory miniature-dogsled-and-team necklace. "I do own long skirts—I need them for the Iditarod awards banquet in Nome, for one thing," she explained, and then said, "Oh, *shoot!* I wish I'd brought my qiviut dress." She was wearing that dress—qiviut is the underwool of the musk ox—last March when she received first prize for the 1987 race, and also the year before when she picked up the trophy for the 1986 Iditarod. That was the race in which she set the world record (eleven days, fifteen hours, and six minutes), and it made up for the previous year, when a rogue moose attacked her team, killing three of her dogs and forcing her to drop out. "No one was going to beat me in 1986," she told us. "I was really determined."

Susan said that her first dog, Cabee, was a Labrador mix, and her second dog was an Alaskan Husky, and all her dogs since have been Huskies. She first mushed dogs in Massachusetts, where she was born, and she kept at it when she moved to Colorado and shared a house with a woman who had fifty Huskies. By the age of nineteen, she was sure enough of herself to know that she wanted to live in the wilderness with a lot of dogs, and that there was nowhere in the Lower Forty-eight that would satisfy her. "At first, I wanted to build wooden boats," she went on. "I really loved carpentry, and I wanted to sail around the world, because at the time I thought the ocean was the only place I could go to get away from people. But then I tried to figure out what I'd do with twenty or thirty dogs on a small boat." When she moved to Alaska, in 1975, she lived in a "fly-in"—an area accessible only by plane. Then her work as a dog breeder, trainer, and racer made living near a road necessary, so she and her husband (they were married in 1985) and the dogs moved to a slightly less remote spot, a hundred and fifty miles north of Fairbanks and twenty-five miles from the closest village (Manley, pop. 62). She still hunts moose for food, but now there's a gravel road to her cabin. "Where we're living is very downtown to me," she said. "We chose it because it's good for mushing. There are very strong winds and it's stormy, and that's good, because it's the kind of weather you get during races. I just don't like city living. We do have a radio, and David likes to listen to it, but I don't. He likes to read newspapers. I like to burn them for firewood."

Someone passed out auction brochures—Fortuna was listed under the heading "Luxurious Fun"—and then a man who was wearing a World Boxing Hall of Fame tie clip and belt buckle, and who had the cauliflower ears of a boxer, grabbed Susan by the elbow and said, "Are you the girl that did that thing on the dogsled?"

She nodded and said, "Eleven days on a sled in the Alaskan wilderness."

The man turned to someone walking past and exclaimed, "I couldn't do the thing she did! I can go into the ring and get bashed up, but I couldn't do that thing she did!"

FANS

ONE OF THESE DAYS, Leo Herschman is going to clean up his shop, the Modern Supply Company, which is on the third floor of a narrow building near City Hall. In the meantime, Modern Supply, where Mr. Herschman has been selling nothing but ceiling fans for more than thirty years, has the look of a Swiss village all but obliterated by an Alpine rockslide. "We're jammed to hell in here," Mr. Herschman was complaining the other day as he extracted an order form from a pile of boxes, flyers, fan catalogs, newspapers, and stationery on his desk. "I keep planning to get this place organized. When my late wife and I opened Modern Supply, in 1932, we had a beautiful store on Fulton Street. We sold all manner of appliances—refrigerators, ovens, everything. But the Fulton Street building was torn down for the World Trade Center, and we moved to this lousy place. We brought what I would call the minimum from Fulton Street—

fans and motors. Now all I sell is ceiling fans. It's still too crowded in here. A designer was here once buying a fan, and he said to me, 'Sir, would you care to retain me to redesign your store?' I said, 'What are you planning to do, set fire to it?' "

Mr. Herschman likes to say that he became an adult at the age of eight, which means that he has been an adult for eighty-one years. He is short and wiry, with strong cheekbones, a certain amount of smooth gray hair, and a voice that is very easily heard. He wears black-rimmed eye-glasses on his forehead or at the conventional angle, depending. His eye-brows are in a constant state of arch. He is fitter and livelier than many people his age, but he likes to punctuate his workday with moments of pri-vate reflection. This means that people who come to Modern Supply hop-ing to have a consultation about fans with Mr. Herschman, who is described in his advertisements as "Leo Herschman, Famous Expert," are sometimes disappointed. Interest in fan consultations usually increases with the onset of hot weather, but so does the number of Mr. Herschman's private moments. "That's fine with me," Mr. Herschman said, shrugging. "I can't stand the general public. I make no effort to be courteous to them. I also don't stand for any undue familiarity. We get a lot of me-generation people in here, and I try to get rid of them as fast as possible. My assistants can take care of most issues that people come to have us resolve. There's not that much to know about fans, but I suppose I am the famous expert. I know that makes me sound like a big ham. When a guy comes in and says, 'Hey, are you the famous expert?' I say, 'Well, big boy, I'm lying. I don't know a fan from a bucket of mud.' "

Before becoming big in ceiling fans, Mr. Herschman excelled in a few other careers. "When I do something, I do it all the way," he told us. "I had a lot of pep in the old days. I was a boxer and a runner. I went to sea. I was a tough guy. I was a real musician—a jazzman, not one of these drug-laden psycho-rocker types. When I was fourteen, I spent time in the printing and advertising business. The boss was a hand shaker, a Babbitt, tight as the devil—he didn't give me a raise in ages. Then he fired the production man—he was an idiot—and I moved up in the business. I tried to enlist during the First World War. Boom! Then came the Armistice. I worked as a rivet heater on a ship after the war, with a crew of tough little brats who taunted me. I said to them, 'Excuse me, I know you don't mean any harm even if you are bums. If you bother me any more, I'll knock your skulls to-gether.' Then I knocked their skulls together, and they said, 'Hey, this fellow's all right!' Then I wangled a transfer to the pipe-fitting crew. After that, I went to sea."

Just then, three apparently athletic men wearing T-shirts cut off above their navels walked in and eyed the fans hanging from the ceiling: There were twenty-one of them—white, brown, black, bright brass, and antique brass, with blade spans of thirty-six, forty-two, forty-eight, and fifty-two inches—and half were on, filling Modern Supply with what Mr. Herschman calls horizontal thrust. One of the athletes said, "Hey, do you sell ceiling fans, or what?" Mr. Herschman ignored them.

"Then I had my own printing outfit," he went on. "That's when I met my future wife. She was a little hundred-pound girl from Philadelphia. I helped her set up her own business, because she had been working for a terrible guy. I said to her, 'Jean, you're working for a terrible guy. He's got an obsequious manner. You should go into business for yourself.' She was going to be selling all discount goods—refrigerators, ovens, everything. I suggested the name Modern Supply, because we would be anticipating future needs. I'm good at anticipating booms. For instance, I anticipated the lawn mower boom on Long Island. Eventually, I was doing so much work for Jean that I said to her, 'You can't afford to pay me what all this is worth, so let's get married.' I didn't have any silly romantic notions. We were absolutely the same kind of people, my wife and I. We both loved to work. It was almost an obsession."

In the early sixties, Mr. Herschman said to himself that there was going to be a boom in ceiling fans. "We had been selling fans occasionally, and then I realized that we would be having a boom. When the price of electricity went up and air-conditioning became expensive, the whole thing skyrocketed. We now sell fans to a variety of, shall I say, *characters*, but I do not pay attention to anyone who comes in who is of a weird or unusual nature. In the old days, the men bought the fans, and they'd choose brown. Now women do most of the choosing, and four times out of five they pick white. They like white fans to go against their white ceilings, because it has less of a discordant effect. Some people come in here thinking a ceiling fan is the do-all and be-all of everything. It is not. It is a *cir*-cu-la-tor. It will *cir*-cu-late air and cool an object, including a person. People have asked me to build them noisy fans to drown out noisy streets. A psychologist who had, shall we call them, *patients* once asked me to build a device to block sound from traveling into his waiting room. We had a fellow named Slater, a hypnotist, who had me build one that made a sound that helped get people hypnotized. He didn't want them to think there was anything unnatural going on, even though quite obviously there was."

It is Mr. Herschman's opinion that the world is going down the drain and that the ceiling fan business has been a reasonably good position from which to observe its downward direction over the last six decades. From time to time, he issues updates on the finer points of this opinion. That afternoon, among the matters he addressed were brands of ceiling fans besides the brands he sells ("Let us not concern ourselves with the fact that three-quarters of the fans out there are trash"), his career at present ("I prefer building and fixing things, which I used to do. I could still build things if I were compelled to, and sometimes I get sentimental"), most space shuttle experiments ("Very disappointing"), lawyers ("Robots"), accountants ("Robots"), and academe ("Maybe there are a few professors who know something, but that's only because they had a job before they went to school. We are often approached by professors about ceiling fans, and they do not grasp the reality or realistic attitudes of the problem— that's the fault of their college training").

Mr. Herschman's assistants, Theresa Carriman and Lindsay Noel, waited on the athletes, and then they told Leo that they were leaving for the day, and turned off the fans. The shop instantly became stuffy. "I don't have any fans at home," Mr. Herschman said, pushing his glasses up and squeegeeing the bridge of his nose. "I live in the Village, in a concrete building, and it's as cool as can be."

FISH WINDOW

SOME OF THE PEOPLE who admire Fernando Lara's window displays at the Citarella Fish Company, at Broadway and Seventy-fifth, think the prehistoric-monster tableau he made one day last week was among his finest efforts. A plastic Godzilla clutching a real boiled lobster reared up on a slab of swordfish that had a face of black-olive eyes and a mushroom nose and was resting on a field of finnan haddie and jumbo shrimp. About half a dozen people stopped by to photograph the window that day. Others— purists, probably—prefer Mr. Lara's nonrepresentational displays, which might feature a rosette of gray sole over a cascade of scallops; or concentric circles of brook trout, red snapper, sea squab, and stone-crab claws; or an elaborate mosaic of lobsters and clams and haddock. Mr. Lara's windows—a spectacle of color and texture and fish forms—have become one of the most popular art exhibits on upper Broadway, and there is usually a school of appreciators trolling outside Citarella in the morning as soon as he finishes preparing the day's display. Mr. Lara, who makes up a new window every day but Sunday, doesn't publicly favor one of his styles over another, but he admits to liking to deploy a plastic prehistoric creature along with the fish whenever possible, especially if he can get dry ice for a smoke-pouring-out-of-nostrils effect.

"Sometimes, before I come to work, I sit and think of my design," Mr. Lara said the other day. "I want the window to be nice every time. I just wish I had more time to do it." As he was talking, he put two pails—one full of salmon steaks and one of halibut—on a shelf at the back of the window, smoothed the shaved ice in front, and calculated where to begin. He planned to edge the window with fish steaks, layer sea squabs and scallops beside them, put a pile of shrimp in the center, and poise melon boats on either side of it. He was also preparing a few mackerel for the next day, when he intended to prop three of them up like miniature porpoises leaping out of a sea of other seafood and balance a rubber ball between their noses. "Sometimes I'll ride my train in from Astoria and I'll have the design in my head, but they won't have the fish I planned on," he said. "Then I have to change my ideas really fast. I get ideas from watching television, and sometimes I see a picture in a magazine that I like, and I come to work and make it out of fish. Sometimes I can't believe I can make all this just out of fish."

Mr. Lara, who is thirty-two years old and came here from Mexico in 1979, had never done any artwork or arranged fish in any manner until eight months ago. He was working as an icebox man at Citarella then, and started getting ideas about the window display, so he asked Ricky Oviedo, the manager, if he could give it a try. His only relevant prior experience was a childhood habit of playing with his food. "We had a different sort of window before Fernando started doing it," Ricky Oviedo told us. "We just sort of threw everything in."

A tiny elderly woman made her way up to the counter, asked for a nice piece of white snapper, not too big, and then peered over the back of the window at Mr. Lara's half-finished arrangement. "I come here every day to look at the fish window," she said, "and I tell you, he's an artist." Her companion, a tall woman with a soft Caribbean accent, said, "We never miss a single day coming to see the fish. I loved it when he used the Godzilla."

The tiny woman waved her hands. "I don't know about that one," she said. "But I love the pretty way he arranges the fish."

Mr. Lara grinned and turned back to his pails. He didn't care for the way the salmon steaks were buckling, so he picked up a piece of wood he uses to shove the fish around and whacked the steaks with it. They stopped buckling. As it happens, salmon is his favorite material to work with, because of its good color, density, and form, and because it doesn't smell bad after an hour or two in the window. "I like to go around and look at other store windows," he said. "I like seeing how they arrange clothes and shoes and things. But I've never seen one with fish that I've liked." He added that he was disappointed that the day's delivery hadn't included any good heads. He likes working with heads, and once stuck a salmon head on a sturgeon body. He also painted a lobster and a loaf of bread black once and constructed a giant spider out of them.

The display needed vegetation, so Mr. Lara made a trip to Fairway for eleven heads of green leaf lettuce, three red peppers, an acorn squash, two cucumbers, and a head of broccoli. He washed them all and whittled them into funny shapes and arranged them around the fish. "I'd like to paint," he said, "but I don't have the time. I've never really done it. I'm always thinking of new designs for the fish. The only thing I don't like is when the customers come in and want one of the pieces in the window. It's like if you painted something, you wouldn't want anyone to touch it." He picked up a gooey sea squab and looked it over. "I don't eat fish," he added. "I don't like it. My favorite meal is fried meat."

A few months ago, Mr. Lara found that all he could think about, day and night, was his fish windows. It got on his nerves, so he told Mr. Oviedo that he thought he should stop doing the window. "I said to him, 'Fernando, you do a good window. Stick with it,' " Mr. Oviedo told us. Mr. Lara capitulated, and returned to his morning routine. From eight to ten, he does the window, and the rest of the day he spends behind the counter weighing and wrapping fish for the customers.

This morning, he finished his design by spreading ten pounds of scallops alongside the salmon, crowned the whole thing with a starfish that had come in by chance with the fish delivery that morning, and stood back to survey his handiwork. One of his regular fans, a tall, freckled man, stood on the sidewalk admiring the arrangement. He nodded his approval to Mr. Lara, and hollered, "Fernando, wonderful texture today!" To a passerby he said, "Boy, what that guy can do with fish. I'm telling you, he ought to get an agent."

THREE-DIMENSIONAL

ONE OF THE THINGS the new Steve Urkel doll says when you pull its voice cord is "Got any cheese?" We don't know why he says this, because we are among the few Americans who don't watch *Family Matters,* the allegedly warm, wonderful, hilarious television comedy featuring a character named Steve Urkel, who evidently spends a great deal of his time inquiring about cheese. One of the things that Wayne Charness, a vice president of Hasbro, Inc., says about the introduction of the Steve Urkel doll is "I hope you're as excited as we are!" In this case, we know why *he* says *this. Family Matters* delivers the highest share of viewers aged two to eleven among all prime-time network programs, and this means that the Steve Urkel doll, which Hasbro will be bringing out this fall, is bound to be a very high-margin piece of entertainment hardware.

At a press conference at the New York Hilton the other day, we found out pretty much everything else about Steve Urkel and the official Urkel product line that we had been wondering about. We had been wondering, for instance, how the whole Urkel licensing campaign had been going. A representative of LCA Entertainment, the licensing company orchestrating the Urkel licensing campaign, was sitting behind us at the conference, and he provided this interpretative account: "For one thing, the apparel is blowing off the shelves. I mean *blowing off.* The boxer shorts are really hot. And the sheets, by the way, are incredible." The people at LCA also wanted to mention this: If you yourself do not have a wild and wondrous neighbor like Steve Urkel, you will soon be able to make up for it by purchasing Urkel sweatshirts, T-shirts, twill jackets (screen-printed), belts, suspenders, pajamas, robes, sweaters, fleece coordinates in boys' sizes 2 to 18, sleeping bags, backpacks, beach towels, bedding, trading cards, posters, handheld electronic games, video game watches, tabletop games, buttons, Lucite key rings, mini-stickers, poster books, calendars, jigsaw puzzles, 3-D reels, and Do the Urkel: The Risk and Roll Game That Lets You Be Urkel, not to mention the amazingly lifelike Steve Urkel doll.

Jaleel White is the fourteen-year-old actor who plays Steve Urkel. Like the Steve Urkel doll, Jaleel has big brown eyes, gigantic dimples, a pointy chin, and a sprightly body with rubbery joints. In character, he wears a nerdy shirt, nerdy pants, nerdy shoes, suspenders, and oversize eyeglasses on a nylon cord. In real life, he wears other outfits. Jaleel had this to say about becoming a doll: "A lot of very important people of our time have been dolls." At the press conference, Jaleel made a short speech in the nerdy voice he uses for Urkel, embraced an Urkel doll, and demonstrated the Urkel dance to the adoring overflow crowd. (We have misplaced the dance instructions that were in the press kit, but we seem to remember that they began with the phrase "Hitch up your pants.") Then Jaleel was introduced to Roseann Radosevich, a director of girls' toys design at Hasbro, who supervised the development of the doll. "He skewed a little older than preschool," Ms. Radosevich explained to us after the encounter, because we had, in fact, been wondering how Urkel skewed. And how about his adorability quotient? "He's very, very three-dimensional," Ms. Radosevich said. "It's easy to see how he could be a toy."

Here's something else we'd been wondering about: What do seventeen eager press photographers say to a living doll? This much we could make out: "Jaleel, can you shuffle a little again?" and "Hey, Jaleel, redo the Urkel dance!" and "Jaleel, do the Urkel!" and "Jaleel, over here, babe!" and "This way, Jaleel." Also, "Do the thing with your foot up, babe." Jaleel's reaction to the hubbub: "I've been in the business since I was three years old. I know how to communicate with the press. I've grown into the press. Also, I've been on Carson." And how about describing his approach, as an actor, to the Urkel character? "To be honest, it was destiny."

Basically, a press conference announcing the introduction of a multi-million-dollar product line involves a small hotel room filled with a lot of people in good moods about their upside potential answering questions from other people about that upside potential. This was the case with Urkel: The Press Conference. Someone from *Teen Beat* wanted to know whether the Urkel doll was likely to be bigger than the New Kids on the Block products, and whether Urkel was a multidimensional sort of thing, and what Jaleel's dream date would be like. (We were wondering about the last item, too. She would be—this is direct from the source—"not a shallow person, who has ambition, and who would not be ashamed to ride around in a car that wasn't a Mercedes-Benz.") Iris Burton, Jaleel's agent, wanted to know if she sounded too nasal in her interview. A reporter from Long Island wanted to know how long Urkel-mania was likely to last. Grace Garland, the gossip reporter from WBLS Radio, wanted to know if Jaleel's father, a dentist who lives in Los Angeles, had done Jaleel's teeth. Someone sitting beside us wanted to know if we had ever eaten fried dough. A reporter from a Philadelphia television station wanted to know if Jaleel had heard the rumor that he was more intelligent than all five New

Kids on the Block put together. Someone without a name tag wanted to know whether a comparison between Jaleel and the young Jerry Lewis had been made before. We wanted to know how we should feel about getting a press release saying "Urkel-mania Takes the Country by Storm," considering that until the press conference we had never heard of Steve Urkel. Grace Garland, when she had finished complimenting Jaleel's teeth, wanted to know if we wanted one of her business cards, just because, as she put it, "you never know."

ACCOMMODATING

REPORTER (*which means us, entering a dry-cleaning establishment at the corner of Ninety-seventh and Columbus Avenue*): Pardon me, I was just wandering by and saw the sign in your window that says:

> ANNOUNCING NAT
> OF VALETONE'S CLEANERS
> YEARS OF EXPERIENCE
> EXPERT TAILORING
> AND ALTERATIONS
> HAS JOINED THE STAFF OF
> MANHATTAN VALET

I was thinking that this Nat must be quite something. Most dry cleaners don't announce their tailors with such enthusiasm.

PERSON BEHIND THE COUNTER (*who turns out to be Gary Adler, owner and founder of Manhattan Valet*): What can I tell you? He has an excellent reputation, and he was working up the street at a store that was closing, and I needed a tailor. So we both had needs that needed to be filled. I wanted an authority in the area, and that was Nat. He's very known. After I hired him, I put up the sign, because we're not too shy to say we have Nat now.

PERSON WHO JOINS GARY BEHIND THE COUNTER (*who happens to be his sister Alisa, co-owner of Manhattan Valet*): Actually, Nat came to work here because he's been in love with me for years.

(*Another person now joins Gary and Alisa behind the counter. This is their mother, who introduces herself as Mother Adler.*)

MOTHER ADLER: Alisa, *please*! (*To us*) You can call me Rhoda or Mother Adler. The story of Nat is that we had a tailor before Nat who was from Trinidad, a lovely man, but he wanted to do music. Calypso and cha-cha, and so forth. So he left.

NAT FREUND (*who has stepped out from behind his sewing table and joined the conversation*): What I can't give them musically, I give them in tailoring. Musically, I can't accommodate.

ALISA: Personally, I think he's an incredible tailor.

NAT: (*Embarrassed silence.*)

MOTHER ADLER: Nat, I'm telling you, you don't have to be modest. You don't have to be shy. (*To us*) This is really my kids' business. I'm just the mother. I don't meddle. I don't butt in. I just give suggestions. I just give advice.

GARY: Mother, enough already. On the subject of Nat, I'm not saying this to swell his head, but there are people who simply will not go to anyone besides Nat.

NAT: I used to work for His Majesty the King.

GARY: You're joking. (*Gary exits.*)

NAT: What's to joke? His Majesty King George VI. In other words, the British Army. I worked in a uniform factory. Then for thirty-four years in this neighborhood. I'm known on the avenue.

ALISA: I met a woman at a luncheon once—this is a true story and a really funny story—and I mentioned to her that we had hired a new tailor and she said, "Oh my God! Not Nat! He's the best! I've been *looking* for him since Valetone closed!" (*Commotion at the door. Gary reenters.*) Gary, where have you been?

GARY: I went and got us a little something to eat. I thought to myself, We're talking, we should have a little something. What does everyone like to eat? And then I thought, Butter cookies! Everyone loves butter cookies!

NAT (*eyeing the cookies*): I always say to my customers, "It's easy to take in, it's not so easy to let out." When they keep coming to me for letting out, sometimes I tell them they need a dietitian, not a tailor. Of course, I let my own pants out. Periodically. Since I stopped smoking. Have a cookie! You could gain two ounces, it wouldn't kill you.

MOTHER ADLER: Wonderful cookies. It's a lovely bakery on Broadway. You should try their candy cake if you're having company over sometime. By the way, I should mention that we have specials here all the time—shirt specials, Lotto specials, rug-cleaning specials. This is a real family place. We love to accommodate. When Gary was on his quest for a business, I said, "Gary, find a business where you can accommodate." And I said, "Gary, when times are tough, people don't buy suits, they clean them."

NAT: I can tell you this. Of all the dry-cleaning establishments I've seen in this city, and I assure you I've seen quite a few, this is the most unique one. I used to walk by here four, five times a day when it first opened and just stare in the window. These are progressive young people with a whole new concept about a dry-cleaning establishment. I am not exaggerating when I say that no other tailor in the entire city of New York has a situation like mine. We have a whole department here! We have so much room! There are two of us tailors, me and (*points across the room to a dark-haired young man bent over a sewing machine*) my young friend over here from the Soviet Union. I know the other tailors on the avenue. I consult with them on an informal basis. It's not for me to say they're jealous, but I am sure that I'm the object of some—how would you put it?—envy.

GARY (*leaning over conspiratorially*): That's something else you should know about Nat. A lot of tailors wouldn't work with another tailor. You're dealing with ego, with feelings, with conflict. For him, it's not a problem. (*To Nat*) Nat, would you say you have charisma?

NAT: That's not for me to say. Work is work. I will say I've got a following. I will say I'm known. I will say I have quite a lot of loyal customers. I will say I take care of them. They need me, because they need alteration. Also, I have a family that needs alteration.

SPLURGE

SO THERE'S THIS HUSBAND and wife, and one day they decide to go to Saks Fifth Avenue. They walk over to the store and end up in designer handbags. Before you know it, the wife is checking out the merchandise. Right away, the husband's getting nervous. Suddenly, he notices this pleasant-looking gray-haired woman behind the counter. This woman, believe it or not, happens to be Judith Leiber, the most famous designer of designer handbags, who is making an in-store appearance with her fall collection. For those of you who just recently fell off the turnip truck, a Leiber handbag is tiny, rhinestone encrusted, and shaped like something cute— maybe a bird, or a panda, or a butterfly, or an egg—and is also, we mean to tell you, not cheap. A Leiber panda, say, runs three thousand bucks. Anyhow, the wife falls in love with the panda and then takes a deep interest in an egg bag, too, so the husband starts hyperventilating. Maybe she's a new wife, maybe she's an old wife—what's the difference? He just knows she's getting hung up on these three-thousand-dollar little handbags and he's going to have to do something quick. Finally, the husband—he's sweating now—says to Mrs. Leiber, "Hey, look, if I buy two, would I get a special price?"

Mrs. Leiber looks him in the eye and says, "No, but we would thank you very nicely."

Okay, okay, so there's a priest, a rabbi, and—No, seriously, there's a reporter who walks into Saks Fifth Avenue this same day and heads over to the Judith Leiber counter, jots down a few notes about the handbags, and then goes up to Mrs. Leiber and says, "Listen, I was wondering. You were born in Hungary and learned to make handbags there, and then came to this country in 1947 and went into the handbag industry in New York, and then started your own company in 1963, designing and manufacturing luxury evening bags that have become the must-have status object for certain women, and you have fans who own dozens and dozens of your designs, including a fan in New Orleans who lent fifty of her Leibers for a show at the New Orleans Museum of Art a few years ago. But what I was wondering was: What sort of handbag do you carry?"

So Mrs. Leiber looks at the reporter and says, "One of my own, of course. Either that or a paper bag. And I won't carry a paper bag, so you figure it out."

But seriously, now—another husband and wife come up to the counter. The wife is going crazy for the handbags, and the husband is doing the death grip on his wallet when he notices Mrs. Leiber. So he says to her, "Are you Mrs. Leiber? I've long been an admirer of yours."

Mrs. Leiber says to him, "Oh, really?"

The husband says, "Actually, my wife more than me."

Mrs. Leiber says, "That's good. You shouldn't be carrying handbags. You're not the type."

Could you die?

All right, it's the same afternoon, and this skinny woman in thigh-high boots and a baggy sweatshirt comes up to the counter. She's here to meet Mrs. Leiber, but also she decided when she woke up this morning that life is short and, God willing, today she's going to splurge and buy a Judith

Leiber pillbox. The pillboxes are also tiny and rhinestone encrusted and shaped like pandas and what have you. Anyhow, this hippie type is looking at the pillboxes, and she says to the saleswoman, "Do you have any pillboxes that are bigger? I mean, these are exquisite, but I need something bigger, because I take a lot of vitamins."

So the saleswoman says to her, "We do have one shaped like an egg, which holds quite a lot."

Mrs. Sweatshirt-and-Thigh-Highs looks at her and says, "Hey, maybe I should just *eat* an egg. That way I wouldn't need the vitamins *or* the pillbox!"

You cannot make this stuff up.

Okay, now, the afternoon is rolling along, and Mrs. Leiber is the center of attention—some Japanese women have their picture taken with her, and a lot of Saks brass come to pay their respects, because, after all, she's got a lot of real estate on the first floor. Are you still with us? So two young women in those it-wasn't-enough-for-me-to-have-a-lovely-husband-and-children-I-had-to-have-a-*career* suits come up to Mrs. Leiber, and one of them says, "Mrs. Leiber, you make me so happy. I want to thank you for doing what you do."

Mrs. Leiber looks at her and says, "Please. Don't thank me. Buy."

The other young woman says, "Mrs. Leiber, I just love coming to see your bags. It's like going to a museum."

Mrs. Leiber looks at her and says, "Sweetie, you have it all wrong. Believe me. These are to own, not to be in a museum."

Did you hear, by the way, the one about the Leiber pig bag? This is one of her new designs—a fat little pig covered with pink rhinestones, hinged at the haunches, and with a grin on his face. Hey, you'd be grinning, too, if you cost three thousand dollars, right? Anyway, the pig is the big hit of the day. One woman picks it up and says, "I've got to have this, even if it's *trayf.*" Another one says, "Take a look at this, he's even got cloven hooves. Is that biologically right?" Another one finally puts her MasterCard where her mouth is. She picks up the pink pig and hands it and her card to the saleswoman standing next to Mrs. Leiber and says, "My husband's going to kill me, but I'm going to die if I don't get this, so, the way I see it, I'm going to go one way or the other, right?"

The saleswoman takes the pig and the credit card, and then she pulls Mrs. Leiber over for a private moment and says, "Mrs. Leiber, this pink pig is just a sample. Maybe we should keep it."

Mrs. Leiber looks at her, looks at the pig, looks at the customer, looks back at the saleswoman, rolls her eyes, catches her breath, and finally says, "Darling, *please*. Don't give me a heart attack. Sell the pig. There's more where that came from."

LAST FRONTIER

BELIEVE IT OR NOT, Alan Abel, the man who masterminded that fake $35 million-dollar lottery winner a few weeks ago, pulled the stunt for humanitarian reasons. Mr. Abel is a square-built middle-aged man who has a low center of gravity, gray-brown hair, longish sideburns, pointy eyebrows, and a gigantic, mobile smile that turns slightly sheepish when he drops one-liners like "I've given up smoking until this lung cancer scare blows over." It is entirely possible to imagine him, Art Buchwald, and Allan Sherman in a room somewhere giving one another noogies. Mr. Abel says that he is a fundamentally serious person, however, and one recent afternoon he could be found wearing a sane as anything midlevel-executive outfit—navy blazer, gray slacks, loafers—and looking contemplative as he sat in his office, which is a brick-red train caboose parked in his backyard, in Westport. Mr. Abel retires to the caboose when he wants to devise new pranks. "I find it easy to come up with nonsense," he explained, settling onto a lumpy couch that takes up about half the caboose. "This is a good place to work— it's a good place for me to think about exploring the mind. The mind is the last frontier. I like to play, and my friends and my mind are my toys."

How do the humanitarian considerations fit into the last frontier? It was Mr. Abel's opinion that the public was sick and tired of seeing every lottery jackpot end up in the hands of some pipe-fitter-from-Queens type, and that most people playing the lottery were getting traumatized by always losing—sometimes by just one or two digits—and he figured that everyone would be cheered up if there were to be a young winner with long hair and a glossy smile, so he provided one. Mr. Abel would also like to take credit for the aliens in Russia last summer. He claims he had been sitting around in the caboose worrying that they didn't have any fun in Russia, and that there had never been a UFO spotted there, so he sent detailed plans for a spaceship and aliens to a couple of Russians he had listed in his hoax-lovers Rolodex. "What I do is give people a kick in the intellect," Mr. Abel is fond of saying. "I like a big audience. If I'd been born five hundred years ago, I'd have been a court jester. If I had a lot of money and if I were an evil person, I could take over the world. My hope is that people see the sociological significance of what I do. This is a mental exercise. No banana peels, no buckets of water falling on people's heads, no whoopee cushions—that's low class."

That afternoon, Mr. Abel was still fielding calls from around the world about the lottery prank. To date, he has successfully published his own fake obituary (the *Times*, 1980), passed off phony organizations, including Females for Felons, Omar's School for Panhandlers, Society for Indecency to Naked Animals, and the International Sex Bowl Olympics (many talk shows, many years), and trick-or-treated his own neighbors (Westport, the eighties). He may or may not have put a phony referee in a football game (Super Bowl XVII, Redskins vs. Dolphins, 1983), and brought a faux Salman Rushdie out of hiding (American Booksellers Association convention, 1989). But for some reason the lottery prank has proved to be his biggest hit. "This was the whopper—the media loved it," Mr. Abel said. "They loved having someone pretty and pleasant as a winner, for a change, and Lee Chirillo, the actress who played the part of the winner, was very good at it. When the electronic media jumped in so fast—whew, I honestly wasn't expecting such a big blast. How do you arrange something like the lottery hoax? It's really simple. I just wrote a script and then rounded up my group of merry pranksters, and we each chipped in a hundred and fifty dollars for a room at the Omni Park Central Hotel and champagne, and then we faxed the wire services saying we had the winner. Before we started, I said to my pranksters, 'Look, we'll produce this scenario and we'll party. Whatever happens happens.' Most of my pranksters are actors and actresses with day jobs. I've always got along best with people younger than I am. We had a great time."

Mr. Abel stood up, stepped over to a desk, picked up a set of drumsticks, and began pounding out a beat on a drum pad. "Basic rock beat!" he yelled over the drumming. "Easy as anything! Anyone can do it!" That answered a question a lot of people have about major league hoaxsters like Mr. Abel: How does the guy make a living? "I teach drumming!" he yelled. "I teach a class called Learn to Drum!" He segued into the drumbeat of "Bolero," and then put down the drumsticks and said, "I also teach a class in comedy to people with no sense of humor, called Learn to Be Funny. I show them how to do things like—oh, if they're shy, I suggest they take a bunch of hard-boiled eggs to a party and surreptitiously slip them into people's pockets and handbags. It's an icebreaker. I've composed and published sixteen pieces of concert music. My wife and I directed a very successful movie called *Is There Sex After Death?* starring Buck Henry, and we made a lot of money with that. I've written many books, and I'm working on one right now called *Abel Raises Cain.* I'm in the creative field. I also teach a class called Don't Get Mad—Get Even. My philosophy is that it's healthier to give ulcers than to get them."

Mr. Abel named P. T. Barnum and Jonathan Swift as his greatest sources of inspiration, and went on to say, "My mother had no sense of humor whatsoever. My father, though, was a very flamboyant general-store owner in a small town in Ohio. He'd do things like put a big lump of worthless glass in the window with a sign saying, 'Come in and Find Out About This,' and people would. He'd put 'Limit—Two to a Customer' in front of the things that wouldn't sell, and they'd be gone in a minute. Maybe the learning experience in this is that you shouldn't believe everything you read. I don't. When people tell me I'm crazy, I say, '*Me* crazy? You know what I think is crazy? I think bowling is crazy—taking a ball and rolling it down the floor. *That's* crazy. Exploring the mind is not crazy.'"

EXTENSIONS

BARBARA TERRY'S DREAM: Several years ago, Barbara Terry dreamed she was walking along Seventh Avenue in Harlem and saw dozens of women parading down the street in fancy clothes, looking great except that the backs of their heads were missing. A voice then said to her, "Barbara, you have to do their hair!" Ms. Terry said, "How?" and the voice answered, "You have to braid it." Ms. Terry then woke up, went to the store, bought a sixty-four-ounce Pepsi, went over to her mother's house, woke up her little sister, cut up an old wig, braided the wig hairs into her sister's hair so that it was styled into eight braids, and realized that she had just invented extension hair braiding—the use of synthetic fibers to extend short, broken-off, overprocessed hair and make it more manageable. About that experience Ms. Terry now says, "I'm a person who really gets into her dreams."

HAIR FACTS, ABOUT AND ACCORDING TO BARBARA TERRY: Her grandfather was a barber in the Panama Canal Zone. Her father ran Nelson's Tonsorial Parlor in the Bronx. As a child, Ms. Terry would walk around with a comb in her pocket, and let's say she was talking to you, and your bangs had got messed up—she'd just whip out her comb and fix them for you. As a young woman, in 1961, she invented the Afro when she was rushing out for a date: She didn't have time to hot-press and curl her hair, so she let it dry naturally and fluffed it out, and then found she preferred it that way. People used to stop their cars and curse her for wearing an Afro. She started wearing dreadlocks a few years later, when she was in a hurry to get to Harlem after hearing about the assassination of Martin Luther King, Jr., and decided to twist her hair into separate clumpy sections and let it dry. People used to stop their cars and curse her for wearing dreadlocks. Some friends of hers who live in the Poconos told her recently that putting a circle of hair clippings around the edge of their property seemed to scare the deer away. "I could have made a gazillion dollars by now if I'd been saving hair clippings and selling them to people upstate," Ms. Terry says. "With extension braiding, though, I'm more interested in putting hair on people's heads than in taking it off."

CERTAIN THINGS A PROFESSIONAL HAIR BRAIDER KNOWS FOR SURE: The other afternoon, Ms. Terry was in her apartment, in the Bronx, along with T'Vohnah Benyahmeen, to whom she was teaching extension braiding on a mannequin head named Betty. Betty's hair was chestnut colored with bleached spots; it appeared to have been whacked off somewhat randomly. Ms. Terry's hair, which is about 70 percent her own and 30 percent extensions, was arranged in what she described as "a few hundred individual plaits worn with a little slide bang, with a pompadour and a side ponytail." Ms. Benyahmeen, whose braids had been done by Ms. Terry about a month earlier, was wearing them pulled up into what Ms. Terry described as "a kind of Nordic, I Remember Mama wholesome, cute kind of I'm-not-going-to-misbehave kind of thing." While the two women were braiding monocrylic fibers from a package marked "California Fashions Coarsened Braid" into Betty's hair, they discussed the hair issue as it pertains to some well-known individuals.

Ms. Benyahmeen: "Janet Jackson?"

Ms. Terry: "Not her real hair."

"Whitney Houston?"

"That's not her hair."

"Robin Givens? When she was dating Mike Tyson?"

"That's not her hair."

"Patti LaBelle?"

"Everyone *knows* that's not her hair."

HISTORICALLY AND FACTUALLY SPEAKING: Extension braids can be styled as African string curls, Egyptian twists, Senegalese twists, Nubian twists, basic cornrows, individual plaits, and New York pix, or they can be fashioned using the interlock method, which Ms. Terry happens to hate and doesn't like to do. "I've revised my technique six times," she says. "My system is called the Songa Original Undetectable Extension Hair Braiding Technique. The whole point of it is neatness. When you take a scrambled mess of hair and make an ordered creation out of it, that's a work of art. Woolly hair is very unusual. It can be woolly or straight: If you shape it into a duck when it's wet, it'll dry in the shape of a duck. It's very sensitive to humidity: If you're wearing an Afro on a humid night, you might go to a party looking like Angela Davis and leave looking like Miriam Makeba. Your hair might change shape in the middle of a sentence. Extension braiding gives it length and structure and lets you do anything with it. It takes hours to get braided, but the braids last six or eight weeks, through dozens of shampoos, and during that time you can get on with your life. While I'm braiding, I say to myself, 'This lady has come to me looking like a plucked chicken and I want to help her.' I'm the pioneer extension braider in the country. I've written a book about it, called *Professional Secrets: How to Do Extension Hair Braiding.* I used to have two salons in Harlem, and one was open twenty-four hours a day. While we braiders were working, we'd turn on the television and discuss and debate *Oprah,* or we'd put on old tapes of the show I host on cable television, called *Harlem Here It Is.* I closed my salons when Reagan came into office, because I knew no one would have any money. Now I teach braiders, lecture about braiding, and wholesale my braid-care products, and I'm opening my Songa Too salon franchises in Florida, Ohio, and Chicago. I'd like to open a museum of African beauty in Harlem. Black people ruined their hair pressing and perming it, all because they were trying to look like Donna Reed. That's *over.* Extension braiding is the biggest thing since bubble gum."

LIKELY FUTURE DEVELOPMENTS IN AFRICAN-AMERICAN HAIR AND SOME FINAL COMMENTARY: Ms. Terry thinks that the next trend in hairstyling will probably be baldness. "Toxic chemicals, pollution—no one will have any hair left or any time to fix it," she explains. "In the meantime, I've figured out a way to restore hair to bald heads. I'm forever trying to maximize what people have. I couldn't help but look at someone like Pearl Bailey and think, After all those years, wouldn't you expect her hair to be longer than *that*? That dinky little inch or so? I know I could have done something for her. During your celibate years, you come up with great ideas."

ON DISPLAY

STEVEN JENKINS' GRANDFATHER Adolph Mayer has a big beefsteak tomato named for him. "The Adolph Mayer is a really wonderful tomato," Mr. Jenkins told us the other day when we dropped in at Fairway, the busy produce market on Broadway near Seventy-fourth Street, where he is one of four junior partners. "My grandfather helps the University of Missouri test new vegetable seeds, so they honored him by naming one after him." Being immortalized anywhere, especially in association with an appetizing vegetable, would probably please almost anyone, but for Mr. Jenkins that kind of recognition has special significance. "Would I like a cheese named after me, the way my grandfather had a tomato?" he asked himself. "That sounds great. You bet I would. You *bet*."

Mr. Jenkins' specialty at Fairway is cheese, but his real passion is writing chatty and enticing signs for all the store's products. A few of the Fairway signs just do their job—they say something simple, like NEW CROP YAMS or CRISPY WESTERN ICEBERG SOLD AT COST PRICE—but those are made by the other Fairway partners, who figure that a sign's a *sign*, especially when you're in a hurry and there are crowds stretching from the cash register to the back door. Mr. Jenkins' signs have become something like required reading among shoppers in the neighborhood—they can be informative, argumentative, comic, autobiographical, or sassy—and whatever time he finds between checking cheese orders he spends making them.

The signs are about five by seven inches and are made of white tagboard. Mr. Jenkins hand-letters them with bright-red or orange or blue or purple laundry markers. One of his signs that day said:

HOOP CHEESE: NO FAT! NO SALT!
AN INTRIGUING MARRIAGE
OF WET COTTON AND LIBRARY PASTE

"I'm very opinionated about cheese," he explained to us, and he pointed out another sign, which said:

MIMOLETTE: HARD, BLAND. DE GAULLE'S
FAVORITE,
WHICH FIGURES. I DON'T KNOW WHY,
IT JUST DOES.
WE STOCK IT BECAUSE IT LOOKS LIKE
CHEESE.

His all-time favorite sign is no longer in service, but Mr. Jenkins was so pleased with it that he saved it for display. It's stapled to the store's back wall, and says:

RAW SEX
FRESH FIGS
SAME THING. 69 CENTS

Some of Mr. Jenkins' signs acquaint shoppers with people who supply choice items or who figure in his interest in food. On signs here and there throughout the store are mentions of Ted and Sally (makers of Wieninger cheese), Laura (California chèvre), Jane and Bo (pie bakers), Nana (Mr. Jenkins' grandmother, who introduced him to kohlrabi), Dr. Scott Severns (his dentist), and Al Grimaldi (bread baker). "I think it's important to know where food is from—that's why I name some of the suppliers," he said. "I wanted to write about my grandmother because she really taught me about the value of fresh foods, and my dentist just asked me to order sorrel for him, so I thought I'd mention him, too." Some signs have won Mr. Jenkins gratitude from customers. His treatise NEVER WASH A MUSHROOM! was very popular, for example. Other signs, however, have been controversial. A sign on some Illinois goat cheese asserting that the cheese was exciting but Illinois was really boring offended so many shoppers that for a while he had to post a note beside it admitting that he was from Missouri and considered it even more boring than Illinois.

Mr. Jenkins, who is late-thirtyish, curly haired, blue-eyed, and barrel-chested, told us that he moved to New York fourteen years ago to become an actor. His career went well—he played the Dean & DeLuca counter-man in *Manhattan* and had a shot at a major role in the soaps—but he soon realized that his day job as a cheese man was making him happier than his acting did. He decided to get serious about food, and he discovered that the thing that made him happiest of all was driving around Europe looking at food and finding the villages that his favorite wines and cheeses were named for. He also liked finding towns famous for their sauces. He more or less gave up acting, and seven years ago he joined Fairway. Today, Mr. Jenkins has credentials in cheese—he is America's only Master Cheesemonger, which means he's an elected member of the Guilde des Maître-Fromagers, Compagnon du Saint-Uguzon—and he manages to satisfy his hunger for an audience by making signs. He recently described this professional odyssey in a sign for cornichons:

> WHEN I GOT STARTED IN THIS BUSINESS
> 13 YEARS AGO, I
> THOUGHT CORNICHONS WERE LITTLE
> CORN COBS.
> AND NOW LOOK AT WHAT A GOURMET
> I'VE BECOME.
> MY GOD, LIFE IS AMAZING.

"I think the best way to show off food is to have a big, huge, untethered pile of stuff," he said as he tidied up around his department, straightening a sign that chided the makers of Pecorino Toscana sheep cheese for charging so much. "Then you stick a big, funny, outrageous, eye-catching sign in the middle of it. You say everything there is to say about the product. There are several schools of food-display signs. One is the fancy-shmancy school, where you have a tiny little sign that says 'One-Hundred-Year-Old Quail Eggs, Eight Thousand Dollars a Dozen.' Another school, which is the one I'm in, is where you take a garish sign and staple it to a big stick and you wedge it into the pile of food. It's a real peasant way of life, making your living from food, and I enjoy the peasant quality of putting a sign on a stick into the food. My partners are always yelling at me for spending so much time on my signs, but I love to do it. You can tell the ones I didn't make. They're rather terse."

As he walked past a sign that said:

> HANDMADE STUFFED PEPPERS: WOW!
> HOOO!
> STRANGE BUT TRUE!

FROM RHODE ISLAND. . . . CRAZY
AMERICANS!

he spotted a woman in the checkout line clutching a bottle of olive oil. "Hey, you're not going to buy that, are you?" he asked her. She eyed him nervously. "There's another brand that's better and it's seven dollars less," he explained, pointing toward a shelf. Then, to us, he said, "I do have an urge to communicate. The truth is, my ideas about food are not necessarily commercial, but I think they might help people know more about what they're getting. I think people should come into the store to have fun and learn something. If you're not going to learn something, why get out of bed?"

HER TOWN

A DAY BEGINS IN THE VILLAGE OF MILLER-ton, New York. A man pauses while shaving and says to his wife, "I think I will run for mayor." Down the road, a cow expires mysteriously. A shopkeeper in town has labor pains. The corn begins to tassel, earlier than usual. The agenda for the village zoning board meeting is copied, collated, stapled, and stacked. A family, over breakfast, decides to give up farming and sell its land. A mutt gives birth to ten puppies and then abandons them. Someone makes the high school honor roll. A lawsuit is filed. A guy dies. A barn burns. A car skids. These kinds of things get reported in the town's weekly newspaper, the Millerton *News*. A woman cracks her husband over the head with an inexpensive piece of pottery. This will probably not be reported in the Millerton *News,* unless she kills him. If she does, it will indeed be big news in Millerton, and big news in the Millerton *News*—bigger than some recent stories like TEENS UNINJURED WHEN CAR CATCHES FIRE AT INTERSECTION and RASHES RUNNING RAMPANT DURING BAD IVY SEASON and KENNETH HANLEY NAMED JIFFY LUBE MANAGER, but less enduring than the Pet Parade (a photo spread of adoptable pets, which runs in every issue of the paper) or the local crime blotter (every issue) or the Seniors Menu at the community center (most issues) or the list of the new books at the library (anytime any new ones come).

The village of Millerton is two hours north of New York City, in the town of Northeast, in the northeast corner of Dutchess County, and is set in the middle of slumpy hills and wavy alfalfa fields and pastureland as soft and rumpled as someone's lap. The houses in the village are solid and modest. Many of them have gardens blooming with fat, old-fashioned, costume jewelry flowers, like dahlias and peonies and mums. In the village, you can sometimes pick up Manhattan radio stations, but you can also shop on the honor system for tomatoes and honey and pattypan squash that people leave on stands out in their yards. About nine hundred people live in the village and about two thousand more in the surrounding area. They are dairy farmers, prison guards, antiques dealers, schoolteachers, organic-vegetable growers, mechanics, store owners. Overwhelmingly, they are Republican. Once, a woman visiting in town gave birth ahead of schedule, and the baby grew up to be the famous Chicago White Sox second baseman Eddie Collins, whose major-league career began in 1906, but other than being the accidental birthplace of a Hall of Famer the village has never rocked the outside world. On the other hand, the people of Millerton have given birth, argued, voted, married, grown things, built things, burned things, and died often enough to fill their own newspaper for the past hundred years.

The reporting staff of the Millerton *News* has usually consisted of one person. The front page of each week's edition features seven or eight stories and two or three photographs. Each story has a byline, and each photograph has a credit. The front page of the June 15 edition carried these stories:

ELEMENTARY STUDENTS
LEARN ABOUT DIVERSITY
by Heather Heaton

MORE ANSWERS NEEDED
ABOUT ASSESSOR'S JOB
by Heather Heaton

EGG ROLLS, BAGELS
COMING TO RR PLAZA
by Heather Heaton

FESTIVAL WAS JUST THE BERRIES!
by Heather Heaton

WEBUTUCK BOARD ADDRESSES
CONCERNS RAISED AT WORKSHOP
by Heather Heaton

DOC BARTLETT REMEMBERED
AS "ALL-ROUND GOOD MAN"
by Heather Heaton

FUNDS STILL NEEDED
FOR FIELD REPAIR
by Heather Heaton

There were also three photographs: one of second graders dressed as leprechauns and fairies; one of a fake thermometer indicating how much money had been raised so far to restore the town's Eddie Collins Memorial Park ball fields; and one of little kids eating strawberries and ice cream at the Strawberry Festival in the nearby town of Amenia. The shots of the second graders and of the Strawberry Festival were credited to Heather Heaton. This meant that there were nine mentions of Heather Heaton on the front page of the paper—the Millerton equivalent of having your picture appear on the Sony Jumbo-Tron in Times Square. I have been a reader of the Millerton *News* for several years, and that day, somewhere between the berry festival story and the obituary for Doc Bartlett, I realized that the big news was that someone named Heather Heaton had just become the incarnation of the Millerton *News*.

Recently, I went to Millerton to spend a week with Heather. It was the thick of summer, just after the raspberry season and just as the sweet corn had started to ripen, shortly after the local American Legion post's chicken barbecue and not long before Millerton Days, the annual town celebration, which was dedicated this year to Eddie Collins. I'd thought it might be a week of dog days, but Heather told me that all sorts of things were going on: The elementary school principal, Steve O'Connell, had resigned unexpectedly; the Millerton Gun Club was testing a new trapshooting machine; McGruff the Crime Dog was going to visit the village swimming pool; a local man had been killed by a train on the railroad tracks south of town; a cold front was about to collide with a warm front and create a gigantic thunderstorm; the author of a book about ponies was coming to speak at Oblong Books & Music, on Main Street; a woman whose family had been dairy farming in Millerton for three generations was submitting a request for rezoning so she could turn part of the farm into a gravel mine; and executive sessions of the village government would continue to be held downstairs in the town hall rather than upstairs, because one of the commissioners had a sore hip. Also, the village clerk had just quit, and the mayor, who owns an accounting practice in town, was refusing to comment on it. Unexpected things would probably happen, too. I've spent many summer weekends near Millerton, and it had always struck me as a tiny, quiet place, but knowing that all these things were happening made it seem to swell and expand like one of those pop-up sponges.

BY NOW, almost everyone in Millerton knows what Heather Heaton looks like, because anyone who appears on Main Street more than a couple of times gets noticed by almost everyone else in town. Heather is leggy, lean, and a little pigeon-toed, and she has a peachy complexion, a scatter of freckles across her nose, and fine brown hair with loose, loopy curls, which she wears pulled back from her face. When she blushes, which is often, she blushes from above her eyebrows all the way down the front of her neck. Her gaze is mild and disarming, and her voice is wobbly and sweet, like Tweety Pie's. The day I met her, she was wearing a long flowered jumper and a cotton top and a pair of beige sling-back sandals. The next day, she wore a pair of cutoff sweatpants and a T-shirt. The day after that, she wore a blouse and a dotted skirt, and after work that day she was going to be fitted for a firefighter's uniform, because she serves as a volunteer on the squad in Canaan, Connecticut, the town where she lives.

Heather is twenty-two years old. She grew up in Amherst, New Hampshire, which is not much bigger than Millerton, and graduated this May from the University of Connecticut, in Storrs, where she majored in journalism. She had interned at the Hartford *Courant* and had imagined that she would work for a big daily after finishing college, but then one of her professors told her about the opening at the Millerton *News*. She had never been to Millerton until the day she came to be interviewed for the job. She started work in early June. The first few nights, she went back to a room she rents in a farmhouse in Canaan and felt like crying. Since then, she has fallen in love with one of the other Canaan volunteer firefighters, has met a good proportion of the people in Millerton, and has written about sixty front-page stories for the *News*. Her EGG ROLLS, BAGELS COMING TO RR PLAZA article is framed and displayed on the counter at the Bagel Café. Heather still hopes to work on a big-city daily someday, but she's afraid she may be spoiled by all the exposure she's getting on the front page of the Millerton *News*. In the meantime, she's getting settled in Millerton. Once, while we were talking in her office, I could hear the rasping of an emergency services scanner in the background, and I asked her what was being reported. "Bee sting in Staatsburg," she said. "But I wasn't really listening. After all, it's not my town."

THE MILLERTON *News* used to have its offices on Main Street in Millerton. In 1972, the owner of the Lakeville *Journal*, a weekly in Lakeville, Connecticut, which is just a few miles to the east, bought the Millerton *News*. The two papers are now like Siamese twins: They share an office in Lakeville, and their dozen or so inside pages are virtually the same mixture of community announcements, columns, service articles, church news, and advertisements for tractor dealerships, horse farms, and plant nurseries, but the front pages are different, depending on which town the papers are being distributed to.

Though Lakeville and Millerton are only four miles apart, they are not much alike. Lakeville is rich and sleek and full of summer houses; Millerton is more of a working town. They are connected by Route 44: It is Main Street in Lakeville and then Main Street again in Millerton, and, in between, it is a sharp-curved two-lane country road with a view to the north of a huge dairy farm. After the road crosses the Connecticut–New York state line, it passes the Millerton Burger King, a car wash, a fancy restaurant called the New Yorker, and a house that Heather pointed out to me because the woman who lives there displays a collection of dolls on her lawn; Heather said she plans to write a story about her someday.

On the first day of my week with Heather, we drove from Lakeville past the dairy farm and the doll lady's house and into Millerton. Heather has a big brown beater of a Pontiac with bumper stickers lauding her college soccer team. As she drove, Heather told me she had decided against living in Millerton because she wanted to volunteer on the fire and rescue squads wherever she lived, and she felt that if she was on the Millerton squads she wouldn't be able to write about them objectively. Living in the town you cover has its perils. Once, there was a Millerton *News* reporter who lived in the village, and his girlfriend came to visit him, bringing along her pet six-foot-long python. During the visit, the snake got loose and wiggled its way into the walls of the house where the reporter was renting a room, and his landlady became loud and hysterical until the snake was found. The incident gave rise to some local discussion. Not long afterward, the reporter quit and left town.

In Millerton, we stopped to buy out-of-town newspapers at Terni's, a fishing tackle/newspapers/camping goods/candy store on Main Street. The day before, Millerton had celebrated Phil Terni Clean-Up Day, in honor of the store's owner, who is famous in town for sweeping up around his store every morning. Heather had subsequently written a front-page feature about the event and had taken a picture of Phil to accompany it. Phil was behind the soda fountain when we went in. The store's counter is made of cool marble, and the wood of the cabinets is old and silky. Years ago, when Millerton still had a milk-processing plant, the farmers would bring their milk cans to town every morning, drop them off, and then head for Terni's to get cigars and newspapers before they went back to their farms. Now the milk-processing plant has been converted into an apartment building, and some of the grandchildren of the dairy farmers work at Hipotronics, a small electronics plant that is just outside the town, beside fields of sweet corn and hay. "Nice article, Heather," Phil said. "You know, you wrote every single article in that paper."

"I know," she said. "I'm supposed to. Hey, I hope you sold a lot of them."

"Sold out," he said. "I'll order more today."

A few doors down from Terni's is Oblong Books. One of the owners of Oblong, Holly Nelson, is the head of the town planning board. Up the street is an appliance store called Campbell & Keeler; Heather planned to call Jimmy Campbell, one of the owners, about a story she was going to write on the dangers of lightning. Campbell was also one of the organizers behind Millerton Days, so she'd be in touch with him about that, too. Heather told me that not long after she started reporting in Millerton, she called a village board member named Glen White, and then called a schoolteacher named Glen White, and was about to call someone named

Glen White about a third story when she realized that there weren't three men named Glen White—there was one Glen White who was involved in three different things. To some people, this state of affairs is what makes a small town seem monotonous, but to others it is what makes a place seem anchored and secure, even as it bumps around and changes. In small towns like Millerton, the same people pop up over and over in slightly different positions, but they always stay tied to the same deep place, like buoys.

THE WEEK BEGINS at the Millerton *News* on Thursdays, when Heather and the staff of the Lakeville *Journal*—Charlotte Reid, Marsden Epworth, and Tim Fitzmaurice—meet with David Parker and Kathryn Boughton, the editor and managing editor of both papers, to talk about their stories for the upcoming issue. That Thursday, Heather told David she was working on the O'Connell resignation, the Scoland Farm gravel mine hearing, and the story about safety precautions during electrical storms. She also said that she was hoping to borrow a cache of Eddie Collins photographs for a pre–Millerton Days feature, but added that the local man who had most of the Collins memorabilia didn't seem eager to lend the photographs to the paper. She said she'd keep trying.

"Great," David said. "What else?"

"Well, as soon as I get enough information, I want to do that big story about how Dutchess County is changing."

"Your 'dying farmers' story?" Kathryn Boughton asked.

"I changed the description of it on my list," Heather said, glancing up at Kathryn. "I didn't actually mean 'dying farmers.' I meant 'dying farms.' "

Over the next few days, Heather and I drove from Lakeville to Millerton, to Amenia, and back to Millerton, to the elementary school, to the Gun Club, to Terni's for the papers, to the sheriff's substation in Amenia for the weekly crime report, back to Lakeville, back to Millerton, to the Burger King for lunch, to the town hall, to the village hall, around the fields and the farms, back and forth through the center of Millerton— around the bend in the road where the low, square buildings of the village huddle—and to the ends of town, where the buildings thin out and finally disappear. Covering a town keeps you busy. At the elementary school, Steve O'Connell was packing to leave. The school is perched on a bald gray hill, and in the summer stillness it felt a little forlorn. Steve was in a great mood because of his new job, in Westchester County. "I read the description of your new school," Heather said to him. "It sounds like a country club."

"Well, it's gorgeous," he said. "It's gorgeous, Heather. I'll tell you all about it, because I know you're not from New York. I know I'm talking fast, but that's the kind of guy I am." At the end of the interview, Heather took half a dozen pictures, because she suspected that the story would end up as her lead.

The next stop was the village pool, to cover McGruff the Crime Dog's presentation. Angela White, who is married to Glen White and is the Millerton recreation director, was waiting, with an unhappy look on her face. "I spoke to McGruff this morning, Heather," she said. "He canceled. He said it was so hot yesterday that he almost passed out. I thought there was a fan in his costume, but I guess I was thinking of Smokey Bear." She said he had promised to reschedule, but meanwhile there would be no MCGRUFF COMES TO TELL HOW TO PREVENT CRIME—at least, not until the following week.

"I think I'll just take pictures of the kids swimming," Heather said. "The only trouble is, I have a lot of pictures of cute little kids this week."

The days had a jerky rhythm. After the canceled McGruff appearance was a stop at the town hall to get information on the Scoland Farm rezoning. It was a local tale without whimsy: an old farm, a fire that destroyed barns and silos, a son killed in a car accident, a family belt tightening, a petition to mine gravel from dairy land. We went to the pig races at the agricultural fair, in Goshen, where the master of ceremonies announced the contestants as Roseanne Boar, Tammy Swinette, and Magnum P.I.G. Back at the office, after Heather called the medical examiner about the outcome of the autopsy of the man killed by a train, she explained the small-town rule on obituaries: "Everyone is an avid *something*. An avid gardener, an avid walker. Charlotte told me we once had someone who was an avid coupon clipper." Another rule: If you crop the Pet Parade photo so that the animal's ears poke out of the frame of the picture, the pet will be adopted more quickly. Everyone at the paper got distracted for a while, listening to reports on the scanner about an ex-convict engaged in a gun battle with a local deputy sheriff. Heather called several appliance stores to catch up on her electrical storm story. And after that she drove to the Gun Club, where three chubby old men smoking Tiparillos were shouting a conversation—"His goddam blower went out!" and "I don't know what the hell he paid for it!" and "Well, he's tougher than whalebone!"—and firing shotguns at neon-orange clay disks. Heather chatted with them, mentioning the fact that she wouldn't be able to come to the Gun Club clambake. The men looked sad for a moment, then resumed shooting. One of them cocked a thumb at the trap and said, "You girls shoot? Oh, no, you're reporters."

"Tell me about your gun," Heather said.

He patted it and said, "Darling, it's a 12-gauge Browning."

"Nice," Heather said. "How do you spell that? Like the food brownie?"

"Exactly," the man said. "You're learning."

Near the end of my visit, Heather went to talk to a shiny-faced young man named Todd Clinton, who was on the organizing committee for Millerton Days. Todd is a local banker, a Lions Club member, the treasurer of the volunteer fire squad, a Chamber of Commerce vice president, and the husband of the woman who owns the new seamstress shop on Main Street. He was in his office, at the Salisbury Bank & Trust Company, and he had a lot of information for Heather about Millerton Days. "We're doing Sno-Kones and cotton candy," he said. "There will be clowns. And 50 percent of the proceeds are going to the Eddie Collins ball field restoration. We've hired a Mickey and Minnie—wait, don't say that. Say, 'There will be a cute mouse couple.' We don't want to get in trouble with copyright people at Disney." Heather scribbled. Todd called his secretary to find out who was lending the freezers to store the ice for the Sno-Kones. She told him that it was Jimmy Campbell, of Campbell & Keeler. Todd said that one of the local restaurants would be donating tablecloths, but that there weren't enough tables yet for the Millerton Days clambake. Heather said, "I could put in 'Please call Todd if you have tables.' "

"Great," Todd said. "Because it's a little bit of an issue with the tables. Oh, and for the antique tractor show you can put in that anyone interested in showing their tractor can call me."

Heather said, "Sounds like I have it all. I just have one question. Will the clowns be free?"

Todd nodded and said, "Absolutely free."

IT WAS ALL THERE in the Millerton *News* the next week: O'CONNELL LEAVES FOR POST AT ARDSLEY MIDDLE SCHOOL and STORM CLOUDS REQUIRE PRECAUTIONS TO PROTECT HEALTH AND PROPERTY and MAUREEN BONDS ENDS WORK AS VILLAGE CLERK and PREPARATIONS PICK UP FOR MILLERTON DAYS, and a late-breaking story about a lawsuit filed against the town board of

Amenia. A few stories had evaporated, and Heather had saved a few others for a later week. It turned out that the man who had squirreled away all the Eddie Collins memorabilia died over the weekend, and the paper had been able to get the pictures for the special Eddie Collins section from his widow. His avidity for local history was noted in his obituary, which also ran that week. By then, I had left Millerton and was back in Manhattan. Heather sent me the paper, and when I had read it I called her. I could hear the hum of the newspaper office in the background. We talked for a while, and then she said she had to go, because she was expecting another busy week.

KING OF THE ROAD

*W*HAT AMAZES BILL BLASS IS AMAZING. LAST year, he was in La Jolla, California, and someone took him to a supermarket, which was somewhere he had never been before in his life; he found the supermarket, and especially the do-it-yourself ice-cream-sundae bar, amazing. In Nashville, where I joined him recently for a trunk show—an in-store event, when a designer's entire collection, and sometimes the designer himself, are on display—he caught me admiring a blazer, made by the designer Richard Tyler, that cost $1,859; even though some of the ensembles in the Blass couture collection cost more than $6,000, he found the price of the Tyler blazer amazing. He is someone who seems fascinated by something or other much of the time. He is a virtuoso of the high-pitched eyebrow and the fortissimo gasp. These give him a puckish air, without which he might seem irritatingly regal. Blass is classically good-looking in the manner of a country gentleman, with a wide forehead, a boxy jaw, a direct gaze, and a chest like a kettledrum. Almost any time you see him, there will be a cigarette in the corner of his mouth, bouncing like a little diving board. He usually stands with his hands poked into his pockets and his jacket hitched up around them. No matter where he is, he looks as if he might be standing on the deck of a big sailboat. He is now seventy-one years old, fond of candy, and settling into leonine stateliness; as a young man, he was long necked, blade thin, and so wolfishly handsome you could weep. I love to hear him talk. His voice is rich, gravelly, and carefully inflected, like a film narrator's. He also has a wonderfully intimate and conspiratorial-sounding whisper. At times, he can sound like an American schooled in Britain, but in fact he is a Depression-era kid from Fort Wayne, Indiana, who came to New York at seventeen and has never left. Like all elegant people, he curses with charming abandon and to great effect. Like most successful, wealthy people, he knows how to deploy a sort of captivating brattiness, to which other people quickly yield. One of the funniest things in the world is to sit in his office at his showroom and listen to him bellow questions to his staff without moving a muscle, or even an eyeball, in their direction.

Universal adoration is one of the reasons Blass goes on trips to places like La Jolla and Nashville. Most stores don't buy a designer's entire collection but will hold trunk shows, during which customers can see samples and place orders. There are trunk shows going on all the time, all over the country. Sometimes the trunk show is brought to the store by a sales representative. Sometimes the designer sends along a model, who throughout the day will stroll around in outfits from the collection. Occasionally, the designer himself escorts the clothes, in which case the store often stages a fashion show and luncheon for good customers. After lunch, while the customers are trying things on, the designer may hang around and editorialize. This year, Bill Blass's collection traveled with salespeople to Boston, Houston, Dallas, Fort Worth, St. Louis, Palo Alto, Midland (Texas), San Antonio, Beverly Hills, Pasadena, Tulsa, San Diego, New Orleans, Cleveland, Cincinnati, Baltimore, and Pittsburgh; he appeared with it in Atlanta, New York, Chicago, Philadelphia, Washington, San Francisco, and Troy, Michigan. Couture clothes cost a fortune, but they have a tiny market and seldom make any money. What they do is endear a designer to those customers whose clothing choices are newsworthy, and this in turn makes the designer famous. Then, when he is famous enough, the designer can sell other companies the rights to manufacture profitable items like underpants and perfumes under the designer's name. Bill Blass was one of the first designers to travel with their collections, and he's one of those who have done it the most. He is generally regarded as the king of the trunk show. His clothes are rarely thought of as artistic or trendsetting or remarkable, but his customers have never abandoned him; they turn out at the trunk shows, and the trunk shows have kept him famous, by fashion standards, for a remarkable number of years.

At a good show, he does a lot of business; two weeks ago, at a trunk show at Saks Fifth Avenue, he sold over half a million dollars' worth of dresses, and that is the most any American designer showing at Saks has ever sold. He does bigger business, though, just selling his name and his designer's eye. Blass licenses fifty-six products, including Bill Blass belts, ties, handkerchiefs, jeans, sheets, shoes, pajamas, outerwear, evening wear, watches, and window shades. For sixteen years, Ford manufactured a Bill Blass Lincoln Continental Mark IV; Blass chose the interiors, paint colors, and trim. Blass's trunk show philosophy: "You don't want to be on the road so much that the novelty wears off, but you want to get to know your customer and help move the clothes. If you are buying a Bill Blass dress for a couple of thousand dollars, I'd say it's an added attraction to have Bill Blass there saying, 'Babe, that looks great on you,' or 'Babe, that's just awful.' "

BECAUSE BILL BLASS is popular and fashionable, I expected him to have a drifty attention span, but he is actually quite dogged. In Nashville, for instance, after declaring the price of the Tyler blazer amazing, he pulled it off its hanger, inspected its seams, and pinched the fabric, and said he thought the cut and workmanship were amazing; then he asked me to try it on and told me I should buy it. This was at Jamie Inc., the Nashville store where the trunk show and a luncheon were being held. The show had just ended, and dozens of women were milling around the racks, placing orders. When he was able to tear his attention from the blazer, he remarked that he found the women's ardor and stamina amazing. Then he turned back to being amazed by the blazer. He got everyone walking by to stop and take a look at it, because it had him so amazed. When I saw him several weeks later, in Manhattan, he asked me how I'd been and then immediately asked me if I had bought the Richard Tyler blazer. His enthusiasm made me feel that I should have done whatever it took to find a spare eighteen hundred dollars. He looked utterly crestfallen when I told me no.

In Nashville, what he found amazing, to start with, was walking through the airport, looking at people's clothes. We had just gotten off the plane and were heading down an endless concourse, and I was following his gaze. He gestured with his chin at a man and a woman walking toward us. He said, "My God, have you ever noticed how Americans dress? They dress like it's summer all the time." The man and the woman were both wearing pale T-shirts and acid-washed jeans sutured with lots of useless-looking zippers. Blass stopped and watched them walk by. He was dressed in his usual bespoke double-breasted English suit and a loosely knotted tie, and he had a topcoat tossed over his arm. The acid-washed couple passed. Behind them was a fat woman wearing a short red dress, red satin pumps, and a red fez. Blass lifted his eyebrows, shifted his coat to his other arm, and said, "That's an outfit." As she ambled by, he said, "I was the first designer to really go out on the road with my clothes, and I've done it for years and years and years, while the other designers were rushing back the minute they could, to go to New York parties. I didn't do that. I'd stay out on the road for days at a time and meet people and keep my name out there. It allowed me to see what's out here. And I can tell you that, no matter what anyone thinks, there's a huge part of this country that still loves print dresses."

MRS. JACK MASSEY, a friend of Blass's with whom he would be staying in Nashville, called me one afternoon before the trip. "Sunday night, when you arrive, we'll be going to dinner at the Johnsons'. It will be just a little informal gathering of friends, so you can wear—oh, little velvet pants, something like that. Monday night is dinner here at my house, Brook House, and that's not formal, either—it's not black-tie or anything, so you can just wear dressy pants or a little silk dress. At the luncheon and fashion show, you could wear a nice suit. During the day, you can just knock around in a sweater set and pants." Pause. "You know, of course, that Bill Blass is just the most entertaining man to ever walk down the pike. Everybody adores him. He is absolutely the best company in the world."

Bill Blass had never before gone to Nashville with his collection; in fact, he had been in Nashville only twice: in 1985, when he spoke at O'More College of Design, in nearby Franklin, Tennessee, and eighteen years before that, when he was the honored guest at Nashville's fanciest annual social event, the Swan Ball, to which many women in Nashville wear his dresses. There is a picture of him on page 51 of a book called *Reflections: Twenty-five Nights at the Swan Ball*. The text says, "And then Bill Blass, the talented, sociable, and just-too-darn debonair designer, brought the clothes and paraded them around for everyone to die over while dining on shrimp and filet de boeuf."

Blass's own recollection of the visit: "The Swan Ball is a good event, but, my God, it's always on the hottest goddam night of the year."

A grand, formal, larger-than-life-size portrait of Mrs. Massey hanging in one of her parlors at Brook House depicts her in a draped gown of ecru pleated silk with a petal-pink cummerbund, her blond bob swept back, her face set in an idle smile, her fingertips dandling a string of pecan-size pearls. The portrait was commissioned by her late husband, Jack, who was the venture capitalist behind Kentucky Fried Chicken, Hospital Corporation of America, and Volunteer Capital Corp. It was painted by Aaron Shikler, who has also painted Ronald and Nancy Reagan and Gloria Vanderbilt. The dress in the portrait is by Bill Blass. I know this because while he and I were walking around Brook House on the evening of the dinner in his honor, he stopped in front of the portrait to remark on how pretty Mrs. Massey looked. Then he interrupted himself with a gasp. "My God, I think that's one of my dresses!" he said. "I honestly think it is. It's one of my dresses."

There were twenty-eight guests in the house at the time. They had been having cocktails in a vast horseshoe-shaped room with French doors that looked out over a brook and a stone fountain (a boy with a frog) and a big guesthouse and some clipped lawns and hedges, and now the guests were done with cocktails and were brushing past us toward a wing of the house which was too far away to see, but I could hear the scrape and chatter of chairs being pulled out, and I was starting to smell dinner. Several butlers were shooing people toward the dining room, and one of them hesitated behind us, gesturing with a silver tray and murmuring, "Dinner is ready in the east room, sir." Blass went on eyeing the portrait. After a moment, he shook his head and said, "Well, I'll be damned. It is one of mine. I *remember* that dress." He popped me in the ribs with his elbow and said, "Say, that was a good dress, wasn't it?"

JAMIE STREAM, the woman who owns Jamie Inc., had met us at the airport with her limousine and a driver. Jamie is snappy and blond and forty-eight. She opened her store twenty years ago, when Nashville was on the outer edges of the fashion frontier. "We pioneered Oscar and Bill and all those people in Nashville," she once told me. "When I moved to town,

I really didn't know what I'd find here. I come from the ranch country in Texas, where everything is pigskin, Hermès, and tweed." I asked her why she thought that Bill Blass had managed to remain fashionable for so many years, and she said, "Well, this isn't a glamorous thing to say, but Bill Blass is just . . . so . . . *appropriate.* Don't you think? Isn't that a compliment in this day and age, to say someone is always appropriate? And no one can take a little satin skirt and a little cashmere sweater and make it as glamorous as Bill Blass can. You know what I say? I say Bill Blass clothes have good bones."

In the limousine, Jamie was telling us about picking up Yvonne Lopez, the Blass fitting model, and Craig Natiello, of the design staff, who had arrived in Nashville a day earlier. Yvonne and Craig had brought the collection with them on the plane. It filled thirteen trunks. Jamie said, "I had the two of them over to the house for drinks. I said, 'Come over, but I'm warning you, I'm just wearing a sweatsuit.' "

"In which she looks adorable," Blass added.

"Well, that's what they were seeing me in, anyway," Jamie went on. She turned to the driver and called out, "Basil, can you turn up the air-conditioning back here? It's beastly." She squinted out a window. We were driving down a four-lane road in Nashville rimmed with fast-food joints and muffler shops. It looked as if it was about to rain. Jamie said, "Oh, I think we're going to have a loblolly. If it lasts for days, it means I'm going to have to hire some parkers for the luncheon. We've invited seventy-five people, and I'm being very tough—all of them have to already own Blass. That's what I'm telling people who are calling me, because I can't just be throwing invitations around. It's a legacy luncheon for the real Blass devotee."

Blass said, "It'll be intimate. Ten tables of heavy hitters."

Jamie nodded and then said, "I'm telling you, this limousine is a wreck. It's our work car. It's just like a truck. We just use it like a truck when we go up to our Adirondack camp in the summer. When we come home, we just load this thing up to the rafters with everything under the sun."

We passed an enormous pillared building sitting back from the road. Blass sat forward and said, "What's that? What's that building? My God, that's something."

"That's the Parthenon," Jamie said. "It's the world's only full-size replica of the Parthenon."

"My God, I'd want to see that. If there's a full-size replica of the Parthenon in Nashville, I think that's something to see, don't you?"

Jamie pursed her lips, and said, "You've got dinner at the Johnsons' tonight, and the fittings for the models are on Monday, and you've got an appearance on a local television show, and you've got dinner at Mrs. Massey's on Monday night, and the lunch is on Tuesday, so I don't really know when you're going to go."

Blass pushed his hand against the ceiling and said, "My God, I haven't been in Nashville in years, and already I'm so busy that I don't have a goddam minute to breathe."

MONDAY, 12:30 P.M., at WTVF, Channel 5: "Mr. Blass, I'm Debbie Alan, one of the hosts of the show. We'll be talking about romance and clothes. We have a good time on this show, so just cut loose, okay? The other segments are Thanksgiving centerpieces and a guy with some great hair-care products. Hey, would one of you tell the hair guy I'm going to ask if conditioners really cure split ends, and if we have time I'll touch on one of the other products, like maybe the curl enhancers."

A production assistant in front of us is wearing fawn-colored twill jeans, a white poor-boy sweater, and brown moccasins. Blass looks at her and says, "My God, those look like my jeans. Call her over. Those are my jeans." The woman turns and comes over to him, looking embarrassed, and says she hadn't known he was going to be on the show, and didn't wear the jeans on purpose. Blass is examining the jeans and doesn't answer. "That's a nice fabric, that twill, isn't it? It's a nice finish. It looks like suede."

"I love them," she says.

"She's got herself up nicely, hasn't she?" he says to me. "That's a good look."

The show begins, and Debbie Alan announces that the internationally famous designer Bill Blass will be coming up after the commercial. Then she giggles and says, "I have Bill Blass underwear and perfume, because that's all I can afford, and I'm not going to tell you if I'm wearing either of them." Blass, now perched on a tall director's chair, hands in pockets, lets out a beefy chuckle. Once the commercial is over, Yvonne Lopez comes out wearing a slim-cut white jumpsuit piped in blue, followed by a model in a white-gazar-and-black-lace strapless gown. Debbie says, "Will someone scoop this up for, say, the Swan Ball?"

Blass says, "I hope so, Debbie."

Now a model is wearing a Prince of Wales plaid pantsuit overlaid with black lace. Debbie asks whether women in Nashville dress differently from women in other parts of the country. Blass says, "There are wonderful-looking women all over this country, Debbie. I truly have a variety of customers—active, busy women who work or, like Alyne Massey, who are involved in charities, and so forth, and live all over the country."

A few more outfits are shown: a boyish blazer in a granite-print fabric, a floral tiered minidress, and a long gown in the same floral fabric with black illusion sleeves and neck. Then the segment is over. Debbie thanks him for coming. Blass says, "Thank you, Debbie, and enjoy your underwear."

A FEW OF the Nashville models had gotten their breasts done. No one had anticipated this. The models had been discussed before our trip to Nashville: Craig had wanted twenty, but he and Jamie settled on eleven. Blass had said that because they would be local girls he expected them to be "a little plumpy." As it happened, the Nashville models were not particularly plumpy, but they did have big breasts, one pair quite recently enhanced. When we got to Jamie's store on Monday, Craig was fitting them into the samples and doing cleavage checks while three workmen were building a little runway in the store. The luncheon would be in the front room, which has a crystal chandelier, thick taupe carpeting, gilded molding, and plate-glass windows looking out on a small parking lot and then on Harding Road and across to a Kroger's and a strip mall. The rest of the store is broken into separate nooks for different designers; there is also a shoe nook, a fine-jewelry nook, and a lingerie nook. The center of the store is a living room elegantly furnished with an ottoman, a coffee table, and two side chairs. Jamie was saying, "There just aren't any shops like this anymore. Martha in New York—gone. Lou Lattimore, in Dallas—gone. Isabell Gerhart, in Houston—gone. In Nashville, I'm it. Let's face it: In the past, we all used to fly our own planes around and spend a fortune on clothes, and we've all had to cut back. I still wanted to make this a special place. And that takes a little something. Those chairs for the living room— they're oversized French fauteuils with needlepointed leopard upholstery— cost thousands of dollars, but I think it's worth it, don't you? It gives it a homey feel, don't you think?"

Craig was helping one of the models into a gray and white chalk-striped sweater and morning-striped pleated skirt, saying, "Your cleavage, dear." Blass rummaged around in a box of accessories on a counter, pulled out a little shoulder bag, and said to the model, "Put this on. Across your shoulder. Across. Yes. That's good. That'll jazz it up. Craig, use more of this goddam stuff to jazz it up." He murmured to me, "I would never use a bag in the New York shows. I also left out a few of the pieces I showed in New York and added some from the resort collection—flowered things that I think will be big here. A lot of these customers go to Palm Beach for the season, so they need that sort of dress. Everything in New York has to be goddam severe. Of course, in New York they dislike everything anyway, so you give them as little to dislike as possible."

Joyce Preston, Blass's sales representative, walked in and stood next to Jamie, and Jamie said, "Joyce, I'll be disappointed if we don't do a hundred and fifty thousand dollars at the show. Most of the big people are coming, but we've got two Fortune 500s who are out of town and are going to miss the show. So that's disappointing right there."

IT HAD RAINED all day and all night, and then sputtered to a stop just moments before women began arriving for the luncheon. The runway was ready, and tables set with linens, silver, bushy centerpieces, and Bill Blass, Ltd., pencils were now arranged in a semicircle around it. Jamie was dressed in a sharp-looking black wool crepe Blass suit from this fall. Mrs. Massey arrived wearing a suit from the same collection in red. Mrs. Johnson, who had had us over for dinner Sunday night, arrived. Mrs. Hunter Armistead, of the Tennessee Armisteads, and Mrs. Jimmy Bradford, of the J. C. Bradford brokerage Bradfords, and Mrs. James Cheek III, of the Maxwell House Coffee Cheeks, and Mrs. Neil Parrish, of the National Life and Accident Parrishes, and Mrs. Pamela Iannacio, a pencil heiress, arrived. In all, sixty-four guests were there, most of them wearing good Blass luncheon suits, with trim silhouettes, big buttons, smart details. The women were pearly, well coiffed, unglamorous, but timelessly good-looking; there were some mothers and daughters and probably a good span of generations, but for a million bucks I couldn't have guessed anyone's age. Mrs. Massey was seated at our table, next to Blass. Waiters circled the room and placed a papaya stuffed with lobster at each place, and after a few moments the show began. Yvonne came out in a black faille puff-sleeved jacket and morning-striped pants. Mrs. Massey leaned over to Blass and said, "That's very correct, very fun."

Blass said, "That's a good suit. Those are good-looking pants. That's something you ought to have." Mrs. Massey made a note on a pad of paper. Then out came one of the buxom Nashville models, in a floral suit.

Mrs. Massey glanced at Blass, and he whispered, "You should have that, babe. That's very you." She picked up the pencil again.

The next model wore a short black lace dress with black lace stockings. Blass pointed at her legs and said, "Love those stockings. Two hundred bucks a pair and goddam fragile."

Mrs. Massey snorted, and said, "Darling, *never.*"

As soon as the show ended, the women popped up from their seats and headed for the next room, where the sample racks were lined up. Mrs. Massey was at Blass's elbow, saying, "I need something for Palm Beach. Not too severe, because it's for Palm Beach."

People buzzed around the racks. A woman standing near Joyce said to her, "I'm giving something for the Super Bowl. What can you put me in?"

A young woman with a light brown ponytail emerged from one of the dressing rooms wearing an iridescent, mousseline strapless gown that cost $6,040. She said, "I can't breathe, I can't talk, I can't move, but I love it."

Blass looked her over and said, "It's very good."

She sucked in her breath and said, "I think I'll buy it."

I was bumped into one of the racks by someone grabbing my arm and saying, "There was the cutest little girl waiting on me who was Kappa Kappa Gamma at Vanderbilt. Do you know where she is?"

At this point, every dressing room was full, and Joyce, Craig, Jamie, and Jamie's sales staff were bounding from rack to room with the samples. By two o'clock, they had written orders for eighty-five thousand dollars' worth of clothes. Mrs. Massey had picked nine outfits, including a gown for the Swan Ball; they would all be tailored and delivered in a few months. Then she kissed Blass good-bye and left for Brook House.

A few minutes later, the phone in the store rang. Joyce took the call. After hanging up, she said to Blass, "That was Mrs. Massey. We have to protect her. She wants us to protect her especially on the gown and also on the suit." Blass grimaced, and Joyce said, "Bill, we have to. I promised her no one else would have that at the Swan Ball." To herself, she said, "I'm going to have to pull that plaid suit with the lace overlay, too. I could sell six, I'm sure, but I've already sold two, and this town is too small for another one."

WHEN THE TOTAL of orders approached a hundred and fifty thousand dollars, Blass decided he could sneak out to see the Parthenon after all. We called for a limousine. It had a new driver. Mr. Blass looked at him and said, "Good-looking man." The driver, Jim, opened the glove compartment and handed Blass a photograph of himself modeling suits for a local store.

"Very nice," Blass said. "I think we should see the Parthenon."

"You should go see Opryland," Jim said. "The entertainment business is to Nashville what a pinkie with a diamond ring is to a hand."

Mr. Blass settled into the seat and lit a cigarette. When we got to the Parthenon, Jim told us to be sure to look inside at the statue of Athena, because it was the largest indoor sculpture in the Western world. When we saw it, Mr. Blass stopped and stared in amazement. The statue was chalk white, and was wearing a peplos, sandals, and a military headpiece. After a minute, Blass said, "Well, that's the biggest goddam fake job I've ever seen. My God, it's incredible. I've never seen anything so awful in my life. Have you ever seen anything so awful?" We went down to the gift shop, where he admired a T-shirt and then told the cashier her printed-silk bomber jacket was amusing and asked if it was for sale. She said it was. He took a second look and said, "It's a good jacket. It's amusing. But it's really not for me."

TIFFANY

ONE THING THAT TIFFANY, TIFFANY'S MANA-
ger, and the entire Tiffany organization would like you to
know is that even though it may seem too good to be true,
Tiffany's real name is really Tiffany.

"Of course her real name is Tiffany," says George
Tobin, her record producer, manager, and vigilant shepherd. "Her name is Tiffany, just like Madonna's name is
Madonna. You know, I'd actually prefer that you didn't use
her last name at all. No one ever uses Madonna's last
name—it's always just Madonna. I like it to be just Tiffany.
If her name were Mary or something, then we'd use her
last name, but we have a name like Tiffany, and that's perfect, and it's real."

Tiffany, who is sixteen years old and whose debut
album, *Tiffany*, has sold 4 million copies worldwide, says,
"I know Tiffany is a pretty unusual name. It actually was
really unusual when I was born. But then, when I was
about two, it started to become really popular." She rubs
her forehead and then says, "When I was about two, they
even started making Tiffany lamps and even Tiffany rugs.

They even started making Tiffany jewelry. I guess it's just a name that got really popular."

Another thing that Tiffany, Tiffany's manager, and the entire Tiffany organization would like you to know is that even though her success may seem too instantaneous and easy to be true, Tiffany's talent is real.

"She's going to be around for a long, long time," Tobin says. "She's going to have a long career. The whole trip with her is that she's real. It's going to last. We've built a fan base of support, and now we're solidifying it. I'm sure that you'll be writing about her many, many times in the future."

"I'm myself onstage," Tiffany says. "I want to come across as a real person. This is my career. I'd like it to continue for a long time. Or, I guess, I could end up being a manicurist or something, right?"

It is the night before the day that Tiffany will perform at Disney World. For the first time in her life she will be singing with a band before a large audience. Granted, her statistics are impressive: She is the youngest female to have her debut album go to the top of the pop charts, and the youngest person to have the first two singles of her first album ("I Think We're Alone Now" and "Could've Been") hit Number One, and the first person in three years to have two different songs hit Number One simultaneously, one in England and one in the United States. Her record is already multi-platinum. But her only experience in front of crowds has been singing along with tapes in shopping malls.

"I'm not nervous," Tiffany says, her voice mild and somewhat affectless. "Not anymore. I only get nervous in airplanes, and that's just because I'm not in control."

She is sitting with Tobin, his wife, and three of their children in a faux-Italian restaurant a few miles east of Disney World, in Lake Buena Vista, Florida, and she has a plate of black olives in one hand and a portable phone in the other. Black olives are her favorite food. The portable phone is George Tobin's favorite tool. While the Tobins eat pizza and talk about their plans for visiting Disney World tomorrow, Tiffany is working the phone, occasionally popping black olives into her mouth, and mostly solidifying her fan base of support.

"Tiff," Tobin says, pushing a piece of paper toward her, "call this guy first at the radio station. I told him you'd do a phoner."

She tucks the phone under her chin and, after listening for a minute, says into the phone, "Okay, I've got it." Then in a louder voice she says,

"Hi, this is Tiffany and you're listening to WKO . . . uh, oh, I'm a nerd. I forgot the call letters." She takes a big breath and starts again.

"Hi, this is *Tiffany,* and you're listening to—oh, God, I'm a nerd. I'm a *nerd.*"

The table is getting quieter now.

"I'll get it," she says. Her voice is still composed, but her face—usually peachy pale and bloodless—is reddening. "I am *such* a nerd."

On the third try she runs through the sentence without a hitch, and the Tobin family resumes conversation. After finishing his food, George reaches into his briefcase and pulls out a tan plastic gadget, flicks its switch, and shows it to me. "Got it in England," he says, tapping the gadget's little display screen. "Great new toy. It's a real computer! One hundred and twenty-eight K of memory." He pokes a button and the display lights up. "Isn't that something?" he says. "Remembers *everything.*"

AFTER DINNER, Tobin and I ride over to the Magic Kingdom. Tobin mentions that he has been in the music business for decades—he was a staff producer for Motown in the early seventies, has produced Smokey Robinson and Natalie Cole, and now owns recording studios in North Hollywood, where he first encountered Tiffany. A beefy man with shaggy hair and clear green eyes, he has a way of fixing his gaze and stating his case that gives him an unflaggingly imperious manner.

Tonight, though, it's clear that he is anxious. This will be Tiffany's first real concert, and she will have to perform three times—nine-thirty, eleven-thirty, and one-thirty in the morning. This will also be the first time she has worked with a stylist and a choreographer. Moreover, the show is going to be filmed for her next video—two hundred thousand dollars' worth of cameras and crew will be standing around waiting for one good rendition of "I Saw Her Standing There." Plus, there's a matter of prestige. Ray Parker, Jr., Exposé, Regina Belle, and Roger will also be playing in the Magic Kingdom tomorrow night, but they have been relegated to small stages in Tomorrowland, Frontierland, and Fantasyland. Tiffany, though, has been assigned to the most prominent stage—the platform in front of Cinderella Castle, the hub of the Magic Kingdom, which straddles the border between Main Street, USA, and Fantasyland.

As soon as we arrive at the castle, Tobin is set upon by the video director, the road crew, Disney representatives, and the stagehands, all of whom are as anxious as Tobin. Can Tiffany move well on this big stage? Can she follow the band? Can she talk long enough between songs to give the band enough time to reprogram the synthesizers? Can she give the camera crew good stuff even with the distraction of the audience? Look— it's one thing for her to sing to shoppers in malls and to make those slick, sprightly cover versions of old hit records, but this is different. Now there's a lot of money and expectations and a certain critical consideration in play.

Tomorrow night is shaping up as a calculated gamble that this little girl with the big voice isn't just an attractive youngster expertly pushed and packaged, but something for real. And at the moment, on the stage in front of Cinderella Castle, a lot of large adult males are banking on those odds.

TIFFANY IS DANCING in the dressing room. It's Friday afternoon now, only four hours before the show, and she is practicing stage moves with a fake microphone while a choreographer flown in from Los Angeles watches and corrects her.

"Cross your hands like *this*," he says, snapping his wrists across his chest.

She duplicates the move, carefully and somewhat gawkily organizing her long arms and legs as directed. All the while she is staring at herself in the mirror. She is at an age when even a month or two makes a noticeable difference in your looks. Even though the photograph on her album cover is just a year old, she has already lost the placid, babyish look it conveys— her face now tapers more sharply at the chin; her straight red hair is longer and heavier; her dark brown eyes have less of the wounded fawn in them and more of the maturing and somewhat exhausted teenager who has been working nonstop for several months.

"I've got it, I've got it," Tiffany says and then slumps into a chair. "I'm *tired*." She fluffs her hair and sinks down.

For the last forty-five days she has been making appearances to support the record; after Disney World, she will begin an extensive concert tour—playing arenas if the ticket sales materialize—and she will start recording her next album. Even Tobin admits that she is exhausted, but he is the one setting the pace. "We have to build up the fan base now," he explained earlier in the day. "We want as many people to see her as possible. The demand for her is out there now."

Tiffany spent the morning in the Magic Kingdom—the only free time she will have to be a teenage tourist on this trip. "I went on Space Mountain four times," she says, a little morosely. "I should have saved it. After Space Mountain, nothing was quite as thrilling. I guess I'm the kind of person who is always going to go on the best ride and then immediately say, 'What's next?' And unfortunately nothing is ever as good."

Tiffany Darwish met Tobin when she was twelve. The only child of a small-aircraft pilot and a secretary who were divorced when she was two, she grew up in Norwalk, California, a quiet town north of Los Angeles. Her stepfather negotiated her first, albeit impromptu, gig—a few songs with a band that was playing at a barbecue. She was nine years old. By the time she was twelve, she was singing with country bands in town.

That year a local songwriter asked her to sing on demo tapes for a few of his songs and reserved recording time for the session at one of George Tobin's North Hollywood studios. Tobin was producing a Smokey Robinson album at the time and probably would have never noticed the little girl if one of the studio hands hadn't called him over to hear Tiffany sing. It seemed that she was able to mimic anything with her full, elastic voice: all-out weepy country laments, zippy pop songs, even the growls and yelps of rock and roll.

"I was enthralled by her voice," George Tobin recalls. "It was like taffy—you could pull it anywhere. In under ten minutes, I decided to sign her. I had a dream of where she could go. When I do a project, I get totally immersed in it. I got really obsessed with her. I just kept thinking that I *had* to do something with her."

Over the next year and a half, Tobin stayed in contact with Tiffany and her mother and tried to find a manager for her. At first he had intended just to produce her records. "None of the managers I approached were interested in her," he says. "Then I realized I needed a manager for her who could see eye to eye with me, and the only person who sees eye to eye with me is me. I'd watched so many other managers make horrendous mistakes, so I finally decided that I would manage her myself."

In 1986 they signed a seven-album exclusive production and management contract that gave Tobin complete control of Tiffany's records, videos, and performances. Any record company interested in her would have to sign a contract with George Tobin Productions, which would in turn provide the company with Tiffany product. It is far more common for an artist to sign directly with a record company and also to retain separate people to produce her records and manage her affairs, but Tiffany's arrangement with Tobin isn't completely novel—it's a system, a consolidation of control, just like the one Motown has used for developing new and especially young acts. Except this time, the manager, not the record company, is calling all the shots.

"I learned a whole lot working [at Motown]," Tobin says. "Tiffany is signed to *me*—one hundred percent signed to *me*. The record company has no part of her. They deal with *me*."

In the beginning of 1986, Tobin started recording. Tiffany's mother, who according to Tobin declines to be interviewed, had wanted her to be a flat-out country singer, but Tobin started her on a regimen of light pop, loping ballads, and covers of rock and roll standards, because, he says, you have to be in Nashville to do country, and besides, there's so much money to be made in rock and pop.

"Her mother did think covering a Beatles song was sacrilegious, so we just never sent those tapes home," Tobin admits. "But her mother doesn't get involved. The family has decided that I manage the act."

He sent Tiffany's tapes around and was rebuffed immediately—most record companies said they simply didn't know how to promote such a young kid. So Tobin got more aggressive, having Tiffany sing in his studio for small groups of record executives, and he once even sent her to see Clive Davis, president of Arista Records, at his room in the Beverly Hills Hotel, so she could perform for him. "I wanted people to look her right in the face when they said no," Tobin says.

Tobin tells the story of negotiating for her record contract without pulling a punch—such and such record company hated her, so-and-so didn't hear anything in her voice at all—and there's a lot of glee in his voice, the sound of someone who is now savoring the right to say "I told you so." Tiffany is sitting beside him, and rather than seeming embarrassed or hurt by these tales of rejection, she is impassive.

"Remember this, Tiff?" Tobin says and starts to laugh. "I think it was Epic and MCA wanted her, and I think the guy from Epic said, 'What should we do, play poker for her?' " Tiffany shrugs and looks down. "Anyway," Tobin continues, "I wanted to go with a West Coast company, and the main reason I went with MCA is because their offices are one mile from my office, and if I want to get something done, I can drive down there and block their cars on their driveway with my car, which I have done, and not let them out until it's settled."

MCA paid George Tobin Productions $150,000 for Tiffany's record. And it was certainly ready—Tobin had taped forty-eight songs in his sessions with her, from ages fourteen to fifteen.

. . .

BUT UNTIL THE BEAUTIFUL YOU: Celebrating the Good Life Shopping Mall Tour '87 came about, Tiffany's album just sat in the MCA warehouses. "We didn't know how to promote it, how to market it," says Larry Solters, senior vice president of MCA Records. "Radio had been burned by teen stars like Bobby Sherman and Shaun Cassidy. Radio was very tentative about her. Plus, she was only sixteen and the themes on the record are very adult themes. Maybe we got overly analytical about it."

As Solters remembers it, he was stumped for a few months until he thought of sending Tiffany on a tour of shopping malls. He approached Shopping Center Network, a marketing company that sets up promotions in malls; the company's Beautiful You: Celebrating the Good Life Tour, which had such sponsors as Toyota, Clairol, and Adidas, was already under way, and Tiffany was invited to join it. As Tobin remembers it, MCA stalled on promoting the record for a year and a half, so he came to Tiffany's rescue—he threatened to "*ninja* his way into Larry Solters's office" and yank the record unless MCA came up with a promotion plan within the week.

"I don't remember having that conversation," Solters says.

On the Beautiful You: Celebrating the Good Life Shopping Mall Tour '87, Tiffany would stand on small stages set up in the hub of the mall and sing her songs along with instrumental tapes while the tour sponsors spread corporate goodwill with exhibits and giveaways. She performed at ten malls, beginning with the Bergen Mall, in Paramus, New Jersey, during the summer break between her sophomore and junior years at Leffingwell Christian High School, in Norwalk. Tobin videotaped the shows himself and later patched them together to make a music video.

"It was embarrassing at first," Tiffany says of singing in the malls. "People were laughing and giving me weird reactions."

"I loved it," Tobin says, "because it was a new idea, and at least it was an *idea*. It would move her career forward."

That it did. By the end of the tour, this past September, the little crowds had turned into gigantic crowds, and the sixty albums sold in Paramus became hundreds sold in the mall in Littleton, Colorado. The light, palatable music and Tiffany's amiable style first attracted young girls, then young boys, and then an older audience as well. In the fall, two radio programmers, one in Salt Lake City and one in Chicago, started playing "I

Think We're Alone Now," her cover of the 1967 Tommy James and the Shondells classic, which Tiffany, who was born in 1971, remembers having heard once or twice. When the single went to Number One in November, it knocked a Michael Jackson song off the top of the charts.

"I HEARD SHE'S A BRAT," says the small guy in the Disney staff uniform. "I heard she threw some kind of fit over her toast this morning at breakfast."

"She's not a brat at all," his female co-worker answers. "Actually, she's very sweet. She's really very quiet."

The woman speaking is a Disney employee who has been assigned to drive Tiffany, Tiffany's manager, and the entire Tiffany organization around during Tiffany's stint at Disney World. The woman's main job isn't being a VIP chauffeur. "Oh, no," she says. "Most of the time, I'm Pluto. You know, one of the characters in the Magic Kingdom." But all the Disney people pitch in to help the company whenever necessary.

The small guy also works as Pluto and, whenever duty calls, Jiminy Cricket. He was just on his way home after his Pluto shift when he spotted the Tiffany van parked behind the service entrance to Cinderella Castle. It's been all the talk among the employees in the castle—who exactly is Tiffany, this little kid, this little *high schooler,* who has a hit record and will be appearing on the main stage in a matter of minutes?

The woman leans over the steering wheel and says to him, "Actually, I'm not sure I've heard her say very much at all. I can't say I *know* her, but I doubt she'd have a fit over her toast or anything like that."

Upstairs, in the dressing room, Tobin is stalking around with his portable phone. Each time it rings, he answers it by saying, "Penthouse suite, home of the rich and famous!" in a pointedly loud voice. The choreographer is sitting in the corner eating Girl Scout cookies; the stylist, who has also been flown in from Los Angeles, is adjusting Tiffany's new pants.

Tiffany usually wears jeans and sweaters onstage, but because this show will be filmed for the video, she is wearing a special outfit—black leather jacket, black leggings, white crew-neck shirt, and boots. Tobin says he leaves clothes and makeup decisions to Tiffany and the stylist. The stylist says later that the only preference Tiffany has ever expressed was that she wanted to wear black, but a number of people close to Tiffany say privately that Tobin has strict guidelines for her clothes—no flash, no glitter, and nothing that emphasizes Tiffany's fast-maturing figure.

"The trip with her," Tobin said to me earlier in the day, "is that she could baby-sit for you. She poses no threat to anybody. Not to parents, not to other sixteen-year-old girls." He wants nothing to compromise that. "The artist's image has to always be intact. You have to do whatever you can to keep it from being altered." It's the reason he is adamant that she not appear in movies, the predictable jump for a cute, personable celebrity like Tiffany. "It could be confusing to her audience," Tobin explained. "What's a thirteen-year-old girl going to think of Tiffany if she's playing a psycho? Besides, there's a lot more money in being a recording star."

During the last few minutes before the show, Tobin answers a volley of phone calls from his office in Los Angeles, the video director downstairs, and the Disney front office, but all the while he is carefully monitoring Tiffany's preparation. At one point a photographer shoots a picture of her having her eye makeup applied. "Don't take pictures of her having her makeup done," Tobin snaps, "and *don't* take pictures of her eating. You know and I know how that looks."

Tiffany wrinkles her forehead and says in a low voice, "He says don't take pictures of me eating, but that's what I do. I *eat*."

It is the only time—and it seems a nanosecond at most—that she appears to chafe openly at his grip, and it *is* a grip. He talks throughout her interviews, hovers over her during photo sessions, listens to her phone calls. He scolds her if she makes a move without his knowledge. Early this morning he vetoed a shopping trip she and I had planned, saying he didn't want Tiffany to go outside the hotel with me. Later he won't allow me to speak to her on the telephone unless he can listen in.

In spite of all this, she doesn't seem crowded—but then again his brashness and aggression seem to grow in her presence, just as her reserve and passivity do in his. Maybe it's a perfect match—an unformed, talented youngster who has found her mentor—or maybe his unyielding influence on her so early in her life has convinced her that this is the only way that things could possibly be. He has, after all, made her a star.

"It's really nice with George," Tiffany says a little later. Tobin is sitting a few feet away, cradling the phone. "We really discuss things. I do have opinions, but that doesn't mean they're right. There are times I might be right, but that's usually by chance. And there are a lot of times I'll be wrong. Sometimes it's like, maybe I'll be with friends and I'll put on some clothes and they'll say to me, 'Tiffany, that looks *awful.*' I've been very fortunate to have people who will tell me that kind of thing. I'm not going to be difficult. It really hurts the artist to look difficult. I leave that up to George. Besides, George does it really well."

She talks a little about school—a fairly relaxed private Christian high school that has allowed her to come and go as her performance schedule requires. She will be spending more time with a tutor and less in class as the year goes on. Her friends? "Not jealous. If they are, they don't show it."

She says that being in the music business has made her grow up fast, but she recently met some girls who she was sure had already graduated from high school, and she was shocked to find out they were only in ninth grade. She's cautious about having her hopes up, saying that she wants to be prepared for the day that one of her records doesn't do well. She had been doing the dishes when she found out that "I Think We're Alone Now" had hit Number One, and all she said was "Cool."

On religion she is heartfelt but vague. "There must be some reason I've been given this . . . everything. I hope to do something with it. I think of God as, well, sort of a friend or something I need." She hesitates and then says, like a solemn showbiz veteran, "Like the way I need my fans."

Then she talks a little about music. She admires Aretha Franklin, Luther Vandross, and Stevie Nicks, but it's really academic—earlier in the day Tobin, with Tiffany at his side, announced, "I'm one hundred percent dominant with the music. If I like something and she likes it, we do it. If I like something and she *doesn't* like it, we still do it."

Her indulgences to date have been looking for a new house with her mother, going out with boys who are "friends from way back when," and buying a Saab. "I haven't really gotten my driver's license yet," she says a little sheepishly, "so I can't really drive it yet. Actually, I wanted a Pontiac Fiero. My friends have them and told me how fast they are. But that's too tempting for me." She is so used to being controlled that she shies away from imagining what it would be like to lose it.

Then she launches into an anecdote about a cousin who used to resent her when she was the youngest kid around and got all the attention and how she doesn't want to do the same thing to her two stepsisters, who are both younger than she is. It's the only time that she seems to step out of her caution and let a story loose. "My younger sister now always pinches the dog whenever she walks past him, just to be mean," she says. "She's just this little kid, and she needs to *control* something."

. . .

THE SHOW BEGINS on time; the hundreds of kids in the audience begin hollering and clapping on time; the band, a group of experienced session musicians who have never performed together before, is spry and businesslike. George Tobin stalks between the soundboard and the video control room, his face set in determination, his arm cocked to push anyone away who tries to distract him at this critical moment.

Tiffany skips out onstage, deftly switches a dead microphone for a good one, and sings approximately twenty-eight minutes of music. She is a little rushed but mostly on all the cues. She smiles and waves to the audience; between songs she says, "Hi, out there!" and "How are you out there?" She looks cheerful onstage, in a studied but sweet way. It's not a noteworthy performance, unless you consider that she has never done this before. But she will never have a moment like it again.

It is a peculiarly cold and dry night for Florida, no balm in the breeze at all. The trees around the stage are waving, and the Disney banners slap against the castle. In the odd light thrown from the stage floodlights, Cinderella Castle looks enormous and historic—it actually does look like a genuine French provincial castle, complete with spiky turrets and embrasures and arrow loops, built in the fourteenth century, instead of what it is: two hundred feet of fiberglass built seventeen years ago. It's just one of those things that looks absolutely real, but it's not.

A GENTLE REIGN

*K*WABENA OPPONG, WHO IS THE KING AND supreme ruler of the African Ashanti tribespeople living in the United States of America, has a throne in his living room. The throne is a simple wooden armchair, with squared-off legs and arms and a wide, curving back decorated with medallions and baubles made of pounded tin. At each end of the throne's back rail is a metal ornament shaped like a sweet onion. The throne was a gift from the Ashanti king in Ghana, the West African nation that is the home of the tribe, to the Ashanti king in the United States. The two Ashanti kings are in somewhat different situations: The Ghanaian king is royally born, richly rewarded, divinely inspired, and holds his office for life. The American Ashanti king is elected every two years from the ranks of an Ashanti social and cultural organization called the Asanteman Association of the United States of America, Inc. The first Stateside king, Kwadwo Tuffuor, was a plumber. The second, Kusi Appouh, repaired air-conditioners and refrigerators. Kwabena Oppong is the third king; he drives a cab.

At the time he was elected, Kwabena Oppong was given the throne, which he will keep until January, when a new king takes over. He was also given the title "Nana," which is an Ashanti term of respect and means something like "Beloved" or "Your Honor." The people in the tribe now always address him as Nana, and he will be called Nana forever.

When I first met Nana, he was living with his family in a two-bedroom apartment in River Park Towers, a high-rise housing project in the South Bronx, near Yankee Stadium. This is hardly a kingly address, but the apartment was cheery and not without touches of royalty. In the living room, besides a large rubber plant and a furry mustard-colored couch and matching love seat, there were four strikingly large framed photographs—one of the current African Ashanti king, Otumfuo Opoku Ware II, in opulent ceremonial garb, and three of Nana Kwabena Oppong at his coronation celebration, at the Roosevelt Hotel, in New York City. A brass-and-wood plaque that said NANA KWABENA OPPONG CONGRATULATIONS ON YOUR ENSTOOLMENT AS ASANTEFUOHENE OF NEW YORK 23RD MAY 1987 was propped up on a small side table. The throne was wedged between the couch and a color television set.

Nana's four-year-old son, Dennis, greeted me at the door and then ran into the living room, grabbed a bag of Cheetos, and sat down on the throne. The television was tuned to *Jeopardy*. Nana waved to me from the kitchen, where he was standing with the telephone balanced on his shoulder and his hand cupped around his ear.

"One of my people," he said, pointing to the phone. "I'll be done in a minute." He listened for a moment, with a worried look on his face. Then he spoke briefly in Ashanti. The language has a lot of *g*s and *n*s, and seems to erupt from the back of the throat. When spoken rapidly, Ashanti sounds like bubbling stew. When Nana speaks, it sounds like a gentle simmer. He spoke for a few more minutes, and then ended the conversation, looking considerably cheered up. He walked into the living room and handed me a Diet Coke.

"Everyone always has a problem for the king," he said, shaking his head. "That's just the way it is. If you're going to be king, you find that out. Now, let me drink first, please. In Ashanti tradition, the host has to drink first to show he hasn't poisoned the drinks." As he sipped, he glanced across the room. "Oh, Dennis, get off the throne now!" Nana said. Then he let out a deep sigh. "I really can't help it," he told me. "The kids sit in it all the time."

At the time, Nana was in the first year of his reign and was just getting the hang of being a king. "I definitely love *being* the king," he said, after Dennis was dethroned. "But sometimes things aren't exactly the way they seem. This job can be so *bothersome*. Some of the time, I really don't love the bother." He went on to say that as king he is expected to act many roles—to be, in effect, a combination of supreme court justice, party planner, marriage counselor, religious leader, master of ceremonies, diplomat, and icon. He is regarded by his tribespeople here as the surrogate for the king in Ghana, and is often called on to settle personal, marital, and business disputes; he is the central figure at the monthly meetings of the Asanteman Association; he has to travel to important Ashanti occasions in other American cities; and his attendance is expected at all the Ashanti social events in the New York area. Every Ashanti I've met has been either gainfully employed or in school, but the parties come in a constant stream and usually last all night. It's a rare week that goes by without an African holiday or a funeral, a wedding, a picnic, a puberty celebration for a young girl, a sweet sixteen party for an older girl, or an event called an "outdooring," which is a baby's coming-out party. (In old Ashanti tradition, babies were kept inside for a week after birth, so the spirits wouldn't be tempted to snatch them back.) "Africans love to party," Nana explained. "I have to go to all of them. Sometimes at these events, I don't have to *do* anything. I don't speak, eat, or drink at ceremonies. But I have to be there. The king has to be there to make it an event. Sometimes it interferes with my driving the cab." A typical week for him is likely to include fifty hours of driving the cab, thirty or forty phone calls from Ashanti wanting something, a party, and a meeting of the association.

Nana has an entourage of a queen mother (who is neither his wife nor his mother but another association member, elected as second in command, who specializes in women's and girls' issues) and eight or nine elders, including a chief linguist, who is the Ashanti equivalent of a White House spokesman, and a number of junior elders, who oversee various neighborhoods and give counsel. In the long run, though, the headache of being king derives from the fact that Nana is the one who is constantly in demand. That afternoon, for instance, after we had been speaking for only a few moments, the phone rang. Nana went into the kitchen and answered it, listened for a long time, spoke in Ashanti briefly, and then came back to the couch. "That was a member of the club who wants to know how to send the body of his brother back to Ghana for burial," he said. A moment later, the phone rang again: "Someone wants to make sure I'll pour a liba-tion and make a blessing before a wedding."

Later: "I'm arranging a performance of our cultural group, with drum-ming and dancing. That was the guy who is making the invitations."

Later: "That was a man who needs help in getting a loan and also needs a ride to the meeting next week."

Later: "That was another man in the club—he's having a problem with his wife. I have to go over to his house this evening."

Much later: "Someone trying to sell a newspaper subscription. That one wasn't an Ashanti."

Nana has a few other royal accoutrements besides the title and the throne: several robes made of gorgeous Ghanaian fabrics ("I wear them only for special ceremonial times. When I'm not king anymore, I'll have to give them back"); two Advent loudspeakers ("We use those at meetings and for performances of our cultural group. I don't like having them, be-cause I have to take them in my car anyplace the club needs them"); an umbrella of deep-gold silk edged with fringe ("The umbrella is very impor-tant. Ghana is very sunny, and you don't want a king walking out in that sun"); and a small wooden stool filled with the spirits of his tribe's ances-tors. The stool is a representation of the sacred Golden Stool, which, ac-cording to Ashanti legend, was divinely created and delivered to the first Ashanti king as a symbol of his supremacy. When an Ashanti king ascends to the throne, he is said to have been enstooled. The stool gives Nana's wife, Georgina, the creeps, so she keeps it hidden in the bedroom closet and lets Nana bring it out only for ceremonial use.

Nana does not, as Ashanti kings traditionally did, receive gold dust, wives, slaves, or cattle for his trouble, but he has often said that being king has changed his life. "I've learned so much about people that I never knew before," he told me. "I've learned a lot about communicating. Before, I didn't know much about other people's ideas or their actions. Now my knowledge has been broadened. The people give me so much love and re-spect. That's what I've liked most about being king." Although very little in his life up to now might appear to have prepared him for the job, he seems to have taken to it instinctively. He has quickly become comfortable with the attitude of royalty—one of his boilerplate phrases is "A king's greatness is his people"—but if he ever savors the loftiness of his position he has clearly not let it turn his head.

"Everyone knew Nana would be a good king," one of the elders said re-cently. "He's fair, and he loves his people. During his reign, he has got more and more respect. The more we see how humble and warmhearted he is, the more we see the intensity of Nana."

Another one of the elders says, "I wasn't sure what kind of king Nana would be. But Nana has fitted into the job very well. It isn't easy being king. It's a touchy thing. You have to be without any arrogance at all. After all, once you become the king your people look up to you and serve you. Your life changes. You have to act kingly. For instance, even at the height of provocation you can't strike anyone. You can no longer dance, like a common person. You receive special consideration from the rest of the Ashanti. If you walk in the room, people bow their heads. If you go to the airport, your people carry your suitcases."

NANA'S PUBLIC SITUATION has occasionally made him see his private situation differently. For instance, he told me that day that he thought the housing project he and his family lived in was going downhill as fast as his station in life was going up, and he was planning to move as soon as possible. "There are drugs and other problems—it's not the way it used to be here. It's not good for the kids," he said. "Anyway, a king isn't supposed to live in an apartment in the Bronx!" He told me that after considering the options he had decided to buy a house in Teaneck, New Jersey, because the greenery of New Jersey reminded him of the part of Ghana where he grew up.

Ghana is a modern concoction of regions ruled by neighboring but not necessarily neighborly tribes, of which the Ashanti is the largest. During the sixties and seventies, Ghana's economy crumbled, and its government, formed in 1957, when the country (called Gold Coast until then) was granted independence from Britain, followed suit; there are people who say that for a time in Ghana the coups were more regular than the trains. A coup in 1979 put a flight lieutenant named Jerry Rawlings in power. Rawlings calls himself a radical populist and is a member of the Ewe tribe, which has never been in what anyone would describe as total harmony with the Ashanti (although, as it happens, he is married to an Ashanti woman). In the second half of this century, it became fashionable for any Ashanti who could afford it to go to Great Britain or the United States for college. Rawlings's rise to power, combined with the continued failure of Ghana's main crop, cocoa, convinced even more Ashanti to leave. Most have families back in Africa and still think of Ghana as home. There are probably close to ten thousand Ashanti in New York, mainly in

Brooklyn and the Bronx, and about twenty thousand living elsewhere in the United States.

"The Ashanti have become a traveling tribe," an association member named Kojo Nsiah-Amanquah told me after describing his own pilgrimage from Ghana to Temple University, in Philadelphia, to study insurance. But when Nana first announced his intention to move approximately twelve miles, from the Bronx to New Jersey, a certain amount of panic broke out; some members of the tribe worried that a king in Teaneck would be less accessible to them than a king in the Bronx, and insisted that Nana consider their opinions and concerns before relocating.

One of Nana's favorite words is *aggravation,* which he pronounces like a drumroll, with five or six syllables: "ag-gar-ra-va-tion." By his standards, aggravation is a condition that exists in this world in almost unlimited supply, and has almost unlimited negative potential. Aggravation, in its specific Nana-exasperating form, is what happens when something like deciding to move to New Jersey, which comes with its own raft of difficulties, takes on a new load of complications because it is perceived as a matter of royal policy. Nana told me that he considered all the anxiety unfounded, but, as aggravating as it might be, it was his duty to smooth things out and assure everyone that once he was in Teaneck he would be as available as ever to carry out his responsibilities as king. He called a number of the worriers individually and pleaded his case. As another gesture of appeasement, he announced that as soon as he moved he would quit his job as a cabdriver, which keeps him out of reach for hours at a stretch (he admitted that, because of his driving schedule, he was making a lot of royal-related calls from phone booths), and instead take a job in a Laundromat. "A king in Teaneck doesn't seem to be a problem to me, but some of the people are really worried," he said. "I keep telling them, 'There will be no problems with New Jersey. I'll be here for you, just the way I am now. There won't be any problems.' You see, if the king is in New Jersey they can still call anytime. A king in a cab is actually much harder to get on the phone."

WELL AFTER NANA'S REIGN is over, it will live on both in the memories and on the videotapes of the members of the Asanteman Association. A crew of cameramen, hired by the club, films almost every social event, and I got accustomed to receiving invitations like this one:

FLASH! FLASH! FLASH!

THE KING'S WELCOME DANCE IN

HONOUR OF

Osabarima Nana Kodwo Mbra V

Omanhen of Oguaa Traditional Area

MUSIC BY = GUMBE SOUNDS

SUPPORTED BY DISC JOCKEY

VIDEO BY = AGYEMAN RECORDING

STUDIO

SPECIAL ATTRACTION = CROWNING OF

MISS OGUAA

In fact, the first time I went to a meeting of the association, the proceedings were delayed for an hour while members viewed videos of Nana's coronation and then filled out forms to order them. There were two different tapes—one shot in a standoffish, scan-the-crowd, public-television style befitting a House of Windsor affair, and the other more in the manner of a home movie, with a number of blurry close-ups of Nana's left cheek and ear. There seemed to be a lot of enthusiasm for both tapes. "It's important that we record all this for posterity," the queen mother, a tall, bashful nursing home attendant named Ama Asantewaa, said to me as we stood in the group of people watching the monitors. "The Ashanti have a high sense of history, so we like to have records of everything that goes on."

Just then, another Ashanti woman came up to us. "Ama, which are you going to buy?" she asked. "I don't know what to buy. Last week, I ordered the tape of the puberty festival. Now I don't know which of these to get."

The queen mother shrugged and said, "I loved the coronation party so much that I just have to buy both tapes."

Having a face that is television-friendly has never, as far as I know, figured in the Ashanti royal elections, but I have heard it observed during tape viewings that most people believe that the camera favors Nana. He is forty-eight years old, but looks ten years younger. He is about five feet eight and has short brown hair, smooth dark skin, a squarish mustache, small, bright eyes, and a large, well-formed head. On his left cheek is a peanut-size horseshoe-shaped scar—an Ashanti tribal mark given to him at birth. (The practice of tribal scarification is now mostly obsolete.) Nana's voice is sleepy-sounding. The effect of his accent—a mingling of British clip and African lilt—on my midwestern ear has sometimes resulted in unusual conversations. This effect has occasionally been exacerbated by the fact that the Ashanti language has no pronoun genders; when speaking English, tribespeople tend to call everyone a he.

Nana favors casual shirts and slacks when he goes in for Western clothing, but he looks more at home in traditional Ghanaian robes, called *ntoma,* which are worn either like togas, slung over one shoulder and wrapped around the torso, or like sarongs, rolled at the waist and draped to the floor. Most Ashanti I know wear tennis shorts under their *ntoma* in all weather, and heavy sweaters when it's cold. I have never seen Nana wearing anything on his feet except leather thongs—flat soles with toe loops—from Ghana, but he confided to me recently that whenever it snows he wears Western-style shoes outside.

Nana was born in September 1940, in Bekwai, a farming village in the Ashanti region, in south-central Ghana. Kwabena, his first name, is Ashanti for "Tuesday," which was the day he was born. (There are only seven Ashanti first names—Monday through Sunday.) Many of the houses in Bekwai are made of mud and cement blocks and have bamboo roofs, and are without running water and electricity. The Ashanti region has roughly the same boundaries that it had when the tribe ruled over its own kingdom, during the eighteenth and nineteenth centuries, and amassed great wealth trading in gold, kola nuts, and slaves. The Ashanti have maintained an unusually complex royal hierarchy for almost three hundred years, beginning with Osei Tutu, the greatest Ashanti monarch, who was eventually killed by some members of the Akim tribe. The king holds office for life, but can be destooled for a variety of transgressions, including madness, leprosy, fits, excessive cruelty, blindness, impotence, disfigurement, not following the advice of the elders, or being too fond of disclosing the slave origins of some of his subjects. Even after Britain managed, with great difficulty, to colonize the Ashanti territory, in 1901, the monarchy stayed intact, and it has remained in place since independence.

When Nana became king, his father observed that it was obvious even when Nana was a baby that he would be great someday. Nana's family, however, wasn't royal. His father had a small but prosperous cocoa farm, three wives, and twenty-five children. Like most Ashanti with multiple wives, he maintained a separate home for each of them. Nana's mother, though, divorced him sometime in the 1950s, when she became a Christian and found his pantheistic ancestor worship unbearable. Nana is a baptized Anglican but an infrequent churchgoer; he is a fervent believer in the power of ancient spirits and in an omnipresent deity.

After high school, Nana moved to Kumasi, the second-largest city in Ghana. He says he wanted to live where he could see electric lights. In Kumasi, he went to a trade school to become an automotive technician, and then in 1972 he came to the United States to visit a friend and decided to stay. He drove a gypsy cab in the Bronx for a while, got a job as a security guard at the World Trade Center, became the surrogate tribal chief of an informal organization of his kinsmen in Brooklyn, took a job in an electronics store on Canal Street, became a deputy chief of the Asanteman Association, chipped in with a friend to buy a cab medallion, and finally became king. As I spent more and more time with Nana, I came to realize that the hairpin turns in fortune and circumstance which he has experienced, instead of making him dizzy or frustrated, have given him an air of monumental calm. There are times when he seems to have the imperturbability of a very old man or of a visitor from another planet observing and recording impetuous earthling behavior. He is not impassive—he just finds reconciling seemingly unreconcilable things an abiding condition of life. Whenever he talks about the peculiarities of his personal situation, he throws his hands up as if something had just landed in his lap uninvited, and bursts into a laugh that is one part high-pitched wheeze and three parts thunder. "I *know* how strange this is," he said one day, exploding into the laugh. "My life was one way, and then I turned around and everything had changed. I dream of the headline sometimes if I'm driving and I'm getting scared. Really, it just seems so funny! I think, How would that sound—KING KILLED IN CAB?"

THERE ARE ALL SORTS of circumstances in which people find it necessary to call upon the king. Some are merely ceremonial, such as weddings and funerals, but many are potentially litigious. The Ashanti I met seem to have a pronounced lack of interest in using the American legal system to settle conflicts—a characteristic probably owing in part to their two-hundred-year tradition of having most matters decided by kings and elders, and in part to the more modern condition of living under a Ghanaian government where differences of opinion are sometimes resolved before a firing squad. As much as possible, the Ashanti call on Nana to sit in judgment for them, and this is the part of being king he finds most difficult—he likes to say that he finds argument an awkward exercise and rarely engages in it himself. So far, he has been called in to arbitrate eight major feuds, and he hasn't enjoyed any of it.

"It can be very embarrassing to work with these disputes," he says. "It just becomes very embarrassing to me. Sometimes people can be so— *aggravating*. Once, when I was still just a deputy, just an elder, a big fight arose. The king was in Ghana at the time, so I had to handle it. I finally lost my patience with the people who were arguing, and I decided to leave. I stepped outside, and I could hear through the door that they had started to fight with each other. I had to go back inside. Finally, I called the police, because I thought, This is no matter just for a king! I couldn't stand it! There was just so much argument. I was really embarrassed. What aggravation! One man's lip was bitten in the fight. I wasn't scared for my own sake, because you can't bite a king, or even a deputy king. The man wanted to take the guy who bit him to court. We didn't want to see that happen, so the association paid him a thousand dollars for the lip. It was a lot of money, but it was the right thing to do. I couldn't stand to see one of our people in jail in America."

Nana is so discomfited by feuding that he doesn't like even to talk about it, but within the tribe his judicial temperament is widely admired. He is known less as a strict constructionist than as a legal realist—his is more a court of equity than a court of law. "What I like about Nana," an Ashanti microbiologist named Victor Aning told me once, "is that he is a cool-mannered personality. When he judges things, he does it in a cool-mannered way."

One day not long ago, after Nana had just moved to Teaneck, I stopped by at his new house. It was a steamy afternoon; several elderly white men in shorts and undershirts were out mowing their lawns. Nana's street curves through a pretty neighborhood and is lined with small brick bungalows that have peaked roofs and big picture windows; Nana's was the only house with a yellow cab parked in the driveway. When he came to the door, he peered through the screen. "Oh, I have to do something about the neighbors," he said before letting me in. "Some of the people in the club are upset that I haven't let the neighbors know I'm a king. I just haven't thought of how I'm going to tell them."

The house was still: Georgina Oppong was out shopping; their three children, Dennis, Susie, and Mandy, were playing outside; and the Oppongs' niece Florence, who moved from Ghana last year to live with them, was sitting in the den watching reruns of *Lassie* as she folded a pile of clean *ntoma* and socks. The air was full of the sound of cicadas, lawn mowers, and muffled barking. Nana had driven his cab all night—the Laundromat job had come and gone by this time, having proved convenient from his subjects' point of view but barely lucrative from his—and earlier in the week he had attended two Ashanti events that wound up, as most do, around five in the morning. He was exhausted. We talked briefly about his move to New Jersey, and about the general status of the association, and then he told me that a dispute had come up recently that he wasn't able to resolve. "It was a marriage," he said, frowning. "But it was too broken to fix." The question wasn't whether the warring parties were willing to take Nana's advice—the Ashanti who come to him seem prepared to accept his decisions—but whether he saw a solution that was by his standards reasonable. He didn't, and it depressed him. So far, though, the other major disputes of his reign have been resolved more successfully:

A man reported to Nana that he was leaving his wife because there had been no food in the house for two weeks. The wife reportedly answered his questions about the food by saying, "What's wrong with you?"

Nana: "I called the wife. She said, 'It's true, but I'm angry because my husband has been sending money home to Ghana without my knowledge.' I called all the elders, and we decided that the woman was right—he shouldn't have been sending the money home—but we had to go along with the man. We always give the upper hand to the man. In this case, though, I didn't give a formal judgment. I said to them, 'Cool down.' In some cases I give a judgment, and in some I just advise a little patience. In our culture, to get a divorce you have to get permission from your parents, and I reminded them how embarrassing that would be. They did cool down when I told them to. They have to give their respect to me, because I'm the king."

A woman complained that she bought a newsstand for her husband, and the man was apparently working there, but still no money was coming in. Then the woman found a letter he had written to another woman.

Nana: "I knew this was difficult, because they came to see me in separate cars. It was a Sunday evening. What are most arguments about? It's mostly money, money, money. Ashanti who come here work very, very hard. They work harder than they would if they were still in Ghana. In Ghana, there's nothing to buy—it isn't so materialistic. You don't even have to wear shoes. You have your family. They take care of you. Here you take care of yourself. You have no mommy and no daddy. The people have to earn money. Sometimes they're sending money back home, so they need even more money. So they argue about money. When these two came to me, I took the man aside and told him to apologize. The woman started to cry. [*In a woman's voice*] 'Weee, weee, weee, now I feel so bad.' I asked the man to compensate her fifty dollars because of her finding the letter he wrote to his concubine."

A man complained that his sister and his wife didn't get along and were making his life miserable.

Nana: "The man cited three reasons that he was upset. He said his wife was lazy, she had no respect for him and his sister, and she had to get along with his sister and wouldn't. I called the wife, and she was so annoyed that the man had come to me! I fixed a deal for them when they came to my house, but the man was angry and decided to leave. I was upset with him. I said, 'Why are you leaving? You come to my house and your wife comes to my house, and now you won't accept my judgment.' I guess, though, that they got themselves back together. I saw them later at a funeral, and the wife started screaming at me. Screaming at *me*! Everyone was laughing about it, that now she was picking on me, too! Later, the husband came over and apologized for her. I found it very embarrassing."

A man made a loan to a very good friend, who didn't pay it back.

Nana: "Oh, they were *really* fighting about it! They called me up, and I got the money back from the one. I said, 'Why don't you pay it back already?' So he gave me the money, and I gave it to the other guy. I asked them to come over, so I could see them shake hands over it. They came over, but they wouldn't shake hands! [*In a low, blustery man's voice*] 'I won't shake his hand, no!' You know, I know that people don't mean to be aggravating, but sometimes they really are. Finally, these guys shook hands, and that ended it."

A wife went to Ghana and started building a house for her family without telling her husband. She said she was using her own money and so didn't need his approval.

Nana: "I had to call in the elders for this one. We sat with them for four hours. Four hours! It was so aggravating! We finally made an agreement. We advised the man and his wife to open a joint savings account."

ALTHOUGH THE RESOLUTIONS that Nana orchestrates—Solomonic reasoning with overtones of tribal protocol and a shrewd sense of damage control—don't always result in perfect harmony, he has become known as a peacemaker, and his attitude toward squabbling, which is similar to most people's attitude toward the sound of fingernails on a chalkboard, has gained popularity in Ashanti circles. Partly, this may be because Nana has preached harmony as not just an appealing state of being but one that can have tangible results. In an address to the association, for instance, he once plaited together the threads of peaceful coexistence and economic rationalism so intricately that he left the audience breathless. "I have started looking into business opportunities for minorities," he told the group. "This does not rule out the Asanteman Association. An example of this is Korean and Chinese immigrants who have flooded the fish, fruits, and small grocery shops." After a pause, he added, "If we can love ourselves, we may help ourselves to achieve such great business status."

Nana's emphasis on unity and on positive vibrations is a notable change for the Asanteman Association, whose first few years were marked by intense bickering over rules and regulations. The club was formed in 1982, by Adum Bawuah, a lecturer at John Jay College of Criminal Justice, who while working on his doctoral dissertation came to the conclusion that the Ashanti people who had emigrated to the United States had, as he put it, unwisely flung their culture into the melting pot. He decided that a social organization could help fish the culture out before it was too late. The club would be dedicated to preserving the use of the Ashanti language, educating young Ashanti about tribal history, observing traditional ceremonies and holidays, and bringing kinspeople together; and members would be entitled to, among other things, death benefits and the use of the association mailing list for party invitations.

A few other Ghanaian tribes had fraternal organizations in the United States—among them the Ewe Unity Club, the Akan Association, the Okuapeman Association, and the Kwahuman Association—but those clubs had Western structures, headed by chairmen or presidents. Bawuah decided that the Asanteman Association, which now has several branches across the country, would be better off using an American variation of the traditional tribal system—dynastic succession would be replaced by election. Candidates for king would make their cases before the membership, and then a council of elders would vote on a final selection. This curious hybrid of African tradition and democratic process was instantly popular with the Ashanti whom Bawuah approached, and in 1982, with the blessing of Otumfuo Opoku Ware II, the Ghanaian Ashanti king, the club was formed.

Bawuah wanted the American Ashanti king to be chosen from among the common people. "I didn't want the group to be dominated by the intellectual elite," he told me not long ago. "In Ghana, many of the chiefs don't know how to read or write, but they know how to bring people together. My first choice was to have the king be an older person, sixty-five or seventy. The kings have ended up being younger, which has worked out just as well."

As monarchies have long been racked with upheaval and intrigue, so was the Asanteman Association. An early and especially lively disagreement involved the length of the king's tenure. I have heard countless versions of what happened, but, as near as I can make out, one of the first two kings liked the job so much that he proposed he be kept on for life, confirming an observation Bawuah once made to me—something along the lines of "In Africa, once a person takes office he really likes to die in office." Some of the club members thought that the king-for-life concept was a good one, and others thought that it was approximately as good an idea as, say, indentured servitude. Sides were taken, and many prominent members walked out. For a while, it looked as though a rival Asanteman Association might be formed. "A conflict of power, I would call it," one of the junior elders, Johnson Owusu-Manu, has said. "Or, I would say, a struggle for power, or a dispute over power. The main thing definitely was the power."

Nana never really intended to run for king. He had shown a natural capacity for leadership, having founded and headed an informal organization of his clan, the Amansie, before the Asanteman Association was formed, and he served as deputy chief in the early years of the club. When it came to being king, though, he had reservations. "I didn't want to come in, to begin with," he told me. "I had reasons. I thought, You don't get paid to do this. You don't get anything to be the king. Do I want to waste my time? I'm busy with my family and my cab." But the woman who was then queen mother thought that Nana would make a good king, so a few months before the election she approached him and told him he should run. He refused. She came back. He refused again. Then, to make her point, she sent one of her advisers to see him every three days. Finally, Georgina Oppong started to worry that people would think she was keeping Nana from being king. Georgina is also Ashanti—in fact, her family happens to be royal—but, between the children and her night-shift job as a nurse at a Manhattan nursing home, she has never had much time left to participate in the association. "It wasn't Georgina," Nana said. "I just didn't know if I wanted to be so involved. But"—he threw his hands up and started to laugh—"I finally changed my mind!"

Once convinced, Nana campaigned actively on a love-and-peaceful-accord platform. He vowed that he would postpone his formal coronation until the disgruntled ex-members agreed to return to the club. The elders caucused and voted, and in the end Kwabena Oppong became the third king of the American Ashanti. The next day, he went to the house of the ex-king who had been denied permanent status, talked to him for three hours, pleading tribal loyalty and democratic philosophy, and left satisfied that the ex-king and his partisans would rejoin the club. Eventually, they all did. It was a maneuver so deft that it is still discussed by members of the association. After I heard the story of this negotiation, I asked Nana whether he had any ambitions in the greater political arena.

"I'm not a politician," he said.

"Isn't this politics?"

"Oh, no, this is just what a king does—it's different from politics. It's for the people, for our culture. I don't pay much attention to politics. In Ghana, because of the military government, no one wants to think about politics. A lot of Ghanaians left home because of politics." Then he looked at me and beamed. "I did love campaigning, though," he said. "I tell you, it was so exciting! When you're campaigning, you can really express your views and no one gets angry with you."

AS NANA OFTEN SAYS, maintaining peace and harmony—in other words, avoiding aggravation—in this world is a job in itself. It also happens to be one that at times seems largely incompatible with his jobs as cab-driver and as king. He puts a great deal of stock in the soothing word and the deep, so-it-goes sigh, but they have on occasion failed him. Last winter, the elders of a new Asanteman Association chapter in Los Angeles asked Nana and a few of his deputies to come out to California for a formal induction ceremony. One cold Sunday evening, members of the New York chapter gathered in the basement of the Calvary United Methodist Church in the South Bronx to discuss the trip, as well as other tribal matters. When I arrived at the church, close to fifty people were inside. About half were in Ashanti traditional dress, and the rest were wearing things like leisure suits, shifts, and slacks. Ten of them were in a corner practicing on the talking drums for an upcoming performance, and ten more were dancing behind a chalkboard. Everyone else was sitting around in groups, chatting in Ashanti or passing out party invitations and announcements. I was given invitations to two outdoorings and one funeral. A stout woman wearing a turban circled the room selling World's Finest Chocolates for her son's Boy Scout troop. "Nana's going to be late," she told someone. "He had to pick up some of the elders and couldn't fit them and both loud-speakers in his car."

At last, Nana walked in. He was wearing a cinnamon-colored robe over a heavy brown sweater. A line of people formed in front of him before he could sit down. The conversations were all in Ashanti—the association rules require that meetings be conducted in the native language—but I could tell by watching that about ten people were talking to Nana for every one he was able to listen to. Eventually, Nana made his way to a long table in the center of the room and sat down. The chief linguist gave an opening prayer, and a libation of Stolichnaya vodka was poured. Nana began to speak. He first reported on the success of the Christmas dance, then he announced his recommendation that a man who had argued with and in-sulted an elder and later bumped (maybe intentionally) into a female mem-ber of the association be suspended from the club for six months. Then he said how delighted he was about the new Asanteman chapter, and asked the association to pay half of his travel expenses so he could go to Califor-nia for the induction ceremony. He reminded the members that, as officers of the club, he and the elders received no compensation for their time and expenses, and that the trip was important. "I want to see the new chapter spread its wings," he said.

A few people asked questions, and then the group voted to honor Nana's request. Suddenly, a short man in a red robe, who had the bunchy muscles and thrusting jaw of a boxer, stood up and started talking loudly and with mounting agitation. Nana answered him in a low, reassuring voice. The man grew more upset, and eventually jumped up, shouting and shaking his fist, knocked his chair over, and stomped out of the room. The man's outburst and the sound of the metal chair crashing down on the floor were so shocking that they seemed to linger in the air. Nana sat for a moment with his head bowed. Then he looked around at his elders and sighed. They sighed back. After a long, quiet interval, Nana looked at the rest of the association members and swept his hands into the air as if he had been ordered to surrender. The gesture had the effect of a starter's pis-tol on the stunned members, who immediately broke into excited conver-sation and laughter. Nana himself eventually began to laugh. "This is the life of a king," he said to me. "You have to understand that this is the way some people have to be."

Since the argument had been conducted in Ashanti, I had understood only the phrases *"New York Times,"* "Braniff Airlines," "Atlantic City," and "five dollars." I wanted to know the substance of the argument, so a few minutes later I asked Owusu-Manu, who often translated for me, what all the yelling had been about. He looked at me quizzically for a moment, as if he wasn't sure exactly what yelling I was referring to. Then he nodded slowly and said, "Ohhh, *yes*," took a notepad, wrote something on it, and handed it to me. The note said, "A Discussion was going on. The King was beseeching his people."

Forbearance of this order is actually at odds with the Ashanti tradition, which in the course of history has generally weighed in on the side of ferocity and belligerence, but Nana says that it is just as well to let some traditions fall by the wayside. "Some of what we do here is real," he says, "but some of it is just imitation." One evening after that meeting, he invited me to his house for a gathering of the elders. Nana had wanted to have them describe to me how the association was founded, but within a few minutes the conversation had turned to the subject of the legendary warlike spirit of the Ashanti people. One chief elder, an energetic, gregarious man named Emmanuel Kofi Appiah, who is a child-services caseworker for the city, said, "The Ashanti are fighters, you know. In the olden days, we loved to go to war."

"We were the only tribe to defeat the British. We fought them and won many times," another elder said.

"We fought them *seven* times and defeated them *five* times," Appiah said.

"That was the olden days."

"Those were *good* days."

"Oh, yes, we *loved* to go to war."

Another elder leaned over and said, "Our symbol is the porcupine. It is the wildest little animal in the bush. It has a skin of spears. If you pull out one of the spears, a thousand will grow in its place." He sat back and said, "That means if you kill one Ashanti a thousand will spring up to take revenge."

Nana hadn't said anything all this time, but now, looking slightly distressed, he inched forward in his chair and made some portentous throat-clearing noises. "We love our culture," he said once he had everyone's attention. "Parts of it have changed, though. We're not warlike anymore. We also used to have another tradition we don't follow anymore. It used to be that when the king died his entire entourage was killed, so it could accompany him to Heaven." The elders looked down sheepishly.

A gentle temperament was probably Nana's to begin with, but I have been told that it has even been softened since he became king; if so, this is surely one of the few times when a sensational improvement in a person's status in life has resulted in an equivalent upswing in his modesty and self-restraint. No one I spoke to could remember Nana ever getting cranky or harsh, or seeing him swagger around. In many months of spending time with him, I only once saw aggravation get the best of him.

Last winter, the association had been invited to appear at the opening of an exhibition of antique Ashanti goldweights at the Montclair Art Museum. First, the club's cultural group was going to play the talking drums and do traditional dances in a nearby auditorium, and then Nana and his entourage were expected to attend a cocktail party at the museum. Montclair is a forty-minute drive from Brooklyn and the Bronx, so Nana had hired a van and driver to take some of the Ashanti to the show. About two hundred people were in the auditorium for the performance, but forty-five minutes after it was supposed to begin the van had not appeared.

Nana was dressed that day in his most resplendent *ntoma*, which has gold embroidery on dark gold silk; a gold-beaded royal headband called an *abotire*; thick gold armbands and rings; and dozens of strands of gold-colored beads. The outfit was splendid, but Nana looked distraught and was pacing around backstage, ignoring the rest of the club members, who were clustered behind the curtain. His daughters, Susie and Mandy, dressed in bright skirts and also draped with gold-colored beads, were across the stage, practicing for the performance of the *adowa*, an Ashanti dance that involves mincing forward slowly as you sway and scoop the air with your hands.

"Oh, my! Oh, my!" Nana was muttering. "I get the van, and then it disappears. The queen mother is on that van. I'm down. I'm so down! I'm so down! I am so down!" He suddenly noticed Susie dancing. "Susie, come on!" he scolded. "More action!" He started to dance slowly in front of her, scooping his hands deeply beside his hips, his lips pursed. "More *action!*" he insisted. Just then, word came that the van, the queen mother, and the rest of the entourage had been spotted in the parking lot. Nana stopped dancing, clasped his hands to his chest, and squeezed his eyes shut. Later, after the performance, I went to the museum and, in the center of the main exhibit room, saw Nana enthroned on a platform, with his children and several elders seated around him. One elder was standing and holding the royal umbrella over Nana's head. Nana was sitting absolutely still, gazing into the middle distance. He now looked utterly serene and, for a moment, otherworldly. The room was empty except for the Ashanti, and then the partygoers started to wander in, and someone called over her shoulder, "Oh, Bob, look! It's that king!"

EARLY LAST SUMMER, I received an invitation to the funeral of Dr. Gabriel Kofi Osei. The funeral, the invitation said, would have ninety chief mourners, twenty-nine special guests, and a service conducted jointly by the Reverend Dr. Kumi Dwamena and the Reverend J. O. Sarfo; at the organ would be Professor Ok Ahoofe. The rites were scheduled to begin at 10:00 P.M. and end, according to the usual Ashanti schedule, at 4:00 A.M. "We always stay up late. That's just the way it is in Africa," an Ashanti once explained to me. "We love parties, and no one ever gets to sleep."

The funeral was held upstairs in a community hall called Afrika House, in the Bedford-Stuyvesant section of Brooklyn. Downstairs, in another public room, a group unrelated to the association was holding some sort of gathering that had ascended to a level of enthusiasm not entirely in keeping with the funeral soon to take place above it. One of the chief concerns of the Asanteman Association, and one of the things Nana had hoped to change when he decided to run for king, is the difficulty of finding a suitable place to conduct Ashanti business. "We don't have a home of our own, and it's sad—very sad," Nana told me once, looking grim. "We want our own home. We could have classes there, and parties, funerals— everything. We would even like a school there for our children, so that they could learn the Ashanti language and culture." Then he brightened and said, "I think the king could probably have an office there, too." Earlier in the year, a few members of the association had looked into the possibility of buying an abandoned house from the city, but at the moment the expense was too great.

Today, the Ashanti still have to rent halls and meeting places catch-as-catch-can. The monthly meetings are usually held in the Calvary Church basement, where libations are poured onto a yellowing linoleum floor and where, because the basement is used most of the time as a day-care center, the king makes his speeches before a backdrop of cotton-ball snowmen, hand-outline turkeys, or crayoned-in flags, depending on the time of year. In his State of the Tribe address, last January, Nana had said to the members, "Yes, it is true that we need to have a place of our own for our meetings and public functions. I did not promise you this when I took office—I did not, because there was no fund in our cupboard. However, it has never, never gone out of my thinking cap." Afrika House is another frequently used meeting place; everyone had obviously become accustomed to the possibility that something wild would be going on in one room while a solemn tribal rite was going on in another.

On the evening of the funeral, a rainstorm broke out, and when I arrived I noticed many of the association members running into the building and variously grasping umbrellas, funeral robes, and their invitations. The turnout wasn't expected to be especially large; the weather was forbidding, and Dr. Osei, a lawyer who had also been a professor at John Jay College of Criminal Justice, was not well known, or was known mostly as a quirky man—an iconoclast, a disbeliever in Western medicine (he had resisted nearly all treatment of his final illness, which was lung cancer), and a blazing advocate of African nationalism. He was a committed radical, and was openly political in a mostly moderate and self-contained population. Dr. Osei was not even a member of the association, but the members had agreed to give him a traditional funeral.

Nana, the queen mother, the elders, and the chief mourners were seated at long banquet tables set up in a large circle. They were all dressed in billowy black and maroon funeral robes. At each person's place was a small plate holding sugar cubes, pieces of fresh ginger, and mint candies. I was seated next to Ataa Pokuah, a large, exuberant woman with light skin, freckles, and a broad, upturned mouth, who had been the queen mother for three and a half years before Ama Asantewaa was elected. She pushed the plate toward me. "Just like Ghana!" she exclaimed. "These are the traditional funeral foods, bitter and sweet. The only difference is if we were in Ghana there would be doughnuts, too." I had arrived at midnight, when I thought the funeral would be at its peak, but Ataa Pokuah laughed, and said that it wouldn't really get under way until one or two in the morning.

By one o'clock, there were about eighty people in the room. As each person entered, he would shake the hand of every person seated at the table nearest the door and then at each of the others—an Ashanti custom that is collegial and welcoming and at the same time a serious impediment to traffic. At a few minutes past one, the lineup of funeralgoers extended down the stairs and onto the sidewalk. Nana greeted each guest, reaching his right hand out while he pulled his robe back with his left. On occasions like this, he doesn't speak publicly or direct ritual proceedings; his job is to sit in attendance and give his blessing. He is, in effect, a royal chaperon, and has about him an air of reserve and dignity. The job of chairing events and managing their ebb and flow belongs to Johnson Owusu-Manu, the junior elder who is Nana's chief spokesman. A chatty, high-spirited man with a pencil mustache and a puff of shiny black hair, who habitually wears a gold-plated Playboy bunny pendant with his tribal clothes, Owusu-Manu is as much of a natural speaker as Nana is a pacifying presence. He is handy with a microphone and has told me again and again that he loves addressing a group. He is a master of matching his style to the mood of a crowd. Over time, I have been exposed to some of the many moods of Owusu-Manu. There is the Catskills tummler: "It's June, ladies and gentlemen. It rains. It stops. It rains again. You people in traditional clothing are having trouble. I know that. You're getting wet. You're having trouble driving. It's June. Don't blame me."

The hypothesizer: "We can't go forward with the performance because the spear bearer isn't here yet. If we were a subway train, I would say we had a red light."

The theologian: "The Catholics pray to the saints. The Christians pray to Jesus Christ. The Ashanti pray to their ancestors. We are pouring our libation as an offering to our ancestors. If you want any more information, I would be happy to educate you further in the art of libation pouring."

The snake-oil salesman: "May I bring to your attention the videotape of the recent puberty ritual? May I recommend that you order now? I don't—I *really* don't—think you will be sorry. You will be sorry only if you don't order one or two now."

The showbiz emcee: "Ladies and gentlemen! Ladies and gentlemen— here he is, the *king of the Ashanti!*"

At two in the morning, after the handshaking had gone on for about an hour, Owusu-Manu took the microphone and strolled to the center of the room and announced the pouring of the libation. His mood and speech were dark and serious. Nana watched with his head slightly bowed and his arms stretched out on the table in front of him. After Owusu-Manu spoke, someone turned on an eerie, droning, rhythmic chant record, and a group of ten or twelve mourners clustered together and began dancing in a slow shuffle around the room. As they passed Nana, he extended his right hand and pointed at them with the index and middle finger extended—an African gesture of encouragement. A look of immense sadness crossed his face. The dancers circled the room over and over, pausing in front of Nana as he waved his hand.

"Look at that," Ataa Pokuah said, pointing at Nana. "He's saying he accepts them." She looked so wistful that I asked her if she missed her position as a tribe chief.

"Oh no," she said, and grinned. "I *loved* being queen mother, but it really is a hassle. It's important for us to have the whole thing—the king and a queen mother and the elders—but after you do it you see how much time it takes. I think Nana Oppong feels the same way. It's *nice* to be king, but it's so much work. I'm busy. I just finished my eleventh year as a cashier at a D'Agostino supermarket on the Upper East Side. I have things to do at home. If I were still queen mother, it would be hard for me to do what I need to do for myself, because I would be so busy with the people. And I'm so busy all the time! Right now, I have to prepare a big funeral for my mother-in-law. I have to go to Philadelphia to buy a sheep to eat after the funeral fast, and I have to prepare the whole ceremony. For an Ashanti wife, it's one of the most important things you do—to have a funeral for your mother-in-law."

BY THE TIME of Dr. Osei's funeral, Nana Kwabena Oppong's reign was drawing to an end. The council of elders had met several times during the past year to revise the club's constitution, and one of the subjects they had intended to consider was whether to extend the king's tenure from two years to three or four. By Labor Day, though, it was obvious that no changes could be made before Nana's reign was over, and so the election of a new king was expected to proceed as planned.

For Nana, the matter of another term had been a delicate one. Springboarded into office on the strength of his modesty and lack of ego, he admitted to me that he had started to feel that he wanted a little more time as king. "My chief aim as king was to solve the big dispute with the old king, and I did," he told me one day when we were standing on his front stoop in Teaneck. "I wanted more people in the club, and that has happened. I wanted to find a permanent home for us, but that hasn't happened. The time was so short—so, so short. The new king will come in January. At home, a king is forever. I had so many things in mind for the club, and there are many of them I haven't had a chance to do. But if I push it people will think I want to stay, just like the other guy did. That would be a problem. If they just choose for me to stay without my asking, I'll accept it."

In the meantime, he said, he was leaving for a forty-five-day trip to Ghana, his first in almost three years, and he had arrangements to make both here and over there. The trip would be partly an official visit to the chiefs and the king in Ghana to report on the association's status. On top of that, he is building a house in Kumasi for his family, and it still needs a lot of work. "In a few years, maybe five or so, I want to move back to Ghana," he explained. "Maybe, for a while, we'll just travel from here to there every summer before we move for good. It will be a change for us. I want to have a farm when we go back to Ghana. I want to see green things. Georgina can't believe this. She can't believe I want to be a farmer now. It will be a different life again. I still remember when Susie first saw an ant and she screamed and cried for an hour. Wait until she is in Kumasi! And Dennis—Dennis won't speak a word of Ashanti!" He started his big laugh. "Not a *word*! What will that be like? It's as if we had two worlds now." He went on to say that he was so excited about the trip to Ghana that he had started dreaming about it every night.

"I think the transition will be cool," he said suddenly. "I'll appoint an electoral committee when I come back from my trip to Ghana. It won't be like last time. I'll give back the throne and the robes. Three guys are already interested in being king. One of them is the guy I beat last time. I don't mind, really. I love being king, but I'm very tired. Being king is so, so much work. I want to have a rest now. Maybe I'll have a special job with the association. Someone proposed that the old kings have a special job, like elder or adviser. I think it should eventually be changed to a four- or five-year king, though, and I think the king should get a little money, too. It's a very hard job. It takes so much time, and takes a lot of money. My phone has been busy all the time. I've had to drive all over, whenever someone needed me."

A man emerged from the house across the street, waved enthusiastically at Nana, and started into a hedge with ferocious whacks of a clipper.

"My neighbor," Nana said to me in a low voice as he waved back. "When I finally told him I was the king, he said he already knew it. He said he guessed it when I sent him gin for Christmas."

I asked Nana whether he would start driving his cab more once the new king took over.

He shook his head. "You know, my back hurts so much. My legs hurt. I really don't want to drive anymore. I want to work by myself now. I have a new idea. I'm going to open a wholesale beer-and-soda shop in the Bronx. All the Africans love to party, and they can buy all their beer and soda from me," he said. "Maybe I'll call it the King's Place."

THIS IS PERFECT

*G*ETTING ROSE TARLOW TO DECORATE YOUR house is not an easy thing. To start with, you have to be extremely persuasive. Sometimes it is easier to buy a nice house than to talk Tarlow into decorating it. This is what happened in David Geffen's case. A few years ago, Jack Warner's house was up for sale. The Warner house is a big place in Bel-Air, with five bedrooms, a screening room, a sunroom, a nursery suite, and an office; there's eighteenth-century wood paneling in some rooms and Art Deco detailing in others; and there are tennis courts, a neoclassical swimming pool, a golf course, a caddy shack, a maids' house, and twelve acres of woods, lawns, formal gardens, informal gardens, driveways, a pergola, a fountain, classical stone statuary, and panoramic views. Geffen had a long-standing fondness for this house, so when Jack Warner's widow died and her estate put the house on the market he snapped it up for $47.5 million. Easy. Then he started pestering Tarlow to fix it up. "I was absolutely not interested," Tarlow says. "He kept asking. I kept saying no. I think no one ever says no to David, so I kept him intrigued."

Tarlow, a furniture designer, an *antiquaire*, the owner of a tony design shop in Los Angeles, and a person of famously good taste, had decorated only a couple of places before this: a thirty-thousand-square-foot house belonging to a very rich family in Australia; Edgar Bergen's old house in Holmby Hills, which is now owned by a film producer; and Barbara Walters's house in Bel-Air. Tarlow's favorite thing in the world is to say that she is not a decorator. Nonetheless, everyone in Hollywood with a couple of million dollars and some nagging insecurities about furniture wants her to decorate his or her house. She says that because Geffen is a friend of hers she agreed to take a look at the contents of the Warner house—for $47.5 million, it came with some old chairs and stuff—so she gave Geffen her opinion of the antiques, and then she found herself shopping with him for furniture, and then she began drawing plans for building a new pool house and reorganizing some of the bedroom space, and the next thing she knew she was dispatching workmen to tear down walls, rip up plumbing, recess light switches behind hand-carved paneling, cut ceilings for skylights, and stain floors five times to get the perfect golden hue. That was two and a half years ago. She is still working on the house, and figures it will be another year or so until she is satisfied that she has got it right.

Tarlow says that she finally consented to do the Warner house because David Geffen is very charming and very persistent, but the real reason is that if Tarlow is around anything that she doesn't think is perfect, she cannot restrain herself for very long from trying to make it so. Things other people might not mind looking at—telephones, minor Picassos, rolls of toilet paper, and $47.5 million not quite finished fixer-uppers—drive her crazy. She is also so discerning that it's scary. She will glance at what appears to be, say, a bouquet of flowers, a big brown chair, an okay-looking lamp, and an old toy horse, and in an instant declare one awful, one terrible, one a horrible mess, and one just perfect, not necessarily in that order and not necessarily referring to qualities that a less discerning person would have noticed. The unnerving thing is that as soon as she makes the declarations they seem plainly right. During a few days I spent with her, I would try to guess ahead of time which things Tarlow liked and which she found hideously deficient. I would also try to identify themes. I woke up one morning thinking about a few things in her house— specifically, some gigantic paving stones and a pair of big carved horses from Thailand—and suddenly thought, I get it! She likes large objects only! And when I saw her next I mentioned casually that it seemed that her taste was strictly for furniture and objects of monumental scale. She looked slightly impatient and said, "Not *necessarily*. Something small can be perfect. It doesn't have to be big." She dug around on her desk and picked up a palm-size sterling-silver flask covered with woven straw and said, "See this? This is perfect. This is really good. It isn't big, is it?" I conceded that it was indeed not big, and then spent the next hour or so trying to figure out what a little silver flask had in common with huge slabs of French stone and a pair of big white seventeenth-century carved horses. It was a little like taking an IQ test and having to pick out the right pair of twins. I flunked most of my attempts. After guessing that the theme of her taste was loyalty to large objects, I tried rustic, then French, then wooden, and then a sort of meta-theme of "enormous quantities of anything massed together in an interesting way." These were also wrong. I thought that at the very least it was clear that she liked only old things—after all, she had run a distinguished antiques business, and she designs furniture that is adapted from old pieces—and one day I mentioned this in the most off-hand way, since I thought it was so obvious. She raised her eyebrows and then said that the next place she intends to live in is an extremely contemporary house, which she plans to design herself. At that point, I stopped making guesses. Tarlow does love many rustic, French, wooden, old, and massed-together-in-interesting-ways things, but that is not the whole picture—the whole picture is something more subtle and more deeply wired inside her head. If you ask her to explain it, she says, "I like really good things. Simple things. I like anything interesting. I know it when I see it."

TARLOW HAS ALWAYS LIVED in pretty places. She was born in Shanghai, but when she was still a baby her family moved to New York. She grew up in an apartment on Fifth Avenue near the Frick Museum, and in a summer house on the ocean in Deal, New Jersey, which was so big that when it burned down, its yard was used as the site for a beach club and about a dozen ordinary-size houses. Every summer, Tarlow would repaint her bedroom and rearrange the furniture in an effort to get the room exactly right. She also enjoyed assembling things on her mantelpiece in a visually satisfying way. This was when she was a little kid. If you were the owner of a $47.5 million house, you would undoubtedly find it reassuring to know that the person putting it together for you had a good-looking bedroom when she was ten. Tarlow went to boarding school in New Jersey; when she reminisces about her years there, she gets sentimental over the *boiserie,* and the petrified-wood paneling in the bathrooms of the dorms.

Tarlow has the sort of mature aspect of someone who has probably always looked adult. She is now in her late forties. She has smooth chestnut hair, dark arched eyebrows, and an assertive jawline. She once told me she hates being called petite, but she is in fact petite. Her clothes are conservative, dark, tidy, and refined—the clothes of someone who doesn't love clothes but knows what nice ones look like. In a million years, you could not imagine her in a Southern California–style pastel nylon appliquéd warm-up suit, shopping at a mini-mall. She seems to like to be a little mysterious. People who know her have described her to me as prickly and imperious and impatient, but she mainly comes across as nonchalant— someone who is unshakably sure of her own mind. She makes a lot of powerful, definitive statements in a voice of absolutely flat affect, probably because she doesn't expect to have to argue any of her points. In particular, she has an unspectacular way of dismissing what other people might find impressive. This can include her own accomplishments, which she usually waves off as accidental, or as the result of having been coerced, or as something she never intended, or, at the very least, as something that she would now gladly abandon for a life of working on her watercolor paintings or taking her horses for a ride. If her standards aren't met, she can be cavalier about other people's accomplishments as well. Once, she took me to a house that had an extensive collection of paintings, including Picassos, Franz Klines, and Mirós. As we were leaving, she said, "Did you see those paintings?" I assumed that she meant they were dazzling. Instead, she rolled her eyes and said, "They were just awful. Terrible. And all over the place."

ONE RECENT AFTERNOON, Tarlow dropped by to see how the work on the Warner house was proceeding. "It's a big project," Tarlow said. "We've been at it for two and a half years so far, but this kind of house is slow." As she was parking, she motioned toward a row of garden statues and said, "This is going. All this. Awful. All the gingerbread on the outside of the house: going. All of it. We're simplifying. The place was a mess. We're getting rid of all the horrible stuff. When we're done, it's going to be the best house in town."

A workman walked out onto the driveway, holding a piece of wood that looked like walnut. "Rose, come look at this floor," he said. "This is the twelfth sample I've stained, and I think we've finally got the color."

Tarlow got out of the car, examined the piece, remarked that she didn't like the color on one part of the wood, and said to the workman, "Try it one more time. We're close. We're really close. Once more and I think it'll be right." After he left, she said, "I told David when I started this that I was going to spend all his money. He said that would be fine. We have a great working relationship. He's really interested in what's going on." She crossed the foyer and stood in what will eventually be the dining area, with double-height ceilings, dentil molding, inlaid floors, and three walls of windows. Any fewer than twenty people would feel lost in this room. "This is perfect for David," Tarlow said. "He prefers to entertain informally."

She strolled through the "gossip room" (oval-shaped, and soon to include a black marble sink with a foot-operated faucet and a rare Japanese screen), the nursery (scheduled to become the gym), Jack Warner's old office (lined in butter-colored crackled leather, which will be left untouched), dining-room-size bedrooms, bedroom-size bathrooms, and the downstairs screening room. Most of the house is still raw wood, scaffolding, drop cloths, and sawhorses, but it is possible to imagine it turning out to be a good-looking place. After giving some instructions to the floor man and the wall man, Tarlow went outside to inspect a sample of trim that would replace the curlicues Jack Warner had installed under the eaves. "No, no, I don't like it," she told the carpenter. "I want something with more of an angle on the bottom. It has to be like this." She took a pencil from his shirt pocket and marked on the piece of trim in his hand.

"Rose, they don't have anything like that," the carpenter said, looking sheepish.

She cocked her head and said, "Well, then, let's *make* it."

OFTEN, TARLOW HAS FOUND herself in the position of having to make something herself in order to satisfy her taste. When she was a young woman, newly married, in Los Angeles, she decided to get into the antiques business. Her husband staked her to fifty-five thousand dollars toward her first batch of inventory, and she went to Paris to buy. She had, in the meantime, rented a space on a fancy block of Melrose Place, in Los Angeles. She didn't know much about running a business, but she knew she wanted to sell interesting things she really liked. She went to Paris and spent her fifty-five thousand dollars at antiques shops and at the flea market. The shipper, who was responsible for picking up the merchandise and sending it back to her otherwise empty store, took the money, lost it all at the racetrack, and then killed himself. Approximately half of what Tarlow had paid for made its way to Los Angeles, but it was not half a shipment of whole pieces—it was a whole shipment of halves and quarters of pieces: parts of armoires and chunks of chairs. At this point, Tarlow learned very quickly how to build furniture and re-create antique finishes on wood. With the store's opening imminent, she was so far behind and so understaffed and had her hands so full with her two young sons that her hairdresser came in to help set things up. This was 1975, when there were few fine-antiques dealers in Los Angeles, and even fewer who were selling antiques that were half old and half new. As Tarlow remembers it, most people in Los Angeles at that time thought the zenith of interior design was exposed brick, a pool table, English pub signs, and clean towels by the Jacuzzi. In her store, which is known formally as Rose Tarlow / Melrose House, she had an enormous birdcage filled with bright-colored finches, and high-end Oriental and French antiques. Somehow, it was a success from the day it opened.

Tarlow decided that her retailing rule of thumb was to be nice to everyone. One day, she was nice to an unassuming Japanese man who wandered into the shop. He told her that someday he would come back and buy everything in her store. A month later, he came back and bought everything in her store. Another time, a decorator came in and said he was having trouble finding a particular kind of chair, so Tarlow decided to design it for him, because, she says, she thought it would help him out, and it would be fun to try, and she had nothing better to do at that moment. Coincidentally, the European wholesale antiques market was getting wildly inflated: a Régence chair that she used to be able to find for seven thousand dollars was now twenty-four thousand, and to make it worth finding, shipping, and presenting in a store in this country meant marking it up to a price no one would pay. Tarlow discovered that she was good at designing furniture—she would take inspiration from a classic piece and then fiddle with some of the details—and she also discovered that it was more profitable than rooting around for rare and overpriced originals. She now sells much more furniture of her own design than antiques.

After Tarlow and her husband were divorced, they sold their Brentwood house to Linda Ronstadt. The house Tarlow lives in now, in Bel-Air, is on the edge of a sheer hill. When the house was being built, construction material being delivered would have to be off-loaded from a normal-size truck at the bottom of the driveway and divided into loads that would fit on trucks tiny enough to make it up the hill. Tarlow designed the house herself and then had an engineer draft the blueprints for it. It is L-shaped, with huge, high windows, creamy stucco walls, and Boston ivy growing on the interior living-room walls. Most of the furniture and the other objects in the house are ivory or brown or white. Modern necessities, like telephones and toilets, are concealed in antique wooden boxes. The floor in the living room is seventeenth- and eighteenth-century oak, from France, and the one in the dining room is thick old stone from the French countryside. The ceilings are crossed with molasses-colored beams from an eleventh-century church in Kent, England. It took five trips to bring the beams up the hill. The deliverymen left the beams in a pile at the top of the driveway, where they looked alarmingly like a gigantic order of Chinese spareribs. The fact that Tarlow had never taken any courses in architecture did not faze her, but the sight of the family-size order of ribs gave her a start. Overall, the place has the rugged, sunny, otherworldly ambience of an old California mission. After I saw it, I wanted a house just like it. This emotion has overwhelmed other people as well. Some of them have even scraped together the spare change to do something about it. One developer in California recently cribbed her design and built a copy of the house. It occurred to me that in addition to being an antiques dealer, a furniture designer, a textile designer (she is now creating fabrics for the textile company Scalamandré), a tableware designer (she is also making dishes and silverware for Swid Powell), and a decorator, Tarlow might be interested in becoming an architect. "No interest whatsoever," she said. "I only wanted to make my own perfect place."

AFTER TARLOW HAD LOOKED in on the work on the Warner house, she decided to drive out to Silver Lake to check on her finisher. She got lost on the way, and had to call her office from her car phone to have someone there tell her where she was. Eventually, she arrived at the shop. She strolled with the finisher through stacks of club chairs, occasional tables, sideboards, chandeliers, bookcases, desks, bureaus, and knickknacks. Some were old pieces to be tidied up and put in Geffen's house. Others were pieces from Tarlow's line that had been ordered by decorators from her showroom: a big black-lacquered cabinet with chinoiserie detailing, inspired by a seventeenth-century Japanese piece; a Louis XIII–style side chair, which she makes with a wider seat and slightly pigeon-toed legs;

her Regency-inspired dining table, with tapering, reeded legs; a Tuscan-style side table with corkscrew legs; and a straight-legged Louis XVI–style desk, which she makes bigger, sleeker, and less detailed than a true Louis XVI. Ordering upscale designer furniture is like buying couture clothing: It can be altered according to the client's whim. At the finishing shop, for instance, we came upon some tables and consoles of Tarlow's that she had originally produced in burnished dark wood with lacy silver inlays and that were now being made to order for a foreign potentate who wanted them inlaid with gold leaf and painted bright green. The sight of these pieces made Tarlow look, for a moment, a little woozy. The finisher ran his finger over the edge of one of the green pieces, then shrugged at her and smiled. Tarlow smiled back. "This is why I stay away," she said. "I walk through here and I get upset."

On our way back to her showroom, Tarlow showed me a letter she'd got recently from a "competition adviser" who was looking for someone to decorate the new house being built by a computer zillionaire. The letter said, "[Mr. and Mrs. Zillionaire] are preparing to begin the exciting process of design for the interiors of their estate. . . . [Mrs. Zillionaire] will be the driving force behind decision making and shall receive my guidance and council throughout the process. . . . Following my effort to give [Mrs. Zillionaire] extensive exposure to the best design work being done in the country, a list of designers falling within an acceptable range of taste and quality was developed. The selection process will be conducted in a manner that will assure fairness to all invited to participate." The letter was accompanied by a thick, glossy book with color photographs of the construction site.

I said, "Are you going to apply?"

Tarlow looked at me as if I had lost my mind.

TARLOW'S SHOP is in a little ivy-covered building set half a lot back from the sidewalk. It is open only to the trade, and there is nothing fancy about it—just lots of furniture and books of fabric swatches scattered around a big, lofty room. Walking in, Tarlow was met by her design assistant, Jane Eschen, who was overseeing a photographer shooting a picture of some of Tarlow's furniture for an ad. The centerpiece of the arrangement was a towering cinnabar Ming cabinet that cost several hundred thousand dollars. Hanging behind it was a Tarlow-designed mirror with a frame that looked as if it were made of gilded tree branches; the mirror cost nine thousand dollars. Eschen showed Tarlow a Polaroid that had been taken to check the arrangement and the lights.

Tarlow said, "This is awful."

Eschen looked at her. Tarlow tapped the picture. "Look. All the white behind it. That cabinet. It doesn't work at all." Tarlow put down her car keys and walked into the center of the shop, where the photographer was standing on a ladder with a silver umbrella.

"Rose," he said, hesitantly.

"We'll fix it," she said. She stood for a moment and looked around the room. She was dressed in a smart navy suit with a short skirt and a pair of high heels. After a moment, she pushed her sleeves up slightly and then hauled a side chair across the room and put it in front of the cabinet, moved a vase that had been sitting on it, and opened the door of the cabinet to block most of the white wall behind it. The photographer took another Polaroid and then showed it to her.

"I hate this chair," she said.

Eschen grimaced and said, "Oh."

"It's too gold," Tarlow said. "I hate it."

"We've had it in the line forever," Eschen said.

"Well, I hate it," Tarlow said. She pointed at the cabinet and said, "It's not good with that." She hauled the chair back to the other side of the room.

The photographer looked through his viewfinder and said, "Rose, it's great now. You did it."

She took a deep breath and shook her head. She stood back and contemplated the arrangement. Her eyes were squinted and her arms were crossed. Everyone in the room stood still in anticipation. After a moment, she pushed up her sleeves again, strode across the room, moved the cabinet door a quarter of an inch, shifted the vase an eighth of an inch, and then said, "There. It's right now. It's perfect. I couldn't stand it before."

SHORT CUTS

*R*OBERT STUART RAN AWAY FROM HOME when he was a teenager, used to be macrobiotic, worries that Republican welfare reform might lead to urban violence, thinks Hugh Grant is good-looking but not amazing-looking, is a Nietzschean, has been faithful to his wife since they met seventeen years ago, and planned to become a social worker but ended up as a hairdresser. I know all these things because Robert mentioned them the last time he trimmed my hair. Most of what I've told Robert about myself I don't remember, but it ran deep. Robert cuts hair at his own shop, the Robert Stuart Salon, on Amsterdam Avenue at Eighty-fourth Street, in a skinny storefront about the size of a subway car, with strawberry-blond walls and five wide black barber chairs. The place has a pearly sleekness, but it's cozy. If you are sitting on the banquette near the door and you speak emphatically, someone having a hair wash in the back can answer you: Everything in the place is within earshot.

Robert, who is forty-three years old, has been in business on Amsterdam Avenue for fourteen years. For the first ten years, he was in a bigger space, a few blocks south. He moved into his current storefront four years ago. It was previously occupied by Mario the shoemaker, who now has a place up the block. I happen to patronize Mario, too, but our conversations rarely advance past the subject of rubber soles. This is not a reflection on Mario—who is affable enough, although he's never run his fingers through my hair—as much as a reflection on my relationship with Robert and the kind of place he runs. It is a sort of salon of salons, an ongoing symposium involving Robert, his assistants, his clients, and whoever else walks in the door. The majority of Robert's customers are professional people who live in the neighborhood or work nearby—somewhere between Lincoln Center and Columbia University. Many of his regulars are actors, dancers, writers, casting directors, art dealers, or youngish lawyers—people who appreciate stylish haircuts but need to look as if they could hold a job. Many of them are big talkers and don't need much head massaging to open up to Robert or, as often happens, to one another. Robert himself may be the biggest talker of all. He turns out to be a perfect master of ceremonies, in a compact, ideally proportioned forum, in a neighborhood of chatterboxes, at a moment when the success of confessional television shows and call-in radio programs suggests that people are especially curious about one another and are full of their own opinions and raring to talk. Every time I've been in the salon, I have stepped knee-deep into a conversational current that moves swiftly from, say, spiritualism to cream rinse to Oedipal struggle. Between the gushing of his customers, the roaring of the blow-dryers, the trilling of the telephone, and Robert's own conversational flow, the salon is a river of constant noise.

ROBERT THINKS WOMEN are great. Most of his clients are women, although he does cut hair for a lot of men. Whenever men are in the salon, they are expected to act like women—that is, to speak frankly and openly about personal, intellectual, and political matters and, at the same time, make informed decisions about their hair. One day not long ago, Robert was saying that he felt that his cognitive identity was at least as much female as male, which meant, essentially, that he was paying himself a compliment. There were half a dozen people in the salon at the time, including his wife, Valerie, who was working that day as the receptionist. (Robert's regular receptionists are Nancy Bender, a singer who is sometimes hired to perform as a life-size Barbie doll at parties; Roberta Willison, an actress who was in London just then studying with the Royal Shakespeare Company; and Miguel Garcia, a former Eastern Airlines flight attendant who is between jobs.) Robert then said that he'd noticed that in his group-therapy sessions—he has been in every kind of therapy but likes group the most—the women were much more able to open up than the men, and that he considered his sentimental nature and his enthusiasm for conversation to be fundamental feminine traits. He happened to be cutting a guy's hair at the time, and he paused, with one hand steadying the guy's head forward so he could trim the fringe along his neck; his other arm was outstretched, and the needle-nosed silver scissors he held were glinting in the light. A few minutes earlier, Robert had been moderating a discussion of violence in film—he's against it—and saying how proud he was that his fifteen-year-old son hadn't liked *Pulp Fiction*. "Jeremiah and I walked out of *Pulp Fiction*," he'd said. "We went to see *Little Women* instead. I loved it. I cried."

GUY IN THE CHAIR: Really? I thought *Pulp Fiction* was great. Of course, I grew up watching violence on television.

ROBERT: See, I have a hard time with that. Don't you think we're becoming a society that is getting too used to violence? And humor with violence—that really scares me. I don't want to go too, too short in the back today. On the other hand, if it's short on top and too bushy in back, it gets sort of Brooklynish—you know what I'm saying?

GUY: Definitely. The Pentagon did a study of bombardiers in the Gulf War—

WOMAN IN THE NEXT CHAIR (*Having highlights done, her head bristling with tinfoil leaves full of hair dye*): I heard about that study and—well, I'm a television producer, and it makes me really think about my profession and its role in where society is going.

ROBERT: You know, since you're in such a powerful industry, in television, you really affect people's lives. I envy that. Making an impact, that's what it's about, isn't it? Sit still—I'm going to go over your sideburns now.

ROBERT IS SHORT, wiry, and jaunty. He has bright brown eyes, olive skin, and thick, glossy, highly manageable dark hair, which he wears loose and longish, so it hangs over his ears. Ninety-nine percent of the time that Robert and I have spent together, I've been dressed in one of the shop's black floppy robes. A hundred percent of the time, he's been wearing a pair of cotton-twill pants and a rayon camp shirt—usually vintage, and usually the kind that Ricky Ricardo wore around the house on *I Love Lucy*. He owns one suit. I know this because one day the subject came up while he was cutting the curly blond hair of a woman who teaches law and researches feminist legal theory at Columbia.

ROBERT: So, you just got married, right? Tell me about it. How was the wedding? How was your family? Were they supportive? It's so interesting to me that you had a real seriously traditional wedding. Do you think tradition is coming back?

LAW PROFESSOR: You know, I really wonder. I never thought I'd want that kind of wedding, but it really mattered. I thought I'd feel funny, but I didn't. It was great.

ROBERT: I love ceremonies. When our kids were born, we had everything—a bris, a baptism, everything. After I'm done today, I'm going to a Bar Mitzvah. I brought my one suit. It's like a joke in my family: Oh, here's Robert and here's Robert's one suit.

Everything Robert says, he says with overwhelming earnestness. In his presence, you feel that everything is important and everything is at stake—the direction of society, the length of your bangs, the quest for self-awareness. He is a stirring storyteller. His accent is memorable; it involves relocating r's whenever possible, in the old-fashioned New York way. He now lives in Tenafly, New Jersey, but he is a native of the neighborhood. He grew up twenty blocks north of the salon; his father owned a jewelry store on the Lower East Side.

Robert has a handsome, sturdy aspect, but he is also quite excitable. One day, several of us in the shop were talking about anxiety—someone getting highlights done started the discourse by saying she'd lately become insomniac—and Robert mentioned that he'd twice gone to the emergency room in a panic because he thought he was having a heart attack. The first time was when he had a steak after years of being macrobiotic; the heart attack turned out to be gas pains. The second time was before traveling overseas to meet his mother-in-law. Valerie is Filipino, and Robert figured her mother might have never before met anyone Jewish, and then he began obsessing over the possibility that while he was in the Philippines he would be kidnapped by zealous Christians who would try to convert him. This heart attack turned out to be pure anxiety. Robert has a restless mind and what used to be called a vivid imagination. He also happens to be dyslexic, and recently he was found to have attention-deficit disorder. For several weeks after that diagnosis, ADD was the big topic in the salon, and many of his clients became convinced that they might be suffering from it, too. One day, I walked in while he was finishing cutting the hair of a country-

and-western singer, who was describing how she, too, had trouble concentrating. Robert was snipping the last pieces around her ear. "I don't know," she was saying. "I just can't get focused. My mind goes back and forth."

"Exactly," Robert said. "I read the same page in a book over and over again."

Just then, the woman caught a glimpse in the mirror of the tableau that included Robert, his sharp scissors, and her temples. "You, um, *can* concentrate, can't you?" she said, suddenly rigid. "I mean, you're holding blades against people's heads all day."

"Me?" Robert asked. "Oh, not really. I can barely concentrate at *all*."

ONE RECENT SATURDAY, I sat in the salon, got my hair washed, and then sat in the salon for the rest of the day.

ALICE BURRESS, a television commercial director: I'm having a one-step and a cut.

ROBERT: A single process, you mean.

ALICE: That's what I mean. A single. (*To Roberta Willison, the receptionist*): Did you know that my mom comes up every six weeks from North Carolina to have Robert cut her hair? And now she brings all her friends. Robert got them all to get out of those old Southern boofy-dos. Now Robert's got me in one of those *Beverly Hills 90210* shaggy cuts.

ROBERT: I think of it more as Jane Fonda in *Klute,* sort of shaggy-messy. So how are you, Alice? How's life?

ALICE: I'm good. I'm bidding on a Kellogg's commercial in Milan, so I was going to ask you about Italian people, since I know you were in Italy on vacation. I'll be directing people in Italian, but I don't speak Italian. It's an American product, so they want an American director, because they think of Americans as more humanistic.

ROBERT: Do you want to do features?

ALICE (*sighing*): Well, I want to, but I think to do features you need a lot of life experience.

ROBERT: Don't cross your legs. It makes it uneven. Don't you think you have life experience?

ALICE: Oh, *no*—not really. I mean, I've been in school my whole life. I haven't really been out there.

ROBERT: It's really amazing to me that you can say that. It shows real strength that you can see that in yourself. You're so open. That's probably why you're good.

ALICE: I think I get some of my jobs because they want a woman.

ROBERT: Maybe it's the sensitivity that women have that they're looking for.

ROBERTA: Or maybe that a woman wouldn't make as strong a statement. Maybe it's not such a compliment.

RICHARD SCOTT, one of the hair colorists: Roberta, I was just thinking, with your looks and your manner, you're a walking Merchant-Ivory film.

MOLLY HASKELL, the film critic and writer, who is waiting for her appointment: You know, I showed some thirties screwball comedies to my class at Columbia this semester, and they really showed how much power the women of that era had—for example, the power of knowing they could say no. Now women are just expected to be sexually available, and, instead of it giving them more power, it gives them less.

JOANNA WOLPER, a television producer, who has just walked in: Are you Molly? You were my first guest on my television show!

Robert is now done with Alice and is cutting the hair of a ninth-grade girl named Anna Gay, who has also decided to get a Jane Fonda–in-*Klute* hairdo. Anna is watching herself in the mirror and appears paralyzed. Her mother, sitting on the banquette near the door, keeps telling her that she looks great. Robert finishes and says to her that she looks great. She looks as if she is about to cry. "You're going to hate me for a day," he says to her. "But then you'll be okay, because *everyone* will tell you how great you look. You are going to hate me, but I can take it."

MOLLY: Doesn't it kill you to see a girl getting her hair cut? It's such a powerful memory, your haircuts when you were a kid. And the reaction of your mother. My mother is always telling me how she liked my hair better "before," and the "before" is always some imaginary time that never was.

ROBERT: My father had to drag me to the barber, kicking and screaming. Of course, with my family, everything I did I did kicking and screaming.

In comes a pock-faced man selling packages of aerosol pepper spray, which he offers to Robert and Richard, saying, "Gentlemen, perhaps you'd like one as a gift to your wives or girlfriends?" Robert shakes his head, and the man shrugs and leaves. The door opens again, and Mimi Turque, who plays the mother in the Broadway production of *Kiss of the Spider Woman*, enters. She is here to tell Robert that her recent haircut was a success. "My husband fell over!" she exclaims. "The hairstylist for the show fell over! Everyone fell over!"

Robert says, "Oh, oh, oh, oh, I'm just so happy for you," and waves good-bye to her with his blow-dryer.

The salon fills, empties, and fills again. Over the next few hours, the conversation wanders: The feminist art historian Linda Nochlin tells a story—about how she had her hair dyed when she was in Italy and it all broke off and she had to buy a wig—to Tanya Anticevic, an actress and a preschool teacher at Blessed Sacrament, who has just tried dyeing her own hair, which turned green, forcing her to wear a hat to school for a week until today, when she had time to come in and have it dyed back to her own color, which is especially important because she is about to audition for some movie agents; and in the next chair Ruth Kramer, a journalist who is leaving for London tonight to begin a book tour, is getting her hair blow-dried and is half-listening to Linda and half-listening to Robert, who is telling her how smart she is to keep her hair gray, but then he is interrupted by Denise Bethel, an auctioneer at Sotheby's, who has just stopped by to show him an Atget photograph—he loves Atget—and is about to leave when Linda, overhearing her, begins debating with her whether Atget would qualify as "rare" or just "subtle"; and while they are talking, John Winer, a real estate investment banker, shows up for his appointment, and he and Robert begin a conversation about the psychological implications of being touched by service professionals—that is, dentists, hairdressers, manicurists—and John tries to convince Robert that he should get a massage, even though Robert thinks if he had one he might throw up, because he thinks he holds too much inside emotionally; and then Annette Kletter, Robert's banker, comes in—she doesn't have an appointment but she has just found out that her father has died—and after Robert hugs her and commiserates with her she says to him that she thinks that having her hair washed and cut will make it possible for her to face the rest of the day. After she leaves, Mary Ellen Burns, a division chief at the Federal Communications Commission, comes in, and while she's getting trimmed she tries to reassure Robert—he has told her how much he's worried by the conservative juggernaut—that she is certain that Clinton will be reelected, a comment that turns the discourse toward politics and money and class and real estate, which reminds Margaret Tracey, a principal dancer with New York City Ballet, who is trying highlights for the first time, of a ballet fund-raiser she has just attended, which was held in a palatial apartment that used to belong to Marjorie Merriweather Post; and her anecdote leads to a debate about funding for the arts, about whether Bert on *Sesame Street* is going to have AIDS, about why the audience for opera is so old, and about how Dirt Devils are so much better than Dustbusters—this comes up because Margaret's fiancé, Russell Kaiser, who is also with City Ballet, has come in to tell her that he's finished vacuuming the van they've borrowed—and then we talk about where to buy a Dirt Devil, about getting married, and about wedding anniversaries, and someone mentions how, coincidentally, her mother gave her money to buy a Dirt Devil as a tenth-anniversary present; and then somewhere in the middle of this the last customer of the day arrives, an old friend of Robert's named Vincent Liff, who is the casting director of *Les Misérables* and *Kiss of the Spider Woman* and a dozen other Broadway shows, and, after they talk about Vincent's newest project—to find a kid to star in a musical based on the movie *Big*—and about how the neighborhood has changed over the last twenty years and about losing hair and growing up and growing old, Vincent reminds Robert he really should go see *Les Miz* again, because right now there's a particularly affecting Jean Valjean.

AN ENDURING TOPIC in a hair salon, naturally, is how people look. In such conversations, Robert is a master of the thumbnail sketch. The first time he cut my hair, he asked me what we would be doing. I said I wanted it long but not unruly. He agreed, and then said, "On the other hand, you don't want it to be too Upper West Side social worker with two kids and a co-op, either. You don't want Barbra Streisand in *The Prince of Tides*." One Saturday, there were about six people in the salon, and we all began talking about how shocking it is the first time you get bangs, and someone reminded Robert of the time a performance artist came in for her haircut carrying a little casket, and put the locks of her cut-off hair in it. Most people would rather not make their haircuts into quite such a performance. The other day, a woman named Rene Foss, who is a flight attendant on Northwest Airlines and is also half of a comedy team, was telling everyone about how one time at Robert's she'd run into an ex-boyfriend. "Talk about a vulnerable moment," she said. "You're sitting here in this little robe, with your hair dripping wet, and you look awful, and then in walks some guy you'd been seeing."

"What did you do?" someone asked her.

"I tried to tuck my head into the robe," Rene said. "I thought since everyone looks so generic with wet hair and a black robe that maybe he wouldn't notice, and he'd just go away."

"Was that the guy who was driving you crazy?" Miguel, the receptionist who was on duty that day, asked. "The one you said you were trying to avoid?"

"Well, yes, it was," Rene said. "Actually, I had decided I never wanted to see him again for the rest of my life. I did everything possible to avoid him, and I still managed to run into him everywhere I went. I started to think he was stalking me."

"And he's a client of mine?" Robert said, with emotion. "I cut the hair of someone who was stalking you?"

"Not really *stalking*," Rene said. "I just thought it was weird that I couldn't get him out of my life."

The conversation lingered on the question of how to avoid people you've broken up with, and then someone mentioned how irritating it is to still want to look good when you run into the person you've broken up with, and especially how irritating it is if you don't look good but your ex does, and then we talked for a while about those perennial women-getting-their-hair-done topics—love, heartbreak, and romance—and then we made our way to the subject of antioxidant vitamins (Rene was on her way to her homeopath, who had recommended them to her), and then to the effect that flying has on the human body, which everyone agreed was frightening to contemplate, especially after Rene asked if we'd ever carried a bottle of Evian on a flight and then looked at how crumpled and imploded it had become by the time the plane landed. Robert said he didn't trust technology, and Rene said that she had mixed feelings about it, and that, by the way, her chiropractor had her on a regimen of green tea. Just then, on the banquette, two women were discovering that they were both curators—one for the Rock and Roll Hall of Fame and Museum, where she'd just put together the rap exhibit, and the other for a private art collector, for whom she sought out late-nineteenth-century School of Paris paintings. They kept talking, and it soon emerged that one was from Augusta, Georgia, and the other was about to go *to* Augusta, Georgia, for the Masters tournament. As it happened, they were sitting where, a few days earlier, I had sat listening as two women waiting to get blow-drys had discovered, while wandering through an idle, time-killing conversation, that they were both Dutch. This meant that—here, in the middle of Manhattan, on a rainy late afternoon—they could sit and speak Dutch, and punctuate the conversation with gasps of surprise at that pleasant serendipity. Someone else, eavesdropping, had remarked that she thought Dutch sounded exactly like Yiddish, and what followed was a round of discussion about dying languages, heritage, bringing up children, going to estate sales, and the fact that Jordan is now a very popular girl's name. Several good haircuts were achieved in the meantime. It was one of those occasions when the conversation was really rolling; it felt as if it would have rolled on indefinitely, but then came the last haircut of the afternoon, and the end of the day.

FIGURES IN A MALL

ONE OF THE LAST HAPPY MEETINGS OF THE
Tonya Harding Fan Club took place at Nancy Welfelt's
house, around her dining-room table. The meeting had
actually begun at Clackamas Town Center—the mall, in
Clackamas County, Oregon, where Tonya skates—on the
morning of the day before Tonya's on-again, off-again ex-
husband, Jeff Gillooly, began his sixteen hours of interviews with the FBI. That was several days before Tonya
announced that she knew about the plot to attack Nancy
Kerrigan only after it had unfolded, and about a week before Jeff pleaded guilty, but several days after Shawn Eric
Eckardt complained to the Portland *Oregonian* that Tonya
had browbeaten him for not getting around to arranging
the assault as quickly as she wanted. It was a golden moment. It was probably the last moment when the fan club
members could believe that Tonya had been completely
uninvolved.

On the morning of the meeting, January 25, as on most
mornings since all the bad news, some of the club members went to the rink to watch Tonya practice. The ice was

empty except for Tonya, who was bent over in the corner, fixing a skate. She was wearing a stretchy black sleeveless catsuit over a stretchy gray tank leotard. Every contour of her body was outlined in black—her thick back, her strong upper legs, with their blocky muscles. She stood up and started down the length of the rink, her skates cutting feathery grooves in the ice. Her lips were pressed tight, and her chin was thrust forward. Her expression was wan and stubborn. Her ponytail fluttered out behind her. No other part of her seemed to move, but she was crossing the ice with tremendous speed. A snatch of music came over the loudspeaker. At the end of the rink, where a hundred or so people were gathered, she turned sharply, bent her leg, and then spun until the ice beneath her skate began to make a sizzling sound. Suddenly she stopped, skated toward the other end of the rink, spun again, pulled at the waist of her catsuit, then circled the ice once more. For an hour, she practiced pieces of her program—a spin, a leap, a movement of her leg or hand. The pieces were never fused together into something fluid or pretty. They were just explosions of motion between long silent moments, when Tonya would stand alone in the huge, blank rink, kicking at a frosty patch or tightening her skates. She didn't look happy, but she also didn't look rattled or embarrassed or shy. At the end of the hour, when she stepped off the ice, the club members told each other that she seemed composed and steady.

The club was meeting that day because the members had a lot of work to do. Since the attack, and since Tonya's victory at the nationals, the club, four hundred strong, had received hundreds of requests for membership information. Elaine Stamm, the club's founder and president, had printed up more copies of the flyer describing the memberships—ten dollars for adults, one dollar to join Tots for Tonya—and suggesting additional opportunities to support Tonya, by fund-raising, or by giving her cosmetics, hair care, and nail care, or by making calls about her to sports talk programs, or by mailing her encouraging cards. There were also scores of requests for Tonya buttons and bumper stickers, and for tapes of "It's Tonya's Turn," written and recorded by Linda and Greg Lewis, local songwriters who a few years ago composed a hit song about Desert Storm. Linda and Greg had stopped by that morning to make some last-minute arrangements with Elaine about the song. Linda was saying, "We're not skating fans so much, but we're Christians, and we thought this was the right thing to do."

The mall was a good place for the club to gather and get all this done. There really isn't a town of Clackamas. There are acres of Douglas fir forest and grassy idle pastures, and balding hills now sprouting subdivisions, and ranchettes on lawns of chunky red mulch, and squat new apartment complexes with tan siding and shiny driveways, and featherweight trailers perched on rough concrete blocks, and there are tumbledown old farmhouses on weedy tracts waiting to be seized and subdivided, and there are little strip malls and fast-food restaurants and glassy health clubs and tanning salons standing alone in enormous parking lots, and there are bushy fields of huckleberry, blackberry, sumac, and salal, and there are pockets of businesses having to do with toys and mufflers and furniture, but there really isn't any town to speak of, or even a village to drive through. Unlike an old-fashioned town, which spreads out organically, Clackamas County's settled areas look as if they had emerged abruptly, hacked out of the tangle of blackberry bushes and firs. Around the mall, new things are cropping up so fast that the place seems kinetic, as if everything had gone up, and could come down, in a day. Even where the county is overbuilt and busy, emptiness is the feeling it conveys.

Portland is half an hour's drive away from here. It is an old, compact city that was settled by Yankee merchants, who fashioned it after Boston. Portland is the largest city in Oregon, but it is of very little consequence to people like Tonya and Jeff and Shawn, who live in and rarely leave Clackamas and east Multnomah Counties. News reports that say Tonya is from Portland have missed the geographical and sociological point. The world that Clackamas County is part of starts somewhere in the Great Plains, skips over cities like Portland and Seattle, and then jumps up to Alaska—a world where people are plunked down on harsh or austere or overgrown landscapes and might depart from them at any moment, leaving behind only a few houses and some gear. Alaska, desolate and rugged and intractable, feels like an annex of Clackamas County, and Portland seems a million miles away. Alaska, not Portland, is also where many people from Oregon have often gone to get more land, or to make quick money by working for a summer in a fish cannery or on a logging crew. There is a Yukon Tavern in Clackamas County and a Klondike Jewelers, and at the nearby thrift stores you can find old table linens with Alaskan motifs—huskies, oil rigs, Eskimos—and old postcards of Alaskan landscapes and photographs of Juneau cannery crews and of log camps, scribbled with messages to the family back in Clackamas.

The winter weather in this part of Oregon is gray and drizzly, and the light is flat and filtered through a low ceiling of clouds. Occasionally, the clouds bust up, and it will rain in spats—you can be driving around and the rain will pour on your car but not on the car behind you. The most monumental thing in Clackamas County is Mount Hood, a mostly dormant volcano, which is 11,235 feet high and is snow-covered year-round. Mount Hood has several active, constantly creeping glaciers. Otherwise, the only ice regularly found in the county is the skating rink at the mall.

CLACKAMAS TOWN CENTER is a giant mall, the largest collection of retail stores in the state of Oregon; the space it encloses, more than a million square feet, is so much bigger than any other enclosed space nearby that when the mall opened, in 1981, it provoked a little local hysteria. Rumors went around the county that a band of hippies or Satanists was kidnapping children and taking them into the mall rest rooms and either castrating them or cutting off their hair, then painting their faces and letting them go. Psychologists later attributed the rumors to the unease of people who were accustomed to being isolated and outdoors, as they always had been in this part of Oregon, suddenly making regular visits to a place that was crowded and contained.

There is very little irony in the name Clackamas Town Center. Anything that goes on around here goes on at the mall. There are stores, of course, and also conference rooms where community groups like Alcoholics Anonymous and the Egg Artists of Oregon meet. And there is the skating rink, which the developers put in to satisfy local requirements for recreational facilities. In 1988, the developers proposed replacing the rink with a carousel, but at the public hearing on the matter, Tonya, who was only seventeen but already a nationally ranked skater, made a compelling plea to save it. The rink is Olympic-size, with big bleachers along one side. On the lower level of the mall, behind the bleachers, is a branch of the Clackamas County Library; a sign outside the door says, "YES! THIS REALLY IS A LIBRARY!" On the upper level of the mall, ringing most of the rink, is the food court, which may make this the only place in America where an Olympic contender trains within sight of the Steak Escape, Let's Talk Turkey, Hot Dog on a Stick, and Chick-fil-A.

On the morning of the meeting, Elaine Stamm, the president of the club, watched Tonya practice for an hour or so. That morning, when Tonya first came out on the ice, she was carrying a video camera to film the film crews who were in a press corral near the door to the skate shop. "Wasn't that cute?" Elaine said, on her way to the meeting room. "Wasn't that brave?" She was setting out boxes of flyers and tapes and Tonya buttons when someone quietly took her aside to say there was a problem: Somebody else needed to use the room. This was not a development as bad as, say, Jeff's guilty plea would eventually be, but it eroded morale. The club liked the idea of doing its work in the very spot where Tonya had developed into an Olympic contender. Nancy Welfelt, one of the members, suggested reconvening at her house, so the members got their coats, and fanned out through the parking lot to their cars, and formed a small convoy to the Welfelts'.

They drove up Eighty-second Avenue, past the Lovelier You Beauty Salon and the Beavers Inn and the Moneyman and the Junk-a-Rama, and then turned east, past Lincoln Willamette Funeral Directors, which had a digital sign flashing the time, the temperature, and then the message COMPARE! COMPLETE CHAPEL SERVICE WITH CASKET $1,997. A few blocks west of Eighty-second Avenue, on the edge of Multnomah County, is the neighborhood known as Lents. This is one of the places Tonya lived when she was growing up, and it's also not far from where Gary Gilmore lived for a time. Lents was settled first by farmers and then, in the 1930s and '40s, by shipyard and sheet-metal workers; today it consists of narrow, pitted roads that peter out into gravel alleys, with houses so tiny that some look as if they had been built for dolls or chickens, or were really meant to be one-car garages. In the neighborhood nearer the mall, where Tonya lives now, the houses are scant, speckling open acreage that used to be farms and woodlots. In Lents, everything is shoved together; nearly every house is on a parcel the size of a napkin, hemmed with a high chain-link fence, and in the yard there is usually a motor home and a dog kennel, and a tool-shed, and maybe a car chassis that someone has lost interest in fixing. Every block or so, squeezed between the houses, there is a church: New Testament Church of God and Christ, "Preaching a Living Christ to a Lost and Dying World"; the Church of Christ; the Bethel German Assembly of God.

The Welfelts' house is east of Eighty-second Avenue, in the Mount Scott neighborhood, which is on the steep side of Mount Scott, a small extinct volcano. On this side of Eighty-second Avenue, the houses thin out and are newer and nicer, with bright aluminum siding, and carports, and picture windows, and decorative screen doors. The convoy stopped at Nancy's driveway, and the club members lugged in the boxes of flyers and buttons and bumper stickers, and then pulled chairs up to the dining table. Along with Elaine, a former charm-school teacher, who has frosted hair and narrow, square shoulders and a striking imperial posture, and Nancy

Welfelt, who has a cheery face and fading blondish hair, there were four other middle-aged women, and the husband of one of them: a jittery guy with wire-rimmed glasses. He never sat down at the dining table and never even took off his coat, and then suddenly left during the meeting to go visit his parents' graves at the cemetery across the street. Someone complimented Nancy on the view from her living-room window, and she said, "You want to see something? See out there? You can see Shawn's house. Shawn, the bodyguard. He lives behind me, with his parents." Everyone crowded to the window and looked in the direction Nancy was pointing, across the side of the hill and over the tops of some houses wrapped in fog.

One of the other women said, "Have you ever seen Tonya's mother's trailer? It's just up the road here, and it is meticulous. It is lovely. It is tidy. You would never even know it's a trailer."

"Trailer trash is what they call people out here," another woman said to me. She sat down and started tapping on the table with her fingernails. They were long and burgundy-colored, and each one had a different small image painted on it—a shooting star, a sun, a lightning bolt. She said, "There are plenty of people who think we're scum because we live out here on the east side. Well, I live in a very non-scum neighborhood. It's actually a so-called good neighborhood, but it's always going to be thought of as trash, because it's east side." She tapped. Her fingernails clicked: lightning bolt, star, sun.

"I wouldn't say trash," Elaine said. "I would say . . . I would say . . ." She paused. "Well, my heart just went out to Tonya when I first saw her skate. I just see that little gal out there, the abused child spanked by her mother with a hairbrush, and when they would do the up-close-and-personals for the Olympic skaters, they showed Tonya in her jeans at her little house fixing her car, and I could just feel her sink. When I started the club, the people I heard from were women with abusive husbands, and Vietnam vets who had come home and felt displaced, and they'd see that little gal and feel really good about themselves. So it's funny that people would think of her as trash."

"Scum," the nail woman snapped. "That's what they call us. It's a class difference—that's what all this mess is about Tonya. She's just a regular Clackamas County girl. In my opinion, she's a modern gal, what we would call a tomboy. She can hunt, she can fix a car. She calls herself the Charles Barkley of figure skating, and she's right. She's a stud."

Another one of the women said, "I'll tell you, you know who I cannot stand is that Kristi Yamaguchi." Everyone groaned. She rolled her eyes, and went on, "She is just so prissy. Tonya is so tough. She *is* a stud! She really is!"

The nail woman said, "You know, there are a lot of us who look at Tonya and think to ourselves, There's a gal who pulled herself up, who had some tough times with her folks, and whatever, and she still did great by her dreams. I know what it's like to have dreams and to perform. When I was a kid, I was a performer. I was on that radio show *Stars of Tomorrow*, and I got tons of trophies for my singing."

Nancy said, "You were a singer? You sang?"

"All the time—oh, yeah, all the time," she said. "I had just tons of trophies. I don't have them anymore. My dad threw them all out."

Elaine said, "Why did he do that?"

"Well," the woman said, shrugging and tapping, "we just don't get along."

TANYA UTBERG, the Clackamas County Fair and rodeo queen, said to me recently, "I think Clackamas County is a very warmy place," which makes it sound soothing and regular, but often it seems to be a more haphazard and disjointed place than that. The day I talked to the Rodeo Queen, I drove out to the neighborhood where Tonya Harding and Jeff Gillooly used to live, and where Tonya still lives. Her house is in a part of Clackamas County called Beavercreek. Beavercreek isn't shown on any street map—it's just an area, not far from a small city called Happy Valley, which is where Tonya's mother is currently living. Tonya's road in Beavercreek is a skinny rib that runs along a foothill, past a spread of newish one-story houses. Tonya's house, an A-frame chalet, is at the end of a long driveway and is not visible from the road. At the end of her driveway were a white farm gate, a big homemade heart-shaped sign left by some fans, and several No Trespassing notices. A few miles farther along the road, not far from the Savage Mini-Mall, I stopped at a new housing development, and the real estate broker gave me a tour of one of the houses. When it is finished, the development will be called Sunset Springs Estates. The broker didn't know what had been on the property before it was subdivided, but a few scraggly fruit trees out back provided a hint. In bright weather, the Sunset Springs houses will have a distant view of the wolf-fang shape of Mount Hood and a close view of a new development called McBride Estates, and of a woeful old farm undoubtedly in line to have the earth turned up under it so someone can sow some more houses. The broker said, "Sun-

set Springs Estates are going to be real lovely places when they're done."
Then he gazed out the window and said, "It is sort of funny around here.
Everything is such a big mix-match. You have one kind of thing right next
to another kind of thing, like lots of money beside poor. That's what I call
a real mix-match. Things don't always fit together as well as they should."

TUESDAY AND THURSDAY are Cheapskate Nights at the skating
rink—for four dollars, you can rent skates and skate for two hours. A big
banner advertising Cheapskate Nights hangs above the ice, next to one,
paid for by the fan club, that says HOME OF TONYA HARDING—U.S. FIGURE
SKATING CHAMPION. Saturday evening isn't for cheapskates, but it's the
busiest night. On the Saturday after the fan club meeting, the ice was
packed. You can watch the rink from the mall's upper level, standing between a kiosk with a public-service poster that says SUPPORT THE U.S.
OLYMPIC TEAM: GO SHOPPING and a small business called All About Names,
which is set up on a rolling cart. For a couple of dollars, you can get
printed on a number of different items, such as beer steins and key chains,
or on a piece of fancy paper, a little legend about almost any name. I asked
the woman working at the cart to do the name Tonya on pink paper with a
drawing of a fairy castle, and she said, "Tonya? Ton-ya? *Tonya?* I've never
heard of that before. What a nice, interesting name." That morning's *Oregonian* had had a story about Nancy Kerrigan on the front page for the sev-
enteenth day in a row. The woman at the cart punched some buttons on a
computer, and after a moment the paper came out. It said that "Tonya"
was Latin for "priceless," and that a Tonya was "a liberated spirit" who "has
never settled down to any one thing . . . is attractive, lively, and tasteful . . .
sets high expectations and fulfills them." Down below, kids were whizzing
around showing off, or inching along the edge of the ice, clinging to one
another in wobbly packs. A lot of the girls looked like Tonya, with long
multilevel blond hair and a puff of bangs, eyes rimmed in black liner, and
stocky bodies in inexpensive-looking clothes. In the center of the ice, a few
skinny girls in Lycra skating dresses were practicing spins. Until recently,
Tonya sometimes practiced during open-skate hour, picking her way
through the crowd. Now she skates only very late at night, but for a long
time she usually practiced in the mornings, when the ice was empty but
the bleachers were filled with people eating tacos and gyros and Dilly Deli
sandwiches and looking on.

Around here, kids go to the movies, or they drive up and down Eighty-second Avenue, or they hang out at the mall. If they work at it, they can get into trouble. A juvenile court counselor named Steve Houseworth told me that in the last two years, kids in the county, like kids in counties all over the country, have become increasingly hedonistic, defiant, and angry, and that juvenile arrests have boomed. "Our big problem is with antisocial pre-planned deviant behavior," he said. "We've got an explosion of anger, intimidation, and aggression issues. I think we'll see more of it, too, because the county is growing real hard and real fast." The county, he went on, is trying out a privately run anger-management program called Temper Talk, which offers counseling to juveniles charged with Assault 3 or Assault 4—causing harm to a person without intent or with intent, respectively.

The program director for Temper Talk, Derek Bliss, told me, "Kids here are looking for power and they want control. They're angry about dominance. They want to show the image and reputation of dominance." I asked him whether he recognized the likes of Shawn and Jeff and of Shane Stant, the twenty-two-year-old man who had been paid to attack Nancy Kerrigan. "Definitely," he said. "These are the kind of guys who lose their temper but don't know how to *use* their temper. Shane, the one who confessed to actually doing the assault—he's a very big boy. He's not behind physically for his age-group, but he's clearly behind empathetically. I'd bet there was a humongous amount of inconsiderate behavior in their lives before this assault."

On Saturday night, I talked with two young guys, D. J. Dollar Bill and D. J. Fast Eddie, who were standing on a platform beside the skate rental booth, playing tapes over the loudspeakers and calling out for the kids to reverse directions, and then to speed up, and then to get ready to line up for games. Dollar Bill said he was a delivery driver for an auto supply company. Fast Eddie said he worked in the produce section of a grocery store. Fast Eddie also said he could not comment on Tonya. "What I'm about is right here," he said, motioning to the ice, "and here is fun." He put on a Snoop Doggy Dogg song and then said, "We're going to play some great games later. We just finished a big one. It's the favorite around here. We break up into teams and compete in four events—the ringtoss, ice basketball, ice golf, and a finale, which is a snowball race with a snowball on your head. We call it 'The Olympic Ménage à Trois.' "

CELEBRATION NEW SONG FOUR-SQUARE CHURCH, a Pentecostal congregation, meets every Sunday in a room at the Holiday Inn in

Gresham, a town just north of the Clackamas County line. The pastor
of the church, Eugene Saunders, hadn't been seen in three weeks—that
is, since shortly after the night that he was doing homework with Shawn
Eckardt, the heavyset baby-faced bodyguard and self-described foreign
espionage operative, who was a classmate of Gene's in a legal-assistant
training program at Pioneer Pacific College. That night, Shawn had
bragged to Gene that he was involved in setting up an attack on a figure
skater, and played a garbled tape of a planning session for him. It was that
conversation—which Gene repeated first to a Pioneer Pacific teacher, a
private investigator (who repeated it to the Portland *Oregonian*), and then
to the authorities—that broke the case open. The publicity that followed
was so overwhelming and relentless that Gene decided to go underground.

On Sunday, I went to church, and Reverend Saunders reappeared. In
the newspaper box outside the Holiday Inn, the headlines were still all
about Tonya. Inside, nineteen people were gathered in a meeting room,
among them a weary-looking older couple with a strange, thin, shrill-
voiced boy; a young woman with two restless redhaired children; a man
with stringy blond hair that hung to his shoulder blades, sitting with a
pretty woman who wore her hair in cornrows, and was the only black
person I saw the whole time I was in Clackamas County; a ruddy-faced
man with pinkish eyelids and full lips, wearing a worn-out chambray work
shirt and holding in his lap a Bible and a Bible study guide; a man, maybe
around seventy, with greased-back black hair and thick glasses, wearing a
plastic windbreaker and a short striped necktie. In the front of the small
room, a big, bearded man holding a zebra-striped electric guitar began
strumming and singing in a tender voice. Everyone rose, scraping back tan
metal folding chairs. Someone turned on an overhead projector, and a
handwritten lyric sheet flashed in a crooked rectangle across the wall and
ceiling, and then the congregation sang. The room was new and drab; the
floor felt hollow. Outside, it was pouring. The motel was so new that there
was no lawn yet, or even mulch—only mud and construction equipment,
and fresh sidewalks, which looked silvery in the rain. After one of the
songs, the man with the greased-back hair stepped forward and began a
rhythmic declaration from the back of his throat. He was speaking in
tongues, and he went on for several minutes, shouting and sweating and
slapping his thighs. Finally, he paused, wiped his brow, and then translated what he had to say—that Jesus was coming, that Jesus was watching,
that anyone who followed Jesus and resisted Satan would never go astray.

When he finished, Gene Saunders came to the front of the room. He is a handsome, fleshy young man with small, crowded features; he was wearing a dress shirt and suspenders, and holding an open can of Mountain Dew. He said, "I know you've been wondering a lot of things—some of you have known where I've been, but mostly you've known that I just needed to take a break from the publicity. We got calls from around the world. We got calls from Japan about this. I want to tell you folks a few things. First of all, you know that I am not Shawn's pastor. I think some of you read something saying that he was with us—that I was his pastor—and you were thinking, Hey, we don't know this guy. Well, we were classmates in school. I'm not his pastor." He chuckled. "I suppose he could use one now." People nodded, and bumped one another with their elbows. "Also, I want you to know I never changed my story. I always said I couldn't understand the tape. It was a garbled tape. It started getting into press reports that I could understand the tape, and then at the grand jury hearing I testified that I couldn't, and everyone is asking me why I changed my story. I didn't. It was misrepresented that way."

Someone called out, "That was Satan working! That's how the enemy works—confusing us with things we didn't say!" Gene nodded, and sipped from the can. He strolled around the front of the room. "It's been tough for me, because I've had to neglect you and the church business during all of this, and I've had to make choices. I shouldn't say this in front of our treasurer, but I was offered fifty thousand dollars to tell my story to a television show, and I turned it down." From the back of the room, someone said, "Reverend, we could sure have used that money!" and everyone laughed. Gene said, "Well, I turned everything down. We'll just have to keep fundraising for ourselves. But, you know, that was real temptation."

"Why did they do it, Reverend?"

He looked down, kicking lightly at the carpeting. "Bitterness, I think. Bitterness that things weren't going their way."

The ruddy-faced man flipped his study guide open to Luke 14. "All the answers are right here," he whispered to me. He ran a fingernail across the page, to where it said, "Wanting a new car or hoping to be successful in your career is not wrong in itself—it is wrong only when you want these things just to impress others." He closed the book and then closed his eyes.

Gene finished speaking and shook everyone's hand, and said he would be back every Sunday unless things got too distracting again.

THE THREE SISTERS

*I*N BULGARIA, SOME TENNIS BALLS ARE LIKE dumplings. Manuela, Katerina, and Magdalena Maleeva, Bulgarian sisters who are three of the best tennis players in the world and definitely the three best tennis players in Bulgaria, know all about putting topspin on a dumpling. They also know how to park themselves at the baseline and bang back every dumpling that comes over the net. The flabby, bounceless tennis balls in Bulgaria come from Poland, where they are manufactured to international standards and then, apparently, overcooked. This might discourage some players, but the Maleevas are not easily discouraged. In fact, they may be the least discourageable people in Bulgaria. No world-class tennis players have ever before emerged from that country. One year, the three Maleeva sisters made up the entire Bulgarian Federation Cup tennis team. Youlia Berberian, their mother and also their coach, was the team captain. There are no Maleev brothers, so there's never been much of a men's team.

Each of the sisters excelled in Bulgaria, and then each, in turn, joined the WTA Tour, which has about 360 players and runs sixty tournaments in twenty countries. Manuela played on the tour for twelve years (she retired this winter), and was ranked among the top ten in the world for ten years, won nineteen tournaments, and earned $3.5 million in prize money. Katerina joined the tour in 1985 and has also done nicely. Last week, she and Georgi Stoimenov, who now coaches her, were married. Earlier, I had asked Youlia Berberian if Katerina was going to have a fancy wedding. I got the feeling that Youlia considered this a stupid question. She didn't say anything for a moment, while eyeing me with exasperation. Then she shrugged and said, "She's a very rich and famous girl, you know. People in Bulgaria will be *expecting* a fancy wedding."

The three Maleevas and their mother were in Paris in late May for the French Open, which is held on the orange clay courts of Stade Roland Garros. Their goals were (a) to win the tournament and (b) to buy dresses to wear to Katerina's wedding. Regarding (b), Youlia was the most highly motivated, because she lives in Bulgaria, where the shopping is hell. Manuela got married six years ago and lives in Switzerland, where the shopping is not hell, but she thought she'd find something nicer in Paris. Magdalena, who is nineteen and is called Maggie, lives at home in shopping-hell Bulgaria with her parents, but she didn't seem overly concerned about her wedding outfit. During the time I spent with the Maleevas, Maggie wore either tennis clothes or one outfit of street clothes: a pair of tight burgundy-colored jeans, a long-sleeved burgundy T-shirt, and a pewter peace symbol on a short chain around her neck. Also, she had just dyed her hair a color between burgundy and a young Chardonnay. People tend to think that Maggie will turn out to be the best tennis player of the three sisters, because she has the diligence and finesse that made Manuela and Katerina successful, but she is more athletic and aggressive and plays a more varied game. So far, Maggie has been ranked as high as tenth in the world, and has earned close to a million dollars in prize money. She and I were talking one afternoon in Paris and I asked her what she was going to do with all the money she is winning, and as an afterthought I added that I doubted she would spend it shopping for clothes. She was wearing her burgundy outfit at the time. She said, "Oh, no, no, I *love* shopping. You can spend lots of money shopping." I asked her what she'd bought lately, and she grinned and said, "Well, I just got a really, really great pair of combat boots."

. . .

THEY DON'T LOOK anything alike. Manuela, who is twenty-seven, is pale and slender. Her face is tiny and refined and tragic-looking. Because she is fair and narrow, she looks taller than she is—about five feet eight—and slightly translucent. Her voice is high, sleepy, and shy. Her manner is dignified and tender. On the court, during matches, she used to project an air of enormous sorrow, even when she was up five games and was slugging a winner down the line. People in Japan used to camp out in the lobby of her hotel just to catch a glimpse of her. She has a huge fan club in Japan—she's probably the only Bulgarian who can make that claim. Some of this Japanese adoration ebbed after she got married. The 1994 French Open was the first in twelve years that she had watched rather than played in. She says she decided to retire because she had come to hate her suitcase. At the tournament, she wore little white shorts, a lacy white blouse, black Ray-Bans, black mules, and pink lipstick, which made her look like a French television star.

Katerina, who is twenty-five, is meatier-looking than Manuela. She has a square, contemplative face and silky dark hair, which during her career she has worn short and bouncy or long and braided or swept across her forehead and held in a clip; each variation completely transforms her. She has dark eyes and a golden tinge to her complexion. Her gaze is level and so stern that it struck me as something she could use as a weapon on the court. Like all the Maleevas, she speaks English fluently, but her locutions are formal and ornate: "To this, I will have to again say no." "To that, the answer is personal which is how I will be keeping it."

The first time I saw Maggie was in a rainstorm in Lucerne, at the site of the Eurocard Open, a clay tournament that is a French Open warm-up, and I was immediately struck by the interesting color of her hair. She is no bigger than Katerina, but she has a lumbering, pigeon-toed walk that makes her look as if she were a huge person, or as if she had just come a long distance on horseback. On the court, she usually wears a very short white tennis skirt and tight white Lycra bike shorts, which stick out below the skirt. She has hazel eyes and a long chin and a wide mouth. She seems to find herself a curiosity. Describing her nontennis interests, she says, "I'm famous for liking hard rock music. I'm known for liking a band called Nine Inch Nails."

All three of the Maleeva sisters were taught to play by Youlia, so their games have certain similarities—trim ground strokes, neat footwork. Otherwise, because of their different bodies and temperaments and talents, each has her own style. Manuela, for instance, learned to play in the era of Chris Evert, when nearly all women players were baseliners, with methodical, unvarying ground strokes and two-handed backhands and the patience to wait for their opponents' mistakes. Katerina is also a baseliner, but her strokes are especially flat and her swing is taut and compact, and she is very fast on her feet. By the time Maggie, who is eight years younger than Manuela, started playing, baselining was no longer enough to win points, so she learned to move around the court more, to switch between one- and two-handed backhands, to use more topspin, and to dominate points. The three always hated to play one another in tournaments. Nevertheless, there have been fifteen occasions when one Maleeva played another on the tour: Manuela has beaten Katerina eight times, Katerina has beaten Manuela once, Manuela has beaten Maggie twice, Katerina has beaten Maggie four times. In 1993, all three reached the fourth round of the French Open and the U.S. Open—a first in the annals of sibling athletics. That year, the three Maleevas were ranked within four places of one another among the top twenty women in the world.

In some instances, the sisters have teamed up to use their tennis success commercially; all three are represented by the same agent at Advantage International, and all three have had deals with Babolat tennis strings and Isostar high-performance drinks. Katerina and Maggie were also celebrity spokespersons for Balkan, the official airline of Bulgaria.

Occasionally, the number of Maleevas and their longevity and their persistence near the top of the tennis world has unnerved other players. Theories about them abound. One rumor has it that the girls were under strict orders from Youlia never to have a younger sister beat an older one. Ruxandra Dragomir, a Romanian player, who drew Maggie in the first round of the French Open, told me after their match that she thought Maggie had had a bit of an unfair advantage over her. I asked her what it was, and she shrugged and said, "Well, you know, the sisters. She has all those sisters all over the place." Pam Shriver, in a book she wrote several years ago, said that the Maleevas always moped when they played, whether they won or lost, and that Manuela and Katerina (Maggie was not yet on the tour) were known among the other players as Boo and Hoo. There have been other pairs of siblings in tennis, such as Chris and Jeanne Evert, John and Patrick McEnroe, and Luke and Murphy Jensen, but before the Maleevas there had never been a family in which *all* the children were tennis players, there had never been three same-sex tennis-playing siblings, there had never been three tennis-playing Bulgarians, there had never been three tennis-playing Bulgarian sisters, and there had never been three tennis-playing siblings—Bulgarian or female or not—ranked so close together and so high up in the sport. It occurred to me when I met the Maleevas that I had never before met people with so many signifying adjectives you could attach to their names.

I WANTED TO have a dinner with all three of the Maleeva sisters. "Let me know if you can do that," Youlia said to me. "I personally would like to accomplish that sometime. If you get that done, that will be an almost incredible thing." At the moment, Manuela was on her way to Paris from Switzerland with her husband, François Fragnière; Maggie had just arrived from Lucerne, where she had played in the Eurocard Open; Katerina was flying to Paris from Bulgaria, where she had been resting after playing in a tournament in Hamburg; and George Maleev, their father, who is an electronics professor, was at his job in Sofia, teaching school. Nobody knew anybody else's schedule. "You know the way we are," Youlia said. "We can try to have dinner the night after the first round, but I can't guarantee who will be here. The minute—God forbid, God forbid, I won't even say it, God forbid—someone loses, we are gone as fast as we can. We *go*."

Youlia and I were sitting in the lobby of the Hotel Sofitel, in Paris, where many of the players in the Open were staying; a corner of the lobby had been cordoned off as a players' lounge. Youlia was sitting on a black leather couch, eating fancy cookies from a platter on the coffee table. She was wearing a big green T-shirt, paisley leggings, Christian Dior eyeglasses with complicated frames, and tennis shoes. Her feet are very small, and she has lean calves and little ankles. She is forty-nine years old. As a young woman, she was a nine-time Bulgarian women's singles tennis champion. From the knees down, that is still what she looks like. From the knees up, she looks a little more like somebody's mother. Her hair is chestnut-colored and fluffy. She has beautiful pinkish skin; an aquiline nose; a rubbery, downturned mouth; and huge dimples, which crease her face even when she isn't smiling. Her voice is a porous, trilling soprano; it is round and light and girlish, which Youlia is not. After you meet Youlia, the phrase that leaps to your mind is "human dynamo." She is someone who seems very good at getting things done. She says that she is a very tough coach, and that her philosophy is "Winning is everything." I did not directly observe Youlia working with her daughters, but I believe I experienced some of her technique. That afternoon, for instance, I asked her how she happened to start playing tennis as a young woman in Bulgaria.

"Are you familiar with the Ottoman Empire?" she said.

I told her I was hoping that her answer would be somewhat more contemporary.

"I need to explain this to you," she said firmly. She settled back on the couch. "When you understand the Ottoman Empire, and the situation between the Turks and the Armenians, then we will get to the tennis." She began with Alexander the Great's conquest of western Asia Minor, the Battle of Manzikert, and an account of Suleiman II; I found myself listening and taking notes in spite of myself. Players and their entourages were wandering in and out of the lounge. Someone came in and made an announcement about transportation to Roland Garros. Youlia ignored all this and went on. She was somewhere around the 1718 Treaty of Passarowitz when Maggie, who had been jogging with Katerina's fiancé, came in.

"Mom, did my box from Reebok come yet?" Maggie asked. Youlia looked up and nodded. "Anything interesting?" Maggie asked. "I mean, what am I wearing tomorrow?" She poked around on the cookie platter. Youlia answered her in Bulgarian, which sounded like air rushing past an open window. Then she waved Maggie away and got back to the Ottoman Empire.

At some point, she segued into her own history, including her Armenian heritage, which enabled her parents to emigrate to the United States in 1965 as part of Bulgaria's recognition of the Armenian genocide of 1915. Her parents have lived in the United States ever since. In 1965, Youlia was already a star tennis player in Bulgaria and was engaged to George, who was not allowed to emigrate, because he is not Armenian. She went to the United States briefly, then returned to Bulgaria and married George, and continued competing. Because the tennis courts were a nice place to bring babies, after Manuela and Katerina were born she just took them along to the courts.

In 1979, when Manuela was twelve and was just a few months away from being the national women's champion in Bulgaria, Youlia decided to apply for visas to take her to an American tournament. "I heard about this famous Orange Bowl in Miami, so I went for a visa, for which I had to faint and cry and beg and weep and *plead,* which is what I had to do for the next seven years," she told me. "My God, I can't tell you how much I hate the Communists for that humiliation—my God! But we got the visas and went to this famous Orange Bowl and Manuela played, and in the semifinals she had to play Chris Evert's sister, there, in Florida, which was their *kingdom*, and Manuela was such a brave girl, God, she was so brave"—now Youlia was in tears—"playing in her homemade dress, and she only had three racquets, while the other kids had ten and their shiny bright clothes, and the chair umpire made this bad call and she was *robbed*, and she was such a brave little girl. She took it very hard. She cried and cried. She cried at every point. This is when it is hard to be a mother and a coach. But I was so, so strong. I was such a strong person then. I would sit on the side of the court and talk to Manuela the whole time during the match. I would say, 'Manuela, why are you crying? Hit the ball down the line, please. Stop crying, thank you. Use some topspin on your backhand now. Please stop crying. *Thank you.*' "

Just then, a woman working for the tournament came over and said she knew of a store in Paris where she thought Youlia might find a good dress for Katerina's wedding. Youlia dabbed her face dry and thanked her. Then she leaned over to me and said, "You know, I need to find something nice but not too, too nice. I don't want to look like the Queen of England and be too, you understand, too 'up,' because there will be so many relatives and people from the countryside, and I don't want to make some kind of appearance, but I want something nice." She got teary again. She took her glasses off and started drying them on her T-shirt. Then she looked at them and said, "These glasses, you know, I love them, but I didn't even *know* they were Christian Dior until a friend of mine told me. I just thought they were nice. I don't know anything about Christian Dior! I just said to her, 'Well, I love them so much because they feel so nice!' "

Youlia said that the name Maleeva was now practically a trademark in Bulgaria. Then she said, "You know, if we were American we would be huge."

By now, it was quite late, and I said I would have to get going. I mumbled something about how I had planned to go for a run, but supposed it was a little late. Youlia turned and fixed her gaze on me; it said a million things, but all she said was "Oh. Hmm. It isn't too late. Go do your run." She stood up and left. I went upstairs to my room, turned on the television, lay down on my bed, tried not to think about Youlia, got up after about thirty seconds, turned off the television, put on my running clothes, and went out for an hour, racing around and around the hotel. The next morning, I bumped into Youlia on the elevator. I started to say something about the tournament, but she interrupted me. "I have only one question," she

said. "Now I will ask. After you left last night, did you go out and do your
run?"

A TALL SWISS KID with radish-colored cheeks had been sitting next to
me eating cold frankfurters out of a plastic box as Maggie started playing
her third-round match in Lucerne, at the Eurocard Open, the week before
the French Open. The weather was lousy. The matches had been interrupted several times by wild rainstorms, and the doubles competition had
been canceled so that all the courts could be used to complete the singles
draw. The grandstand was mostly empty. Youlia was sitting alone at the far
end of the court, so she could follow the game without moving her eyes
back and forth, which happens to give her a headache. Manuela, who lives
about two hours from Lucerne, had come to town to watch Maggie. She
sat alone, hugging her knees, across the court from Youlia. They rarely sit
together. This is because Youlia gets nervous watching her daughters play,
and her nervousness makes Manuela nervous. Everyone has been getting
nervous lately when Katerina plays, because she has had a tough year on
the tour and has sagged in the rankings. If you ask Manuela about it, her
face crumples like tissue, and she says, "I know all about this. The pressure, the pressure, the pressure. It's very, very, very *tough*. It's mental. It's
in the head. It's not in the hand."

Beating a Maleeva has always paid a big dividend. Because the
Maleevas are highly ranked, any player who beats one of them earns a lot
of points on the tennis-ranking computer, which rewards victories in proportion to the size of the tournament as well as according to the ranking of
the defeated player. On the other hand, the Maleevas have never been
quite as fear-inspiring as some other top-ranked players, like Steffi Graf. In
fact, the Maleevas believe that most of their opponents play the best games
of their lives against them. The family phrase for this phenomenon is "out
of her mind," as in "The girl who beat Katerina usually can hardly hit the
ball, but against Katerina she was playing *out of her mind*." In the third
round in Lucerne, Maggie was facing an out-of-her-mind situation. She
was the second seed in the tournament. The first seed was Lindsay Davenport, a gigantic, scowling high school student from California, with big legs
and big arms and big shoulders, who had just bounded into the top ten. All
the players in the tournament seemed a little afraid of her. They seemed
less afraid of Maggie. In her second round, Maggie had struggled against a
tiny Israeli girl named Anna Smashnova, who was unseeded in the tourna-

ment and is ranked eighty-seven places below Maggie. Youlia was sitting next to Smashnova's coach during the match, and she turned her chair so she could glare at him between points. After Maggie finally won, 3–6, 6–1, 6–1, Youlia muttered to me, "I watched that little girl play yesterday and she hit nothing but moon balls. She couldn't hit anything flat. Then she plays Maggie and boom, boom, *bang!* Everything is flat. She played out of her mind."

In this third round, Maggie was playing Lisa Raymond, a peppy Floridian with a pointy face, a streaky blond ponytail, and four earrings in one ear. At the time, Raymond was ranked fifty-ninth in the world. She has a solid serve, a topspinning backhand, a good slice, and a bouncy stride on the court. As the first set began, Maggie was hitting a lot of her passing shots out, and a few of her overheads were wild and wide; then she steadied herself and began serving well and playing as many volleys as she could off her backhand, which she hits hard and sharply down the line. In contrast to Katerina and Manuela, who rarely move off the baseline, Maggie dashed around the court and came to the net several times. Still, most of the games went to deuce and were decided on errors—Maggie's, usually. Raymond eventually won the first set, seven games to five.

The rain started again. During the break, we went into the players' lounge, a big white tent set up behind the courts. Tennis racquets and racquet cases were piled up near the door. Raymond sat down next to Lindsay Davenport, whose match had also been suspended. Helena Sukova, a Czech player, who started on the tour the same year as Manuela, stood in a corner, dripping from the rainstorm, and flexed her legs. Maggie sat across the room, stretching to keep from cramping, and chatting with the tournament's massage therapist about Jennifer Capriati, who had recently been arrested on a drug charge. "I didn't know her too well, but I thought she was cool," Maggie said. "She was a cool person. I faxed her a letter the other day to tell her I thought she was cool." Manuela and Youlia were at the other end of the tent, faxing a note to Katerina, in Bulgaria, and glancing every few moments at Maggie. A few other players and their coaches were milling around, talking about their travel plans for Paris. Everyone who had lost her match was leaving Lucerne immediately, because the French Open was starting in three days. The losers seemed cheerful. It occurred to me that the best players on the tour are always the last ones to leave, because everyone who loses has either gone home or gone on to the next tournament. No one sticks around just to watch someone else win. Players would rather be early at the next tournament site. Linda Harvey-

Wild, a Chicagoan, was one of the people in the tent. I asked her how long she was going to be in Lucerne, and she said, "Hey, not much longer! I lost! I'm done! I'm out of here! If I can get a flight, I'm leaving for Paris today!"

After an hour or so, the rain let up, and, once the courts had been mopped, the matches resumed. Maggie would hit several strong shots and then a string of reckless ones, and as she got frustrated her body seemed to get disorganized. Youlia was now leaning over the railing of the grandstand. The boy with the frankfurters was gone, so I edged closer to Youlia. The second set went to 3–0, in Raymond's favor, and then it began to drizzle again. We headed back to the lounge. Youlia walked beside Maggie and said something to her in Bulgarian, and then added, in a low voice, "She's playing out of her mind."

"*Mom,*" Maggie said, grimacing.

Manuela walked next to them, saying nothing. The rain stopped after a few minutes, and the courts were sponged dry again. The two players went back onto the court. Raymond had tightened her ponytail, and it seemed to be pulling back the corners of her eyes. She looked fierce. One of her shots nicked the line and was called in; Maggie bounced her racquet on its head and then walked over to the umpire, saying, "What? Are you *craaazy?*" Her accent made the word *crazy* sound lulling and poetic. She did not get the call, did not win the game, and did not win the match. The final score was 7–5, 6–4, Raymond. As soon as the match was over, Youlia stood up, walked quickly to the lounge, and headed for the phone, to call about flights to Paris. Maggie slung her racquet cases over her shoulder and trudged toward the locker room. Manuela followed her in and didn't emerge for several minutes. In the car back to the hotel, Maggie cried a little and then stared out at a cottony fog that had wrapped around the Alps. After a moment, she rubbed her nose and said, "I wish I had won. It's kind of a bummer."

THE RICHEST, most famous sisters in Bulgaria did not have the best time of their lives at the Grand Slams this summer. At Wimbledon, Katerina drew the second seed, Aranxta Sánchez Vicario, in the first round and lost; Maggie beat Shaun Stafford in the first but was upset by an unknown Indonesian player in the second. In the French Open, Maggie had been seeded thirteenth, but she lost in her first-round match against Ruxandra Dragomir. They had played each other many times before in Bulgaria, starting when Ruxandra was fourteen and Maggie was twelve, and Maggie had usually won. Ruxandra admitted to me afterward that she hadn't been too happy when she saw she was facing Maggie in the first round. "I was like, Oh my God," she said. "It was like, I wish I wasn't playing her. But today I was really confident, and she wasn't expecting me to play so well, so she got scared." For the next day or two, I hardly saw Maggie around at all. I asked Manuela how Maggie was. She said, "She had two days that were not very good. That's how it is. She'll be okay." When I finally saw Maggie again, she was wearing her burgundy outfit and did seem okay, although she looked slightly peaked. Unlike other first-round losers, she wasn't packing for home or for Wimbledon, because her whole family, except for her father, was for the moment residing in Paris at the hotel. Also, she had decided at the last minute to play the doubles competition with Katerina.

The evening after Maggie lost to Ruxandra, I'd seen Youlia in the lounge. She was wearing thick-soled sneakers and a T-shirt from last year's Wimbledon. She said that Dragomir had gotten lucky. "Do you remember that one incredible shot she hit? One of her strings was broken, and she hit such a risky shot, a backhand down the line. That gave her such a boost." She sighed deeply, and then said, "This is when it can kill you to be a mother and a coach. This is when it can kill you to have tennis in your family."

Katerina played Linda Harvey-Wild in her first round. During the match, her fiancé, Georgi, sat beside Youlia, but Maggie and Manuela, as usual, sat several rows apart and some distance from their mother. Katerina played an orderly and unyielding game, while Harvey-Wild was batting most of her passing shots into the net, double-faulting, and missing easy overheads. When the match was over, all the Maleevas looked exhausted and relieved. Two days later, in the second round, Katerina played a beefy German named Marketa Kochta. During the match, Kochta's coach sat at one end of the grandstand, and the Maleevas broke with family tradition and sat together at the other end. Katerina won the first set, 6–0, but then lost the next two, 3–6 and 2–6. As the match went on, she looked more and more solemn; in the stands her mother and her sisters sat more and more upright, their faces pulled into frowns. Kochta looked more and more surprised, and when she finally won she looked as if she might faint.

SERIOUSLY SILLY

*F*OR A WHILE, SILLY BILLY WAS OF THE MIND that all clowns were fungible. This was in 1989, when his business as a children's entertainer in New York began growing by leaps and bounds; he couldn't personally satisfy all the requests he was getting to appear at birthday parties, so he decided to add personnel. The first was a social worker he saw doing an impromptu routine at a children's Christmas party. Silly Billy was so impressed that he offered to make the social worker his supplementary clown. He named him Silly Willy and taught him the Silly Billy act, which is a mixture of clowning, magic, balloon sculpture, and wisecracks. If clients called when his own calendar was filled, Silly Billy would offer Silly Willy in his stead. For a year or so, the addition of Silly Willy was sufficient, but the children's party market kept expanding, and Silly Billy eventually had to hire Silly Milly and Silly Dilly. Before they were sent out as Silly Billy affiliates, he taught them the fundamental balloon animals (several breeds of dogs, a duck, a mouse, and a bird) and at least ten good tricks, like Hippety-Hop Rabbits, Farmyard Frolics, Vanishing Ketchup Bottle, Milk Pitcher on Head, and Mixed-Up Santa. For consistency, all the clowns were dressed like Silly Billy—floppy felt hat, red T-shirt, miniature necktie, patchwork pants, rainbow suspenders, mismatched sneakers, no makeup, and lensless plastic eyeglass frames approximately three times normal size—and they all used Silly Billy's magic word, "Googly-googly." This is how Silly Billy came to dominate the clown industry in New York. Not only was he able to supply quality clowns in the Silly Billy mold but he could also diversify price points. If you call his company, The Funniest Clowns in the Whole Wide World, you can request a $100 clown, which would be one of the associate Sillies, or a $150 clown, which would be Silly Willy, or you can go for the top, which means engaging the services of Silly Billy himself, who charges from $250 to $400 and is the preeminent clown in town.

SILLY BILLY TRAVELS HEAVY. On the job, he carries a fiberboard case that is four feet high and two feet wide and weighs about eighty-five pounds. On a busy day—that is, a day when he is booked at five or six birthday parties around the city—he might have to hoist the case into and out of half a dozen different taxis. Cabdrivers often decline the opportunity to assist him. Sometimes they look at his case, then look at his patchwork pants and his tiny necktie and his rainbow suspenders and his mismatched sneakers, with their Mickey & Pals Bow Biters, and then look back at the case and crack "Hey, whaddya got in there, pal, a dead body?" and Silly will slap his forehead, then clutch his chest and say "My God, yes!"

Actually, the case contains his hat, his glasses, a bullhorn, a camera, a ninety-nine-cent plastic poncho, a Kit Kat, cough drops, a Magic Marker, some Sudafed, and an issue of *Magic*; about twenty magic tricks, including Bongo Hat, Drooping Flower, Chinese Sticks, Silk to Egg, Card on Ceiling, Dove Pan, and Soft Soap; a box of little time-killer props (a deck of stuck-together cards, a troll, a fake hand, a whistle, a squeaker); four different magic wands and a movie clapper; two gross of long, skinny balloons; a few inflatable birthday cakes, 144 heart-shaped balloons, and several hundred somersaulting Silly Billy balloons; several hundred cardboard feet for the Silly Billy balloons; concealer makeup to cover his beard late in the afternoon; a Mak Magic French Arm Chopper; and a cellular telephone. His pants have ten pockets. One is filled with notes about his day's schedule. Beside the name and address he jots down whether the mother sounds nice, whether there is a cute baby-sitter he might ask out on a date, whether the birthday kid is shy, and also whether the kid has seen him before. Because Silly has performed for so many thousands of parties since his first, in 1985, this last notation is sometimes a double-digit number rather than a simple yes or no. Recently, Silly did a birthday party for a first grader on the Upper West Side; most of the children at the party had seen him at four other birthday parties that month. One group of five-year-olds who are classmates at the Lycée Français de New York, a private school on the Upper East Side, saw him seven times this fall. There are other prominent children's entertainers in New York—Princess Pricilla, Magic Al, Professor Putter, Pinkie the Clown, and Arnie Kolodner, to name a few—but if you are between three and five years old and have any kind of social life at all, you are probably intimately familiar with Silly Billy's work.

ONE DAY LAST MONTH, Silly was eyeing his case with some despair, because he had a tight schedule, involving multiple taxi rides—the kind of day that makes him complain that suburban clowns have it easy, since they can just drive themselves around. "On the other hand," he was saying, "I have clown friends out on Long Island who sit around all week with nothing to do, because everyone out there only gives parties on weekends." Silly's schedule that day, a Friday, included a party for six hundred children of the employees of Davis Polk & Wardwell, a midtown law firm; a birthday party for a four-year-old girl on Park Avenue; a holiday party that the Japanese Ambassador to the United States was giving for the children of his staff; and a birthday party for a three-year-old boy in Bronxville. On Saturday, he would be doing a party for a three-year-old girl at an Upper East Side children's gym and a children's holiday party at a Locust Valley country club.

We stood on the corner waiting for a cab that wouldn't be scared off by the enormous case or by Silly Billy's costume. At the moment, most of his costume was concealed: He never puts on his hat and glasses until he arrives at a party, and today he was wearing a down-filled parka that covered him to the top of his patchwork knees. From the neck up, Silly is actually a very regular-looking guy. He has silky black hair, a refined mouth, and the sort of huge, dark, satiny eyes that are standard in clown portraits on black velvet. Out of necessity, he has learned to clean-jerk eighty-five pounds, but his build is smallish and wiry. His hands are fine-boned, square-nailed, fluid, and impressively pale. His clown voice and his normal voice are pretty much the same—light, nasal, and slightly sarcastic. He is rather sly. He has the manner of an older brother who first tortures and teases you, then pulls a quarter out of your nose, levitates the kitchen table, and finally cracks you up.

One day, he said to me, "I just realized that before I became Silly Billy there *was* no Silly Billy." Before he was Silly Billy, he briefly considered being Uncle Funny and, even more briefly, Mr. Funny, and, quite protractedly, was David Friedman. He is now thirty-three years old. His résumé, in reverse chronology, goes: children's performer, 1985 to present; street performer specializing in balloon animals, 1984 to 1986; marketing associate at Doubleday books, March 1984 to December 1984; student at Northwestern University, 1978 to 1982; teenager/owner/chief executive officer of Tip-Top Novelties, a magic-trick and novelty business (whoopee cushions, itching powder, Snappy Gum, and so forth), 1974 to 1978.

Arriving in the lobby at Davis Polk, we were met by a slender woman in a navy blue suit. "Silly?" she said, hesitantly. "Bonnie?" he responded. They shook hands. Bonnie had organized Davis Polk's holiday party. Silly had rated her "Nice!!" on his schedule note. She had booked him for the party in early fall, and they had spoken on the phone several times since. One of Silly Billy's business philosophies is that a client should speak directly to his or her specific clown as soon as the date is booked. Bonnie's only special requests were for Silly to do at least one Hanukkah trick and to bring Crazy String. Because this was a big corporate party rather than a private birthday, Silly would be doing a special version of his show: lots of jokes and magic tricks, but not his big finale, in which he makes balloon costumes for all the kids and has them act out a play like *Aladdin* or *Beauty and the Beast*. Bonnie led us to an elevator and then down a hallway lined with attorneys' offices and conference rooms, where popcorn, hot dog, ice cream, and candy vendors were now set up for the party. A juggler friend of Silly's walked by and waved at us. In a big conference room, where Silly was going to perform, several waiters in tuxedos were setting up chairs. Silly started unpacking his case. A patrician-looking man in a chalk-striped gray suit stuck his head in the room and called out, "Silly Billy? Is that you? Are you happy? That is, do you have everything you need?" Silly nodded. A moment later, the man came back, leading a little boy about two feet tall, who was wearing a matching chalk-striped gray suit. They sat in the first row of chairs.

One of the waiters looked over at us and said, "My God—Silly!"

Silly looked up and said, "Ziggy. Small world." He turned to me and said, "Allow me to introduce Ziggy the Clown, the former Silly Willy." To Ziggy he said, "So how was your show?"

"Killer," the waiter said. "I performed for two dozen Yiddish-speaking Orthodox kids, and they loved it."

Silly rummaged around in the case and pulled out a bag of balloons and a prop for the Drooping Flower gag. "Good," he said to Ziggy. "By the way, I'm doing the Underwear trick downtown. For some reason, it works with the kids there and not uptown. It must be a cultural thing. Also, the Multiplying Bananas. Hey, how are your lungs? Blow up a snowman for me."

"What's the Multiplying Bananas?"

Silly stopped unpacking, gave Ziggy a look, and said, "Please don't tell me you work for me and you don't know Multiplying Bananas." He made a dramatic show of exasperation. Then he explained to him how to multiply bananas. Then he began to explain to me how you turn Silly Willy into Ziggy the Clown: "In the beginning, I thought it was a good idea to make all the clowns interchangeable. Then I started thinking that it was confusing to children to see several Silly Billy–like people, and that as an artist I was diluting the value of the name Silly Billy, because there were so many other Silly-whatevers. I needed to keep my identity more unique." He gave the other clowns new costumes and he renamed them. He went through a Loony phase—there is a Loony Lenny, Loony Louie, Loony Loony, Loony Goony, and Loony Lucy—and then he got more free-form. On his staff now, there are Melody the Clown, for instance, and someone named just plain Clarence.

Silly also decided to reserve exclusive use of "Googly-googly" for himself, so he held an interoffice contest for a new, underclown magic word. The winning submission, "Iggy-la-piggy-wiggy," came from Silly Willy, who happened to be the only clown who refused to change his name; he fought Silly Billy for a year over it. Ziggy told me that even though he was tired of being confused with Silly Billy, he had been Silly Willy for three years and had a considerable following of his own, including people who actually preferred his gentleness to Silly Billy's smart-alecky, edgy style. Nonetheless, Silly Billy insisted. Silly Willy, who in real life performed as a social worker under the name Micah Goldstein, finally gave in to his boss and settled on the name Ziggy the Clown. Now the two of them just fight about tricks and gags and whether Silly is generous enough with his praise.

"Basically, we fight all the time, but I'm very loyal to him," Ziggy says of Silly Billy. "After all, he found me. I never planned on being a clown, and then Silly Billy came along. Now I feel like wherever I go I will clown. If I move to—oh, Dallas or something, I will clown. Right now, I still have to do a little catering on the side to make a living, but I would love to do what Silly Billy does—to be a clown full time and have the kind of stature he has. I'm not sure there's room at the top in this city for more clowns at his level. I'm the $150 clown, the upper-middle-class clown. There are millions of cheap clowns out there, and dozens of upper-middle-class clowns, but only one or two at the high end with Silly Billy. He's the crème-de-la-crème clown."

HIGH-END BIRTHDAY PARTIES often have high-end birthday cakes. Silly Billy documents remarkable ones for his own amusement. This is why he carries a camera. He once photographed a cake that was a six-foot-long mocha-butter-cream scale model of an aircraft carrier. The theme of the party was the armed services. During the party, an actual helicopter landed on the front lawn. The birthday boy was five years old. Silly has also photographed cakes shaped like a freight train, a fire engine, a Barbie doll, and a panoramic countryside with spun-sugar streams, meadows, cottages, and a population of Teenage Mutant Ninja Turtles. Another popular cake is one decorated with a portrait of Silly Billy: Many children are so fond of him that they request him for dessert. Recently, a parent hired an artist to produce a marzipan portrait of Silly on a large sheet cake. Silly provided a snapshot of himself for the artist to work from. The snapshot had been taken late in the afternoon, and the artist was extremely faithful to it, so the birthday cake ended up decorated with an almond-paste Silly Billy wearing a five o'clock shadow.

Sometimes the birthday cake is just a grocery store variety and the party is in a housing project and there are no gingerbread place cards or Barney tablecloths or mountains of presents: There is just Silly Billy or one of his clowns. Once, Ziggy was telling me about the first shows he did after Silly Billy trained him. His debut was in front of thirteen six-year-old Hispanic girls in Spanish Harlem. His second party was held at a McDonald's in the Bronx, but he was tossed out before he could perform, because McDonald's didn't allow clowns on the premises. In the middle of this story, he interrupted himself and said, "You know, people think only rich parents would have a live entertainer at their kid's party, but we do lots and lots in humble surroundings. I think that for a lot of people having a clown at their kid's birthday party is really important. It's become part of the American dream, like owning a VCR."

SILLY BILLY DOES NOT plan to become an old-man clown. He and Princess Pricilla, who specializes in fairy-tale performances, are brainstorming a Silly Billy–Princess Pricilla television collaboration; he has also started doing performances at parties for adults, under the name David Friedman. For adult parties, he does magic, and he has developed expertise in the field of off-color balloons. He has mastered a balloon man with a rising and falling erection, and believes he will soon have a breakthrough involving ejaculation. He told me this on the Long Island Rail Road while we were riding out to the country club party in Locust Valley. He had been explaining the advance in balloon technology that took place in the sixties—when the introduction of long, skinny balloons meant that animals could be made out of a single balloon, instead of being pieced together from several separate ones—and absentmindedly he began making a few balloon men, causing certain parts of them to inflate and deflate in very interesting ways. An elderly man sitting across the aisle fixed his eyes on us and, for the remainder of the forty-minute ride, did not once look away. By the time we got to Locust Valley, there was a pile of aroused figures on Silly's seat. As we were getting ready to go, Silly started to gather up the balloons, then gave me a sly look and whispered, "I think we should leave them all on the train."

THE WILCOX PARTY, at Park Avenue and Eighty-first: seventeen four-year-olds, some with mothers, some with nannies. Chloe, the birthday girl, dressed in an Empire-waisted midcalf red velvet jumper, has been described by her mother as "not shy"—that is, willing to be Silly Billy's assistant in the participation tricks. Silly Billy is familiar with the apartment, which is big and bright, because he has done parties for all the Wilcox children. Before he sets up his props, he asks Bruce Wilcox if he can use the phone. Bruce Wilcox scowls, and says, "Well, don't stay on long. I'm in the middle of a trade." Silly makes a quick call and goes back to setting up his props on a coffee table in the living room. The children stare at him, transfixed. He starts with his warm-up—inflating a dozen balloons to be used later, during the play, and allowing every third or fourth one to escape and fly screeching and whistling across the room. He calls Chloe to come up. He tries putting a hat on her head; she balks. He asks her to hold his magic wand; she balks again. He says, "Okay, Chloe, why don't you say, 'Ladies and Gentlemen!' " Chloe stares down. Silly says, "Do you want to talk? You don't want to talk? Okay, we'll do the nontalking tricks." Chloe, looking relieved, sits down. Silly gives her an inflatable birthday cake, which one of her guests, Nicholas, grabs, saying, "I already have one of those." Silly rolls his eyes and says to the mothers, "Four years old and he's already jaded."

In the cab, leaving the party, Silly pulls out his Wilcox party notes. He always rates his own performance—the scale is "Great Perfect," "Great," "Very Good," or "Good." He also writes "All Knew" if all the kids knew him from earlier parties, or "All New" if they are first-timers. This was a "Most Knew. Great" party. "I know Chloe didn't do the tricks with me, but she had fun," he said. "She was there with me the whole time."

At the home of the Japanese ambassador: twenty-three adult women, in fancy blouses and skirts; thirty children, the boys in blazers and the girls in velvet dresses; and one man, in rumpled pants and a cardigan, who sits alone on a big couch. The man on the couch is the ambassador. The house is grand and formal. Silly decides to do one of his favorite tricks, Card on Ceiling, in which he shuffles a deck of cards and the top one mysteriously shoots upward and sticks to the ceiling. Once it is on the ceiling, it is more or less a permanent part of the plaster. The effect is spectacular in houses with very high ceilings. Silly likes walking past houses where he has performed this trick and checking on the cards months after the party. At the ambassador's house, the deck explodes and the card flies upward. For a moment, no one says anything or moves, and then the mothers start murmuring nervously, and glance at the ambassador, who is staring at the card. Finally, he applauds. Silly lets out a small sigh, and then says to the children, in Japanese, "I don't know how to speak Japanese." On his notes: "Great. ½ Knew." From there we go on to Bronxville.

On Saturday, we go to Gym Time, on the Upper East Side, for what Silly Billy calls a fully loaded party. "First, they have you, then the bagels, then Snow White is coming," the Gym Time aide says as she leads us to the party room. "Thank God, there's no Barney. Although I'm sure if they were going to have a Barney they would have got the really good Barney. Anyway, after Snow White the kids are going to play Munchkin Tennis for a while. They've rented the gym for two and a half hours." The birthday girl is turning three today. Her mother pulls Silly Billy aside and says, "Remember, Silly, if you do the Three Little Pigs, she wants the wolf to be *nice.*" The party room is large and low-ceilinged and has a cushiony rubber floor. A buffet with platters of smoked fish, trays of fruit, and baskets of bagels and pastries for the adults is set up against one wall, and in the middle of the room is the children's table, set with Snow White tablecloths and plates, minibagels, People Pops, Gummi Bears, Junior Juice, and gift bags. On a separate table, there is an enormous cake in the shape of an English Tudor castle inhabited by the Seven Dwarfs. This is a cake that will go into Silly's photo book. Two mothers are admiring the cake. One says, "My God, the baker really outdid himself on this one, didn't he?"

"Incredible," the other says. "I heard he screwed up on the cookies. Look at this cake, though. It's too pretty to eat. Maybe it's, you know, a little *done.*" She gestures toward the children, who have swarmed over Silly Billy. "Look at my kid. Look at him. He's got a hangover. He's been to five birthday parties this week. He's beat." The hungover party boy has started tackling one child after another. His mother says, "I'm telling you, he's just *exhausted.* Look at him!" The boy grabs Silly Billy's leg, and then spots a ball, which he begins kicking around the room. "Brian," his mother calls out. "No soccer now, honey. No soccer!"

After the show, as we are on our way out through the lobby of the gym, we see a pale young woman in a long cape coming in. Silly watches her for a moment and then says, "You know who that is? That's Snow White."

At the show in Locust Valley, which is at a country club called The Creek, there are seventy-five children of all ages. The clubhouse is mahogany-paneled and leather-upholstered. An infant wearing a navy blue double-breasted gold-buttoned blazer and no pants crawls across the carpet as Silly Billy begins the show. Looking down, Silly says, "Who is this person? Does anyone know this person?" The parents are milling around in the back of the room, holding cocktails and chatting; the blazered baby crawls away. Silly wants this to be a "Great" show or even a "Great Perfect" show, because he's never been hired by the club before. It is the end of a week in which he has entertained at twenty parties, and he's losing his voice, but he droops his flower and shoots his card to the ceiling as if it were the very first time. At the end of the show, he gets a standing ovation, a check saying "Pay to the order of Silly Billy," and assurances that the club would like him back.

On the train home, he says, "Sometimes, when I think about it, I realize that thousands and thousands of kids in New York have grown up watching Silly Billy and saying 'Googly-googly' as their magic word. It really makes me think. That's what goes on in a clown's mind. The big issues are what it means to deal with so many kids, whether I will ever figure out how to make a recognizable Barney balloon, and what is the meaning of life."

LA MATADORA
REVISA SU MAQUILLAJE

....

(THE BULLFIGHTER
CHECKS HER MAKEUP)

I WENT TO SPAIN NOT LONG AGO TO WATCH
Cristina Sánchez fight bulls, but she had gotten tossed by
one during a performance in the village of Ejea de los Ca-
balleros and was convalescing when I arrived. Getting
tossed sounds sort of merry, but I saw a matador tossed
once, and he looked like a saggy bale of hay flung by a
pitchfork, and when he landed on his back he looked
busted and terrified. Cristina got tossed by accidentally
hooking a horn with her elbow during a pass with the cape,
and the joint was wrenched so hard that her doctor said it
would need at least three or four days to heal. It probably
hurt like hell, and the timing was terrible. She had fights
scheduled each of the nights she was supposed to rest and
every night until October—every night, with no breaks in
between. It had been like this for her since May, when she
was elevated from the status of a novice to a full *matador de
toros*. The title is conferred in a formal ceremony called
"taking the *alternativa*," and it implies that you are experienced and talented and that other matadors have recog-

nized you as a top-drawer bullfighter. You will now fight the biggest, toughest bulls and will probably be hired to fight often and in the most prestigious arenas. Bullfighting becomes your whole life, your everyday life—so routine that "sometimes after you've fought and killed the bull you feel as if you hadn't done a thing all day," as Cristina once told me. When Cristina Sánchez took her alternativa, it caused a sensation. Other women before her have fought bulls in Spain. Many have only fought little bulls, but some did advance to big animals and become accomplished and famous, and a few of the best have been declared full matadors de toros. Juanita Cruz became a matador in 1940, and Morenita de Quindio did in 1968, and Raquel Martinez and Maribel Atienzar did in the eighties, but they all took their alternativas in Mexico, where the standards are a little less exacting. Cristina is the first woman to have taken her alternativa in Europe and made her debut as a matador in Spain.

There was a fight program of three matadors—a corrida—scheduled for the Madrid bullring the day after I got to Spain, and I decided to go so I could see some other toreros while Cristina was laid up with her bad arm. One of the three scheduled to perform was the bastard son of El Cordobés. El Cordobés had been a matador superstar in the sixties and a breeder of several illegitimate children and a prideful man who was so possessive of his nickname that he had once sued this kid—the one I was going to see— because the kid wanted to fight bulls under the name El Cordobés, too. In the end, the judge let each and every El Cordobés continue to be known professionally as El Cordobés.

The kid El Cordobés is a scrubbed, cute blond with a crinkly smile. Outside the rings where he is fighting, vendors sell fan photos of him alongside postcards and little bags of sunflower seeds and stuffed bull souvenirs. In the photos, El Cordobés is dressed in a plaid camp shirt and acid-washed blue jeans and is hugging a good-looking white horse. In the ring, he does some flashy moves on his knees in front of the bull, including a frog hop that he times to make it look like he's going to get skewered. These tricks, plus the renown of his name, have gotten him a lot of attention, but El Cordobés is just one of many cute young male matadors working these days. If his knees give out, he might have nothing.

On the other hand, there is just one Cristina, and everyone in Spain knows her and is following her rise. She has gotten attention far outside of Spain and on television and in newspapers and even in fashion magazines; other matadors, even very good ones, fuse in the collective mind as man-against-bull, but every time Cristina kills a bull she forms part of a singular and unforgettable tableau—that of an attractive, self-possessed young woman elegantly slaying a large animal in a somber and ancient masculine ritual—and regardless of gender she is a really good matador, and she is being painstakingly managed and promoted, so there is no saying where her celebrity will stop. This is only her first season as a full matador, but it has been a big event. Lately El Cordobés or his publicist or his accountant has been igniting and fanning the rumor that he and Cristina Sánchez are madly in love, with the hope that her fame will rub off on him. She will probably be more and more acclaimed in the four or so years she plans to fight, and she will probably be credited with many more putative love affairs before her career is through.

Before the fight in Madrid, I walked around to the back of the bullring and through the *patio de caballos,* the dirt-floored courtyard and stable where the picadors' horses and the donkeys that drag away the dead bull after the fight relax in their stalls and get their hair combed and get fed and get saddled. I was on my way to the bullfighting museum—the Museo Taurino—which is in a gallery next to the stalls. It was a brilliant day with just a whiff of wind. In the courtyard, musclemen were tossing equipment back and forth and unloading a horse trailer. Another twenty or so men were idling in the courtyard in the few pockets of shade or near the locked door of the matadors' chapel, which is opened before the fight so the matadors can stop in and pray. The idlers were older men with bellies that began at their chins and trousers hiked up to their nipples, and they were hanging around just so they could take a look at the bulls for tonight's fight and see how they were going to be divvied up among the three matadors. Really, there isn't a crumb of any piece of bullfighting that goes unexamined by aficionados like these men. I lingered for a minute and then went into the museum. I wandered past the oil portraits of Manolete and Joselito and of dozens of other revered bullfighters, and past six stuffed and mounted heads of bulls whose names were Paisano, Landejo, Mediaonza, Jocinero, Hermano, and Perdigón—they were chosen for the museum because they had been particularly mean or unusual-looking or because they had killed someone famous. Then I stopped at a glass display case that had in it a picture of the matador Juanita Cruz. The picture was an eight-by-ten and looked like it had been shot in a studio. Juanita Cruz's ivory face and her wedge of a chin and her pitch-black hair with its tiny standing waves were blurred along the edges, movie-star style. She looked solemn, and her eyes were focused on middle space. In the case next to the picture were her pink matador kneesocks and her mouse-eared matador hat and one of her

bullfighter suits. These are called *traje de luces,* "suit of lights," and all
toreros wear them and like to change them often; Cristina has half a
dozen, and Juanita Cruz probably owned twenty or so in the course of her
bullfighting career. This one was blush pink with beautiful gold piping and
sparkly black sequins. It had the classic short, stiff, big-shouldered, box-
shaped matador jacket but not the capri trousers that all matadors wear,
because Juanita Cruz fought in a skirt. There is no such thing as a matador skirt anymore—Cristina, of course, wears trousers. I looked at the skirt
for a while and decided that even though it looked unwieldy it might actually have been an advantage—in a skirt, you can bend and stretch and
lunge with a sword unconstrained. On the other hand, a skirt would have
exposed so much fabric to the bull that in a fight it would have gotten aw-
fully splashed and smeared with blood. Every matador has an assistant who
is assigned to clean his suit with soap and a toothbrush after every fight.
Juanita Cruz was popular and well accepted even though she was an anomaly, but late at night, as her assistant was scrubbing her big bloody skirt, I
bet he cursed the fact that she had been wearing so much fabric while
sticking swords into bulls.

I WENT TO VISIT Cristina at home the morning before she was going
to be fighting in a corrida in a town called Móstoles. It was now a week
since her injury, and her elbow apparently had healed. Two days earlier,
she had tested it in a fight in Cordobés and another the following day in
Jáen, and a friend of mine who reads Madrid's bullfight newspaper told me
Cristina had gotten very good reviews. It turns out that I was lucky to catch
her at home, because she is hardly there during the bullfighting season—
usually she keeps a rock star schedule, leaving whatever town she's in with
her crew right after she fights, driving all night to the next place on her
schedule, checking into a hotel, sleeping until noon, eating lunch, watching some television, suiting up, fighting, and then leaving again. She was
going to be at home this particular morning because Móstoles is only a few
miles from Parla, the town where she and her parents and sisters live. She
had come home the night before, after the fight in Jáen, and was planning
to spend the day in Parla doing errands. The corrida in Móstoles would
start at six. The assistant who helps her dress—he is called the sword boy,
because he also takes care of all her cutlery—was going to come to the
apartment at five so she could get prepared and then just drive over to
the bullring already dressed and ready to go in her suit of lights. Parla is an

unglamorous place about forty minutes south of Madrid; it is a kernel of an old village that had been alone on the wide-open plains but is now pick-eted by incredibly ugly high-rise apartment buildings put up in the mid-sixties for workers overflowing the available housing in Madrid. The Sánchez apartment is in a slightly less ugly and somewhat shorter brick building on a busy street, on a block with a driving school, a bra shop, and a bank. There is no name on the doorbell, but Cristina's father's initials are barely scratched into a metal plate beside it. These days it is next to im-possible to find Cristina. The nearly unmarked doorbell is the least of it. Cristina has a magician press agent who can make himself disappear and a very powerful and self-confident manager—a former French bullfighter named Simon Casas—who is credited with having gotten her into the biggest bullrings and the best corridas in the country but is also impossible to find and even if he were findable he would tell you that his answer to your request to speak to Cristina is no. He is especially watchful of her international exposure. Simon Casas didn't know I was coming to see Cristina in Parla and he might have disapproved simply to be disapproving, and after I saw him later that afternoon in Móstoles, prowling the perime-ter of the bullring like an irritable wild animal, I was that much gladder I'd stayed out of his way.

Anyway, Cristina wasn't even home when I got there. I had driven to Parla with my translator, Muriel, and her bullfighter husband, Pedro, who both know Cristina and Cristina's father, Antonio, who himself used to be a bullfighter—if it sounds like just about everyone I encountered in Spain was or is a bullfighter, it's true. No one answered the doorbell at the apart-ment. Cristina's car wasn't around, so it looked like she really was gone. A car seems to be the first thing matadors buy themselves when they start making big money—that is, when they start getting sometimes as much as tens of thousands of dollars for a major fight. The bullfighter car of choice is a Mercedes, but Cristina bought herself a bright red Ford Probe, which is much sportier. She also bought her mother a small business, a gift store. We decided to wait a bit longer. Pedro killed time by making some bullfight business calls on his cellular phone. Just as we were debating whether to go looking for Cristina at her mother's store, Mrs. Sánchez came around the corner, carrying a load of groceries; she said Cristina was at the bank and that in the meantime we could come upstairs. We climbed a few flights. The apartment was tidy and fresh-looking and furnished with mod-ern things in pastel tones, and in the living room there were a life-size oil painting of Cristina looking beautiful in her suit of lights, two huge photographs of Cristina in bullfights, one of her as a civilian, a large photograph of the older Sánchez daughter getting married, and a big-screen TV. On almost every horizontal surface there was a bronze or brass or pewter statuette of a bull, usually bucking, its withers bristling with three or four barbed harpoons called *banderillas,* which are stuck in to aggravate him before he is killed. These were all trophies from different corridas and from Cristina's stint as a star pupil at the Madrid bullfighting school. Lots of Cristina's stuff was lying around the room. On the dining table were stacks of fresh laundry, mostly white dress shirts and white T-shirts and pink socks. On the floor were a four-foot-long leather sword case, three hatboxes, and a piece of luggage that looked like a giant bowling-ball bag, which is a specially designed case for a matador's twenty-thousand-dollar suit jacket. Also, there was a small black Kipling backpack of Cristina's, which cracked me up because it was the exact same backpack that I was carrying.

Mrs. Sánchez was clattering around in the kitchen, making Cristina's lunch. A few minutes later, I heard the front door scrape open, and then Cristina stepped into the room, out of breath and flustered about being late. She is twenty-five years old and has chemically assisted blond hair, long eyelashes, high cheekbones, and a tiny nose. She looks really pretty when she smiles and almost regal when she doesn't, but she's not so beautiful that she's scary. This day, she was wearing blue jeans, a denim shirt with some flower embroidery, and white slip-on shoes with chunky heels, and her hair was held in a ponytail by a sunflower barrette. She is not unusually big or small. Her shoulders are square and her legs are sturdy, and she's solid and athletic-looking, like a forward on a field hockey team. Her strength is a matter of public debate in Spain. The weakest part of her performance is the very end of the fight, when she's supposed to kill the bull with one perfect jam of her sword, but she often doesn't go deep enough or in the right place. It is said in certain quarters that she simply isn't strong enough, but the fact is that many matadors mess up with the sword. When I brought it up, she shook her head and said, "People who don't understand the bullfighting world think you have to be extremely strong, but that's not the case. What is important is technique and experience. You have to be in good shape, but you don't have to match a man's strength. Besides, your real opponent is the bull, and you can never match it in strength."

Her mother came in and out of the room a few times. When she was out, Cristina said in a low voice, "I'm very happy with my family, but the time comes when you have to be independent." The tabloids have reported that she has just bought a castle on millions of enchanted acres. "I bought a small piece of property right near here," she said, rolling her eyes. "I'm having a house built. I think when I come back from my winter tour in South America I'll be able to move in."

What I really wanted to know was why in the world she decided to become a bullfighter. I knew she'd grown up watching her father fight, so it had always been a profession that seemed normal to her, even though at the ring she didn't see many girls. Plus she doesn't like to sit still. Before she started training to be a matador, she had worked in a beauty parlor and then as a typist at a fire extinguisher factory, and both jobs drove her crazy. She is a very girly girl—she wears makeup, she wants children, she has boyfriends—but she says she was only interested in jobs that would keep her on her feet, and coincidentally those were jobs that were mostly filled by men. If she hadn't become a matador, she thinks she would have become a trainer at a gym, or a police officer, or perhaps a firefighter, which used to be her father's backup job when he was a bullfighter, in the years before he started advising her and became a full-time part of her six-person crew. She didn't become a woman matador to be shocking or make a feminist point, although along the way she has been shunned by some of her male colleagues and there are still a few who refuse to appear in a corrida with her. Once, in protest, she went to Toledo and instead of having a corrida in which three matadors each killed two bulls, she took on all six bulls herself, one by one. She said she wants to be known as a great matador and not an oddity or anecdote in the history of bullfighting. She simply loves the art and craft of fighting bulls. Later that day, when I saw her in the ring, I also realized that besides loving the bullfight itself, she is that sort of person who is illuminated by the attention of a crowd. I asked her what she'll do after she retires from the ring in three or four years. "I want to have earned a lot of money and invested it wisely," she said. "And then I want to do something in the movies or on TV."

She mentioned that she was eating early today because she had a stomachache. With a fight almost every night for months, I suppose there would be nights when she felt crummy or wasn't in the mood. Cristina laughed and said, "Yeah, sometimes you do feel like, oh God, I don't have the slightest desire to face a bull this afternoon!" Personally, I'm not a huge coward, but the phrase "desire to face a bull" will never be part of my life, any afternoon, ever. I figured that nothing must scare her. She shook her head and said, "Failure. My greatest fear is failure. I'm a woman who is a fighter and I always think about trying to surpass myself, so what I most fear is to fail."

Just then, Mrs. Sánchez came into the room and said the sandwiches were ready, so Cristina started to get up. She paused for a moment and said, "You know, people think that because I kill bulls I have to be really brave, but I'm not. I'm a sensitive person, and I can get superterrified. I'm afraid of staying home by myself, and I get hysterical if I see a spider." I asked if bulls ever haunted her dreams, and she said, "I don't dream much at all, but a few times I've dreamed that a bull was pursuing me in the ring, up into the stands. And the night before my debut in Madrid, I did dream of bulls with huge, twisted horns."

I HAD SEEN the first bullfight of my life a few days earlier, on that night in Madrid, and it was a profound education. I learned that I should not eat for several hours beforehand and to start looking away the minute the picadors ride in on their stoic-looking blindfolded horses, because their arrival signaled that the blood and torment would begin. At first, in Madrid, I had been excited because the Plaza de Toros is so dramatic and beautiful, and also the pageantry that began the corrida was very nice, and when the first bull galloped in, I liked watching it bolt around the ring and chase the matador and his assistants until they retreated behind the small fences around the ring that are there for their protection. The small fences had targets—bull's-eyes, actually—painted on them. The bull would ram into them with its horns and the fence would rock. The more furious bulls would ram again and again, until the matador teased them away with a flourish of his cape. The bulls were homely, with little heads and huge briskets and tapered hips, and they cornered like school buses and sometimes skidded to their knees, but they had fantastic energy and single-mindedness and thick muscles that flickered under their skin and faces that didn't look vicious at all and were interesting to watch. Some of the fight was wonderful: the matador's flourishes with the shocking pink and bright yellow big cape and his elegance with the small triangular red one; the sound of thousands of people gasping when the bull got very close to the cape; the plain thrilling danger of it and the fascination of watching a bull be slowly hypnotized; the bravery of the picadors' horses, which stood stock-still as the bull pounded them broadside, the flags along the rim of the ring flashing in the late-afternoon light; the resplendence of the matador's suit in that angling light, especially when the matador inched one foot forward and squared his hips and arched his back so that he was a bright new moon against a sky of sand with the black cloud of a bull racing by. I loved the ancientness and majesty and excitement of it, the way bull-fighting could be at once precious and refined yet absolutely primal and raw. But beyond that I was lost and nauseous and knew I didn't understand how so many people, a whole nation of people, weren't shaken by the gore and the idea of watching a ballet that always, absolutely, unfailingly ends with a gradual and deliberate death. I didn't understand it then, and I doubt I ever will.

IN THE LITTLE BRICK BULLRING in Móstoles, Cristina killed two bulls well but not exceptionally—for the first kill the judge awarded her one of the bull's ears, but for the second she got no award at all. A once-in-a-lifetime sort of performance would have earned two ears, a tail, and a hoof. After that second fight Cristina looked a little disgusted with herself, and she hung back and talked for several minutes with her father, who was standing in the crew area, before she came out and took the traditional vic-tory walk around the ring. She was clearly the crowd favorite. People wave white handkerchiefs at bullfights to indicate their support; in Móstoles it looked like it was snowing. As she circled the ring, men and women and lit-tle kids yelled, "Matadora! Matadora!" and "Olé, Cristina!" and tossed con-gratulatory sweaters and flowers and shoes and blazers and sandwiches and a Levi's jacket and a crutch and a cane, and then a representative of a social club in Móstoles stepped into the ring and presented her with an enormous watermelon.

After the fight, Cristina left immediately for Zaragoza, where she would have her next fight. I went back to Madrid to have dinner with Muriel and Pedro. Pedro had just finished his own fight, and he looked very relaxed and his face was pink and bright. The restaurant, Vina P, was practically wallpapered with old and new fight posters and photographs of bullfighters and some mounted bulls' heads. Its specialty was slabs of beef—since the animals killed in bullfights are butchered and are highly sought after for dining, the specialty of the house might occasionally be straight from the bullring. Pedro said Vina P was a bullfighters' restaurant, which means it is the rough equivalent of a sports bar frequented by real athletes in the United States. Before I got to Spain I imagined that bull-fighting was an old and colorful tradition that was preserved but isolated, a fragile antique. Cristina Sánchez would be honored, but she would be in the margins—it would be as if she were the very best square dancer in America. Instead, she looms, and bullfighting looms. There are tons of restaurants in every city that are bullfighter and bullfight-aficionado hangouts, and there are pictures and posters of bullfights even in the restaurants that aren't, and there are bullfight newspapers and regular television coverage, and every time I turned around I was in front of the headquarters of some bullfight association. At a gas station in a nowhere place called Otero de Herreros the only bit of decoration I saw was a poster for an upcoming fight; it happened to have a picture of Cristina on it. The biggest billboards in Madrid were ads for Pepe Jeans, modeled by Francisco Rivera Ordóñez, Matador de Toros. Mostly because of Cristina, bullfight attendance is up and applications to the Madrid bullfighting school are up, especially with girls. The Spanish tabloids are fat with bullfighter gossip, and they are really keen on Cristina. That night while we were eating dinner, Pedro noticed a gorgeous young man at another table and whispered that he was a Mexican pop singer and also Cristina's old boyfriend, whom she'd recently broken up with because he'd sold the story of their relationship to the press.

I had planned to leave Spain after the fight in Móstoles, but when I heard that Cristina was going to fight soon in a town that was easy to get to, I decided to stay a few more days. The town was called Nava de la Asunción, and to get there you head north from Madrid over the raggedy gray Sierra de Guadarrama and then onto the high golden plain where many fighting bulls are raised. The occasion for the fight was the Nava town fair. According to the local paper, "peculiar and small amateur bullfights used to be done in the fenced yards of local houses until for reasons of security it was recommended to do away with these customs." The bulls were always chased through the fields in the morning so the townspeople could see what they were like. The paper said, "Traditionally there are accidents because there is always a bull that escapes. There is maximum effort put out to be sure that this does not occur, even though it is part of the tradition." It also said, "To have Cristina Sánchez in Nava is special." "The Party of the Bulls—Cristina Sánchez will be the star of the program!" "Cristina Sánchez will show her bullfighting together with the gifted Antonio Borrero 'Chamaco' and Antonio Cutiño—a great bill in which the star is, without a doubt, Cristina Sánchez."

Nava is the prettiest little town, and on the afternoon of the fight there was a marching band zigzagging around and strings of candy-colored banners hanging along the streets, popping and flapping in the wind. Just out-

side the bullring a few vendors had set up booths. One was selling soft
drinks, one had candy and nuts, one had every manner of bullfighter souvenir: T-shirts with matador photos, pins with matador photos, photo cigarette lighters and key chains, autographed photos themselves, and white
hankies for waving at the end of the fights. Of the nine photo T-shirts,
seven were of Cristina. Six were different pictures of her either posing in
her suit of lights or actually fighting. The other one was a casual portrait.
She was dressed in a blue blouse trimmed with white daisy embroidery,
and her blond hair was loose and she appeared to be sitting in a park. A
nun came over to the souvenir booth and bought a Cristina photo-hankie.
Big-bodied women with spindly little daughters were starting to gather
around the booth and hold up first one Cristina T-shirt and then another
and finally, sighing, indicate that they would take both. Skittery little boys,
sometimes with a bigger boy or their fathers, darted up and poked through
the stuff on the table and lingered. After a while, a couple of men pushed
past the throng, lugging a trunk marked C. SÁNCHEZ toward the area under
the bleachers where the matadors and picadors were getting ready. Now
and then, if you looked in that direction, you could catch a glimpse of
someone in a short sequined jacket, and until the band came thundering
by you could hear the hollow clunking of hooves and the heavy rustling of
horses and donkeys.

The tickets were expensive whether you bought one for the sunny side
or the shade, but every row was packed and every standing-room spot was
taken. The men around me were smoking cigars and women were snacking on honey-roasted peanuts, and every few minutes a guy would come
through hawking shots of Cutty Sark and cans of beer. Young kids were in
shorts and American basketball team T-shirts, but everyone else was
dressed up, as if they were going to a dinner party at a friend's. At five-
thirty, in slanting sunlight, the parade of the matadors and their assistants
began. Each of them was dressed in a different color, and they were dazzling and glinting in the sun. In a box seat across the ring from the entrance gate were the sober-looking judge and three girls who were queens
of the fair, wearing lacy white crowns in their hair. Antonio Borrero
"Chamaco" fought first, and then came Cristina. She was wearing a fuch-
sia suit and had her hair in a braid and a look of dark focus on her face.
When she and her assistants entered the ring, a man stood up in the stands
and hollered about how much he admired her and then an old woman
called out that she wanted Cristina to bless a little brooch she had pinned
on her shawl.

The bull came out. He was brownish black, small-chested, wide-horned, and branded with the number 36. Cristina, the other two matadors of the day, and Cristina's picadors and banderilleros spread out around the ring holding hot-pink capes, and each one in turn would catch the bull's attention, tease him into charging, and then the next person would step forward and do the same. It was like a shoot-around before a basketball game. Meanwhile, the matadors had a chance to assess the bull and figure out how fast he moved and if he faked right and passed left or if he seemed crazy. This bull was a sprinter, and all around the ring the capes were blooming. Then two picadors rode out and positioned their horses at either end of the ring, and as soon as the bull noticed one, he roared toward it, head down, and slammed into the padding that protected the horse's flank. The picadors stabbed the bull with long spears as he tangled with the horse. After he was speared several times by each picador, he was lured away by the big capes again. A few moments later, the ring cleared, and a banderillero sprinted into the ring carrying a pair of short, decorated harpoons. He held them high and wide. Eventually the bull lunged toward the banderillero, who ducked out of the way of the horns and planted the banderillas into the bull's withers. Then a second banderillero did the same thing. The bull was panting. The band burst into a fanfare, and then Cristina came out alone, carrying a small red heart-shaped cape. She stood at attention and tipped her hat to the judge—asking permission to kill the bull—and then turned and glanced just slightly toward her father, who was standing between the seats and the ring. The bull stood motionless and stared at her. For ten minutes or so she seduced him toward her, and just as he thought he was about to kill her, she diverted him with dizzying, rippling, precise swings of her cape—first a windmill, then a circle, then a chest pass, where the bull rushes straight toward and then under the cape. As the bull passed her, Cristina's back was as arched as a scythe. When the bull was swooning, she stood right in front of him, rubbed his forehead lightly with the flat of her sword, and then spread her arms, yelled something, and dropped down on one knee. The bull looked like he might faint.

Then she started getting ready to kill him. She walked over to her sword boy and traded him for her longest, sharpest blade. The band was toodling away on some brassy song, and after a moment she glowered and thrust her hand up to stop it. She drew the bull toward and past her a few more times. On one pass, she lost her grip on her cape and her father shot up from his seat and the crew raced in to help her, but without even looking up she waved them away. Then the bull squared up and she squared up. His fat beige tongue was now hanging out, and a saddle blanket of blood was spreading from the cuts that the picadors and the banderilleros had made. Cristina's eyes were fixed with a look of concentration and command, and her arm was outstretched, and she lined up the bull, her arm, and her sword. She and the bull had not seen each other before the fight— matadors and bulls never do, the way grooms avoid brides on their wedding day—but she now stared so hard at him and he at her that it looked as if each was examining the other through and through.

WHEN IT WAS OVER, she got flowers, wineskins, berets, bags of olives, loafers, crutches, more wineskins, hundreds of things shoved at her to autograph, and both of the bull's black ears. The bull got two recumbent laps of the ring, hauled around by a team of donkeys, and there was a butcher with a five o'clock shadow and black rubber hip boots waiting for him as soon as the team dragged him through the door. When the whole corrida was finally over, a leftover bull was let loose in the ring, and anyone with nerve could hop in with him and fool around. Most people passed on that and instead filed out of the stands, beaming and chatting and slapping backs and shaking hands. Just outside the front gate was a clean white Peugeot van with CRISTINA SÁNCHEZ stenciled in script on the front and the back, and in it were a driver and Cristina and Cristina's father and her crew, still dressed in their sumptuous fight clothes, still damp and pink-faced from the fight. Cristina looked tremendously happy. The van couldn't move, because the crowd had closed in around it, and everyone was waving and throwing kisses and pushing papers to autograph through the van's windows, and for ten minutes or so Cristina signed stuff and waved at people and smiled genuinely and touched scores of outstretched hands. It was such a familiar picture of success and adoration and fame, but it had a scramble of contradictory details: Here was an ancient village with a brand-new bullring, and here was a modern new car filled with young and able people wearing the uniforms of a sport so unchanging and so ritualized that except for the fresh concrete and the new car and the flushed blond face of Cristina it all could have been taking place a hundred years in the future or a hundred years ago.

At last Cristina whispered "no más" to the driver, and he began inching the van down the driveway and then out toward the highway, and soon you could see only a speck in the shape of the van. The town of Nava then returned to normal. Cristina was going on to fight and fight and fight until the end of the European season, and then she planned to fly to South America and fight and then to Mexico and fight and then to return to Spain and start the season again. Once someone suggested that she try to get a Nike contract, and once she told me that she would love to bring bullfighting to America. But it seems that bullfighting is such a strange pursuit and the life bullfighters lead is so peculiar and the sight and the sound and the smell of the whole thing is so powerful and so deadly that it could only exist where strangeness is expected and treasured and long-standing and even a familiar part of every day.

It was now deep evening in Nava, and the road out had not a single streetlight. Outside town the road cut through huge unlit pastures, so everything in all directions was pure black. No one was on the road, so it felt even more spooky. Then a car pulled up behind me, and after a moment it sped up and passed. It was a medium-size station wagon driven by a harried-looking man, and there was a shaggy dappled gray pony standing in the back. The man had the interior lamp turned on, maybe for the pony, and it made a trail of light I could follow the whole way back to Madrid.

AUTHOR'S NOTE

Except for minor corrections, the stories in this collection are printed as they originally appeared in the following magazines:

THE AMERICAN MAN, AGE TEN	ESQUIRE, DECEMBER 1992
MEET THE SHAGGS	THE NEW YORKER, SEPTEMBER 27, 1999
SHOW DOG	THE NEW YORKER, FEBRUARY 20, 1995
THE MAUI SURFER GIRLS	WOMEN OUTSIDE, 1998
LIVING LARGE	THE NEW YORKER, JUNE 17, 1991
I WANT THIS APARTMENT	THE NEW YORKER, FEBRUARY 22, 1999
DEVOTION ROAD	THE NEW YORKER, APRIL 17, 1995
AFTER THE PARTY	THE NEW YORKER, MARCH 21, 1994
SHOOT THE MOON	THE NEW YORKER, MARCH 22, 1993
SHORT PEOPLE	"TALK OF THE TOWN," THE NEW YORKER

"Brief Encounter"	NOVEMBER 2, 1992
"Big"	JULY 22, 1991
"Hall of Fame"	FEBRUARY 22, 1988
"Nonstop"	JULY 20, 1992
"Buttons"	MAY 23, 1988

Acknowledgments

This book is literally and figuratively a collective effort, so there are many people to acknowledge. First of all, *The New Yorker, Outside, Esquire,* and *Rolling Stone* were kind enough to have originally published these stories and to have granted permission to reprint them. I am especially grateful to my editors: Robert Gottlieb, Chip McGrath, Tina Brown, David Remnick, and Lee Aitken at *The New Yorker;* Mark Bryant, Susan Casey, John Tayman, and Laura Hohnhold at *Outside;* Terry McDonell and Bill Tonelli at *Esquire;* and Bob Wallace and Jim Henke at *Rolling Stone.* I also tip my hat to the copy editors and fact checkers who worked long hours to make sure everything came out right.

A million thanks to Ann Godoff, my publisher, and a million more to Jon Karp, my absolutely great editor, who is the person who made this book come true. I am indebted to all the people at Random House, and especially Sheryl Stebbins, Alexa Cassanos, Robbin Schiff, and Dennis Ambrose. Richard Pine, agent deluxe, has given me years of wisdom and friendship and has my everlasting loyalty and respect. And speaking of wisdom and friendship, thank you Arthur and Edith Orlean, David and Stephanie Orlean, Debra Orlean and David Gross, Jeff Conti, Sally Sampson, Amy Godine, Celia McGee, Janet Ungless, Diana Silver, Jamie Kitman, Marjorie Galen, Gail Gregg, Lisa Klausner, Patty Marx, Alison Rose, Karen Brooks, Stephen and Rebecca Schiff, Sally Willcox, Ravi Mirchandani, and Tim McHenry. Also, Tshering Wangchuk, who took on the vexing task of actually gathering these stories together. An extra thanks to my boss, without whom I couldn't have written any of this, and who has been my mentor and friend always.

My ultimate gratitude, of course, goes to the subjects of these pieces, who generously and unconditionally gave me so much of their time and their lives.

SUSAN ORLEAN has been a staff writer for *The New Yorker* since 1992 and has also written for *Outside, Esquire, Vogue,* and *Rolling Stone.* She graduated from the University of Michigan and has worked as a reporter in Portland, Oregon, and Boston, Massachusetts. She now lives in New York City.

A NOTE ON THE TYPE

This book was set in Fairfield, the first typeface from the hand of the distinguished American artist and engraver Rudolph Ruzicka (1883–1978). In its structure Fairfield displays the sober and sane qualities of the master craftsman whose talent has long been dedicated to clarity. It is this trait that accounts for the trim grace and vigor, the spirited design and sensitive balance, of this original typeface.

Rudolph Ruzicka was born in Bohemia and came to America in 1894.